IMAGES
of America

SPEARFISH

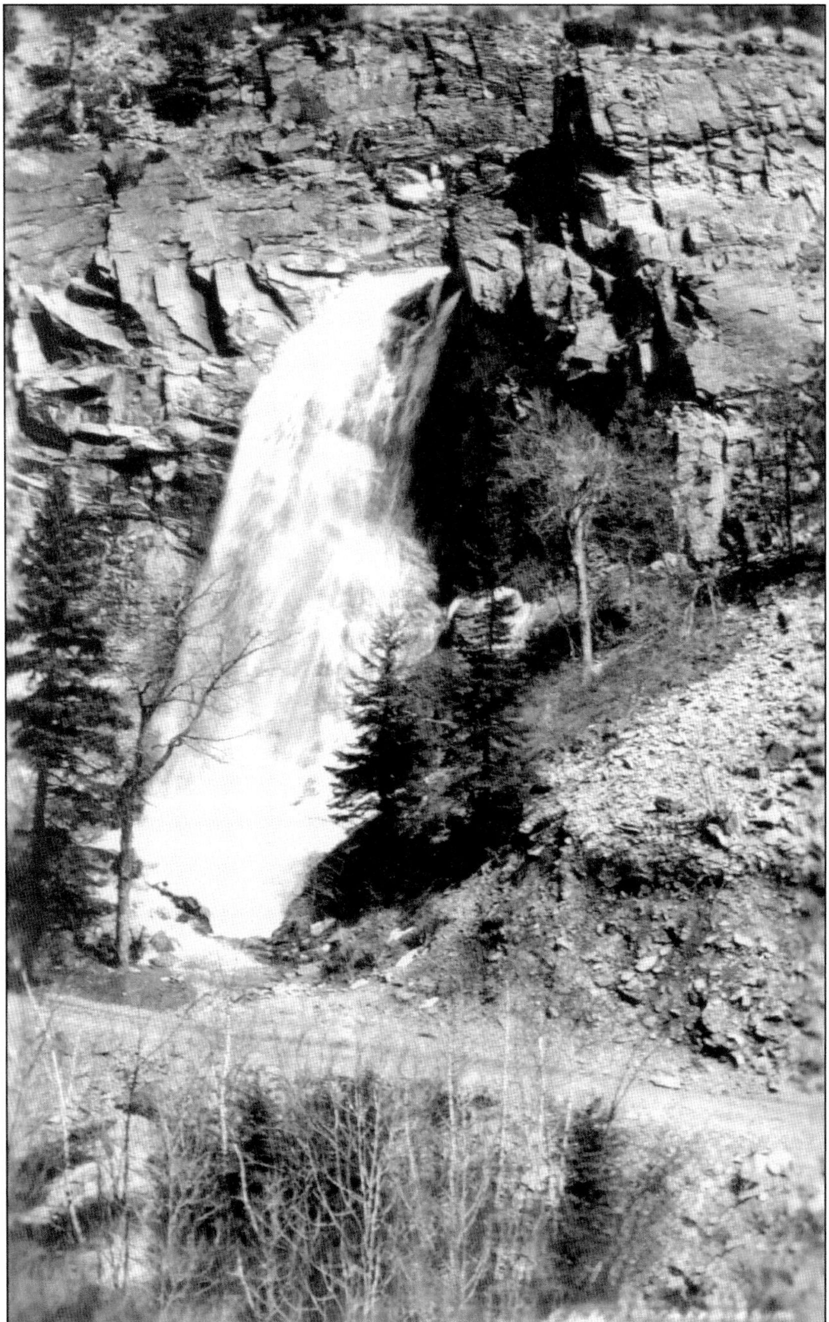

Thomas Odell captured the beauty of Bridal Veil Falls in this early photograph. Bridal Veil Falls is one of several waterfalls found in Spearfish Canyon and was one of the scenic stops on the Burlington Railroad route through Spearfish Canyon.

On the cover: Please see page 41. (Courtesy of the Leland D. Case Library.)

IMAGES
of America

SPEARFISH

Jan Cerney and Roberta Sago

ARCADIA
PUBLISHING

ISBN 978-0-7385-4142-6

Published by Arcadia Publishing
Charleston, South Carolina

Printed in the United States of America

Library of Congress Catalog Card Number: 2006933896

For all general information contact Arcadia Publishing at:
Telephone 843-853-2070
Fax 843-853-0044
E-mail sales@arcadiapublishing.com
For customer service and orders:
Toll-Free 1-888-313-2665

Visit us on the Internet at www.arcadiapublishing.com

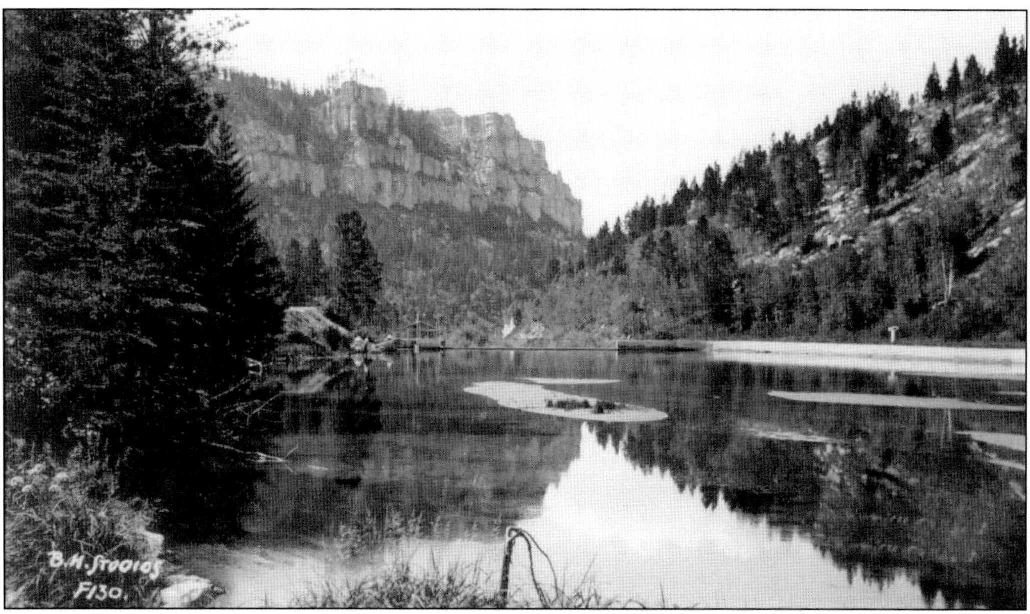

When Frank Lloyd Wright visited Spearfish Canyon in the 1930s he described the canyon as "a stately exposition of what decorated walls on enormous scale can do and be. The Chinese predicted and depicted it. This continued for miles and miles without palling or growing in the least stale."

Contents

ACKNOWLEDGMENTS

The authors would like to thank Charles Haas and the Black Hills Passion Play for their contribution of photographs to this work. We would also like to thank Paul Higbee for his advice and assistance in locating photographs of the Matthews Opera House. This volume would not have been possible without the collections of the Leland D. Case Library for Western Historical Studies at Black Hills State University and their University Archives.

INTRODUCTION

The influx of settlers into the Black Hills began with the discovery of gold in 1874. Very rich deposits were discovered along Whitewood Creek, the site of the future town of Deadwood and, in 1876, miners and merchants flooded to the Northern Black Hills. Unlike neighboring Deadwood, Spearfish did not have vast precious metal deposits. In Spearfish gold was the color green. The lush grasses of the wide valley provided a banquet for cattle driven from Texas and other southern locations. Spearfish also became a center of commerce, helping to provide food and dry goods for the surrounding communities.

Settlement in the Black Hills was a violation of the Fort Laramie Treaty of 1868. This treaty gave the sacred Black Hills to the Lakota people forever and the Lakota defended their territory. The settlers claimed that by not "always living peacefully," as agreed in the treaty, the Lakota had voided it. The flow of settlers could not be staunched. In February 1877, the United States government opened the Black Hills to settlement.

Nestled in the hilly landscape, the fledgling town of Spearfish was especially vulnerable to Native American attacks. Spearfish pioneers built a stockade as a refuge for the dozen or so residents and their livestock in the times of Native American raids in 1876. The stockade remained for two years.

The mystery of how the town was named Spearfish remains unresolved. The story may be a fish tale in itself. It is said that the water was so clear that one could spear the fish in the streams. Although edible, however, the small fish native to the Black Hills waterways didn't provide much of a meal. Another moniker up for debate is Spearfish's nickname, "the Queen City." Some claim it is because the three mountains surrounding the city resemble the points of a crown. Other say it is because Denver did so well with that label. It was thought that the name would bring Spearfish the same growth and prosperity. Many local businesses have adopted "Queen City" as part of their names.

Spearfish has had its share of visionaries and dreamers as well as a few schemers. One who is perhaps the most notorious is former resident Van Buren Baker, the first principal of the State Normal School. He quickly became known as a gambler, womanizer, and skilled marksman. He fled Spearfish after a brief 10-month tenure. He later murdered his wife and mother-in-law in Pennsylvania and was incarcerated for the remainder of his life.

One of the dreamers was Josef Meier of Luenen, Germany. He brought the 700-year-old theatrical production, the Luenen Passion Play, to Spearfish in 1938. After making Spearfish its permanent home, he renamed the production the Black Hills Passion Play. This venture succeeded in prolific proportions. A less successful dreamer was Rudolf Kroll. He ran a small meat market and envisioned Spearfish becoming a major center of the meat-packing industry like Chicago. Due to the considerable distance from major railroads this dream did not become a reality.

Although the periods of growth are numerous, there were a few dark days as well. The post–World War I period brought the influenza epidemic of 1918 when half a million died across the nation. South Dakota saw 1,000 die, and one of the first Spearfish deaths was that of Edna Hare, the wife of a normal school faculty member. Also during that time came the rise of the Ku Klux Klan across the Midwest. This group formed a chapter in the Black Hills. With relatively few African Americans in the area, the Catholics were their primary target, particularly those of Italian descent.

Although few, African Americans were among the first pioneers. Mary Kercherval, a former cook for George Armstrong Custer, arrived in the Black Hills in 1873. She became the matriarch of a Spearfish pioneer family. A young man by the name of Arthur Henry was the first African American student and football player at the State Normal School in 1899.

The spirit of the Spearfish forefathers continues. The city maintains a fascinating balance between agriculture, commerce, natural wonders of the Black Hills like Spearfish Canyon, and cultural attractions.

One

The Thoen Stone

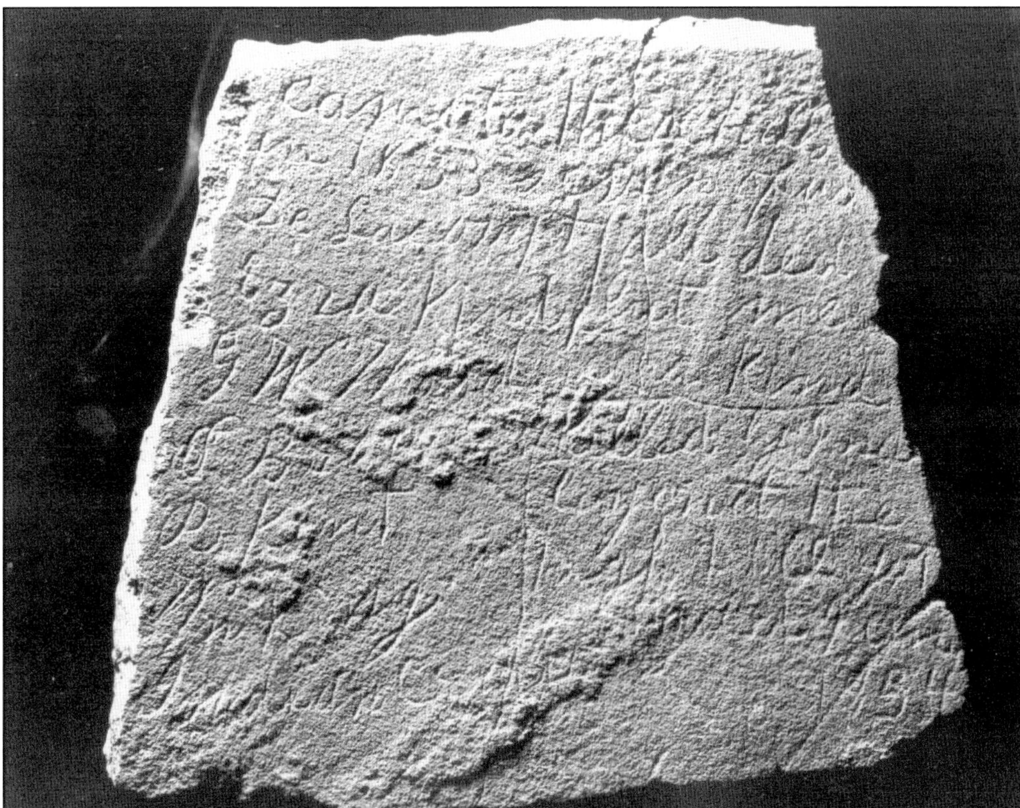

This photograph is of the original stone found by Louis Thoen. In 1887, Louis Thoen, a farmer, miner, and stone cutter, and his brother Ivan discovered an inscribed sandstone slab sandwiched between two large stones at the foot of Lookout Mountain near Spearfish while looking for sandstone to use in a basement that they were constructing. A desperate message had been scratched with a knife deep into the sandstone in June 1834.

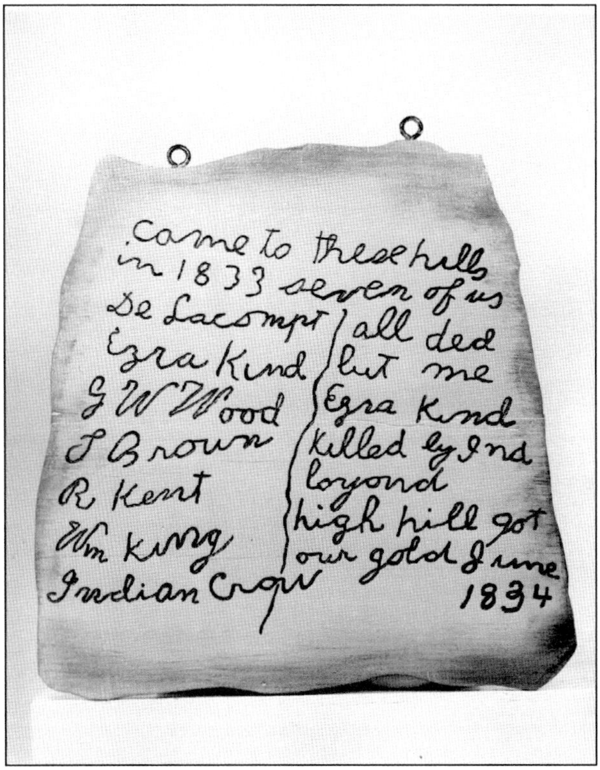

This copy of the original stone reveals the tragic letter scratched by Ezra Kind, the only survivor. Seven men had come to the Black Hills in 1833. They found gold but were killed by Native Americans before they could leave with it. Kind probably later met the same fate as his comrades. The newly discovered stone was displayed in John Cashner's curio store. Cashner had stereotype plates made of the stone and ran a story in the *Detroit Free Press* about the discovery. After reading the story, several relatives contacted him. Today the stone letter is displayed at the Adam's Museum in Deadwood.

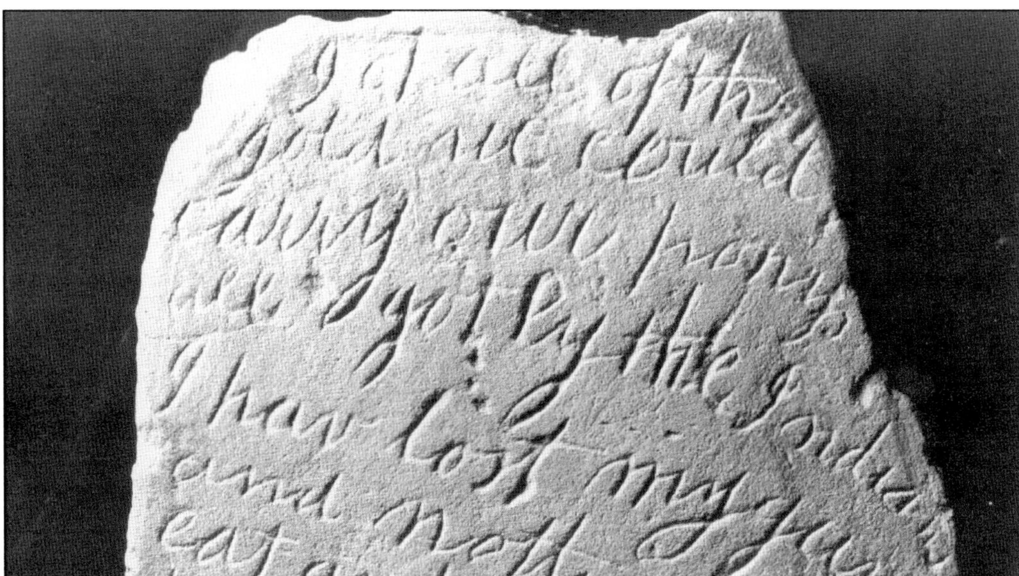

When the stone was discovered, the March 16, 1887 issue of the Deadwood newspaper the *Black Hills Daily Times* wrote a lengthy article concerning the first visitation to the Black Hills by whites. The newspaper wrote that Fr. Pierre DeSmet knew of gold in the Hills in 1828, and prospectors diverted from the California gold rush route in 1849. Rusty relics had been found in addition to rotting cabins, all testaments to early gold seekers. Those venturing forth into the Black Hills were never heard from again.

The stone slab, measuring 8 inches by 10 inches by 3 inches, is of historical importance as it adds to the evidence that gold had been discovered long before the Custer Expedition in 1874. Other prospectors had come to the Black Hills, just as the Ezra Kind party did, but the Sioux Indians were effective in silencing the gold discoveries, keeping the white men out of the Black Hills for several more decades.

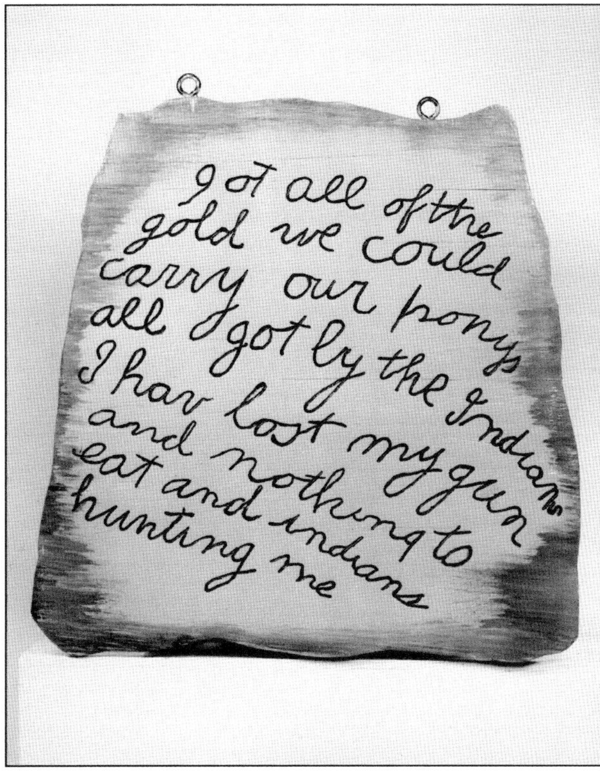

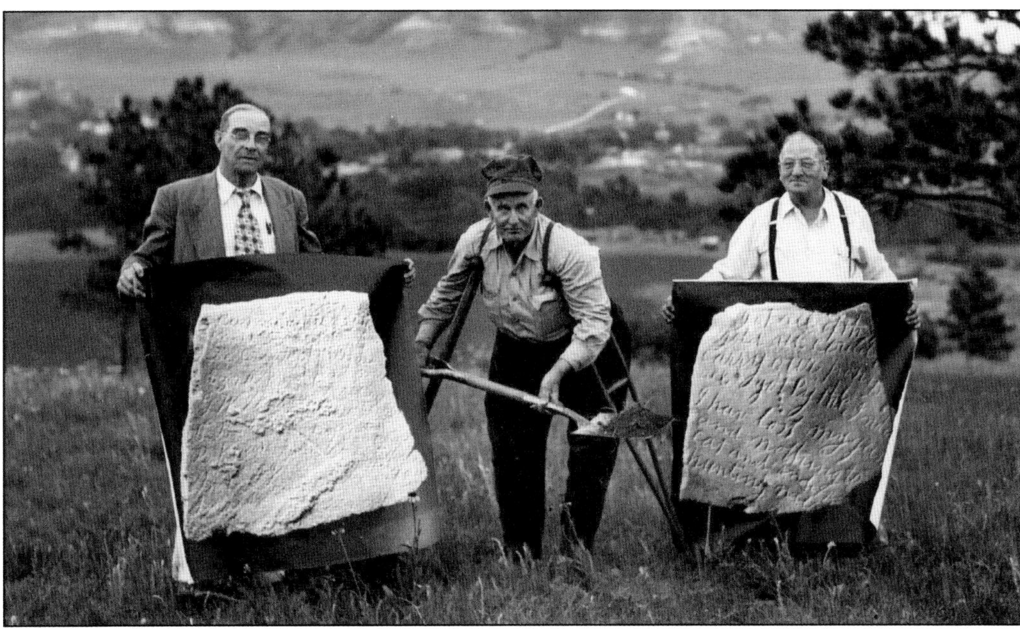

In this photograph, Ernest Lown, Frank Thomson, and Charles Lown break ground for the Thoen Stone Marker. Frank Thomson, a rancher and historian, spent considerable time and energy researching and documenting the authenticity of the Thoen Stone. His search led him to family members of the men inscribed on the stone. He made contact with all descendents of the men except for G. W. Wood.

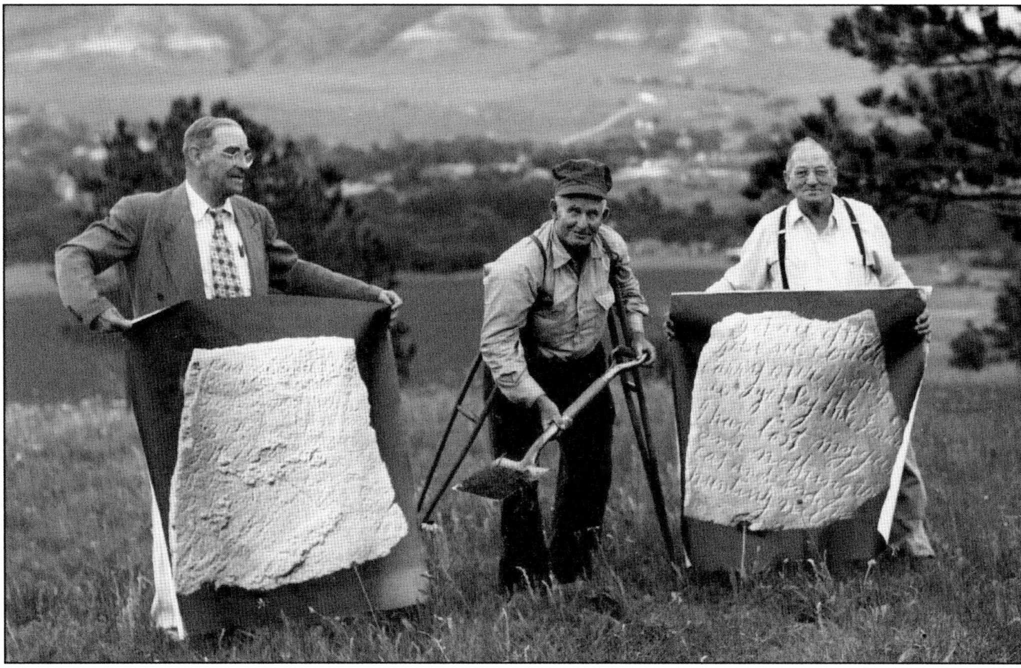

Ernest Lown and Charles Lown display reproductions of the famous Thoen Stone while Frank Thomson breaks ground.

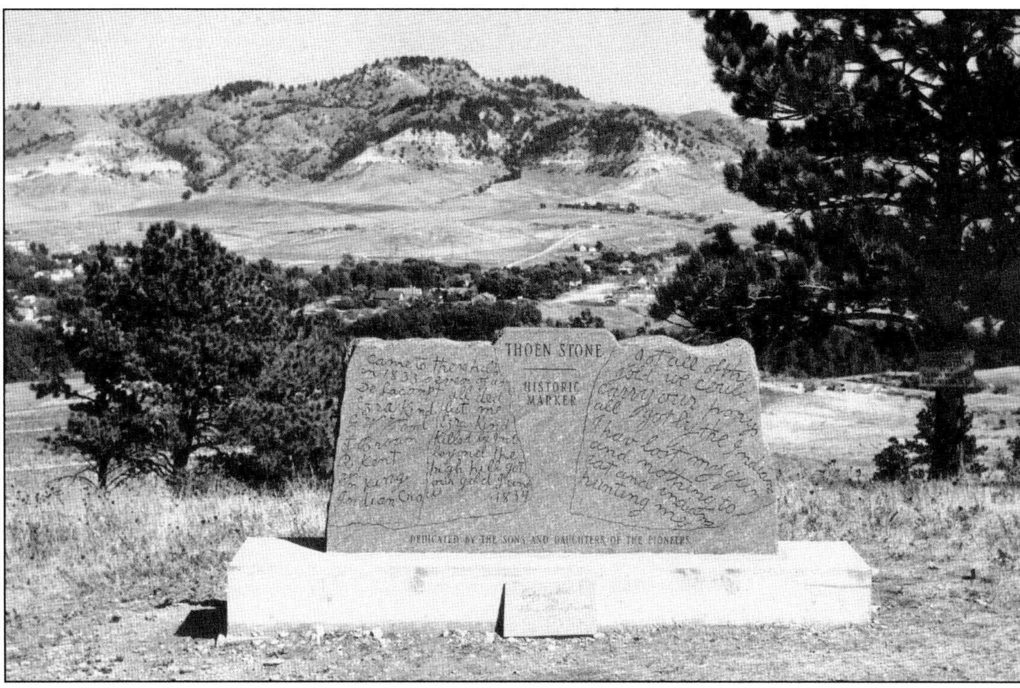

The Thoen Stone Marker stands in the foreground with Lookout Mountain, where the Thoen Stone was discovered, in the background. The marker, made of granite, is an enlarged reproduction of the message Ezra Kind inscribed on a slab of sandstone. Frank Thomson conjectures the original stone was wet, making inscribing easier.

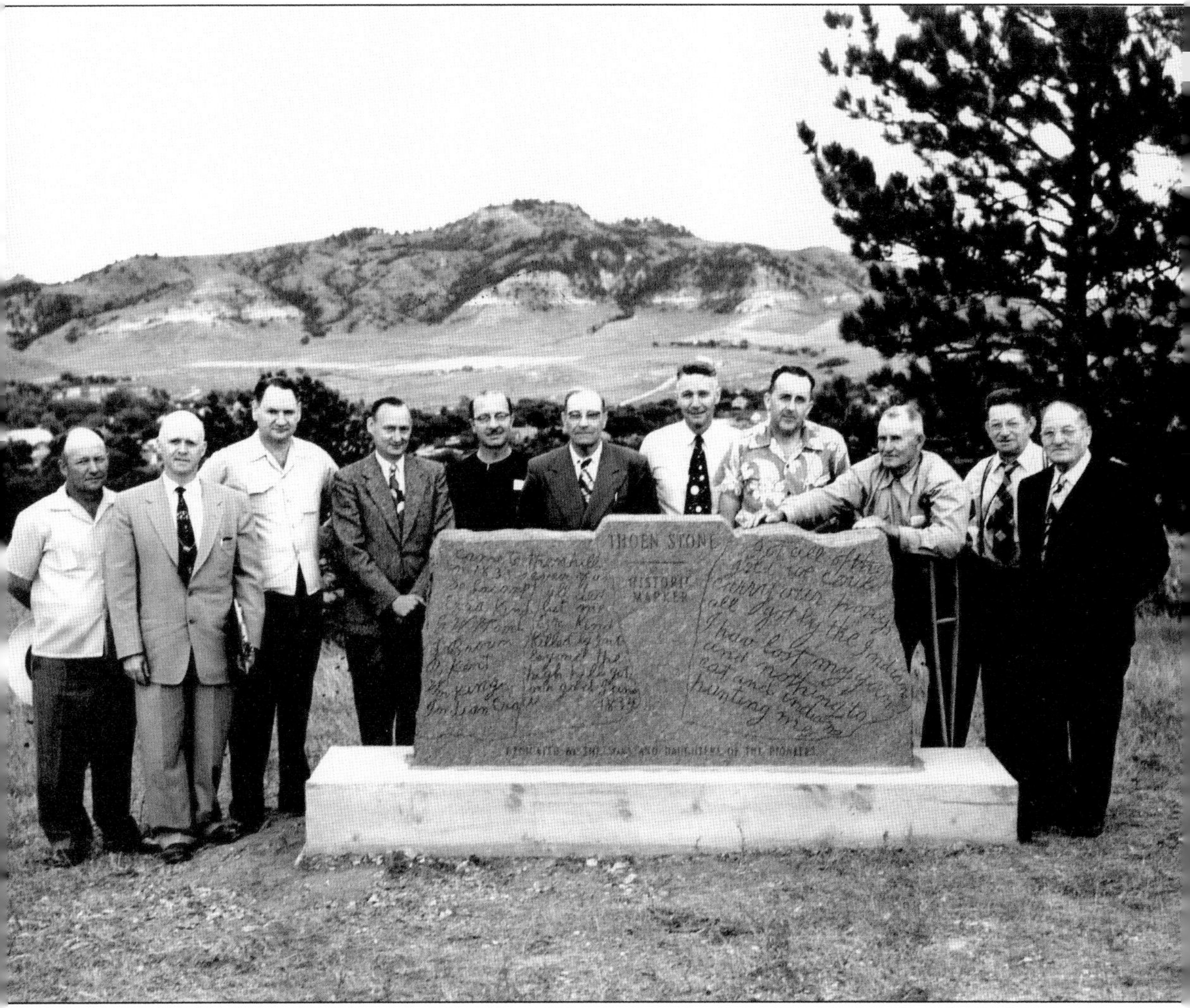

Pictured are members of the Thoen Stone Committee. From left to right are: Orville Banning, Dr. Russell Jonas, Dr. Floyd Ward, Ben Burris, Eldo Trucano, Ernest Lown, Floyd Marchant, Ralph Stordahl, Frank Thomson, Joseph Fassbender, and Charles Lown. Charles Lown, Frank Thomson, Thomas Odell, Lee Hood, James McDermott, Martin Thompson, Roy Cook, and Ernest Lown signed a statement vouching for the authenticity of the Thoen Stone and the honor and integrity of he Louis Thoen family. The authenticity of the Thoen Stone has been questioned.

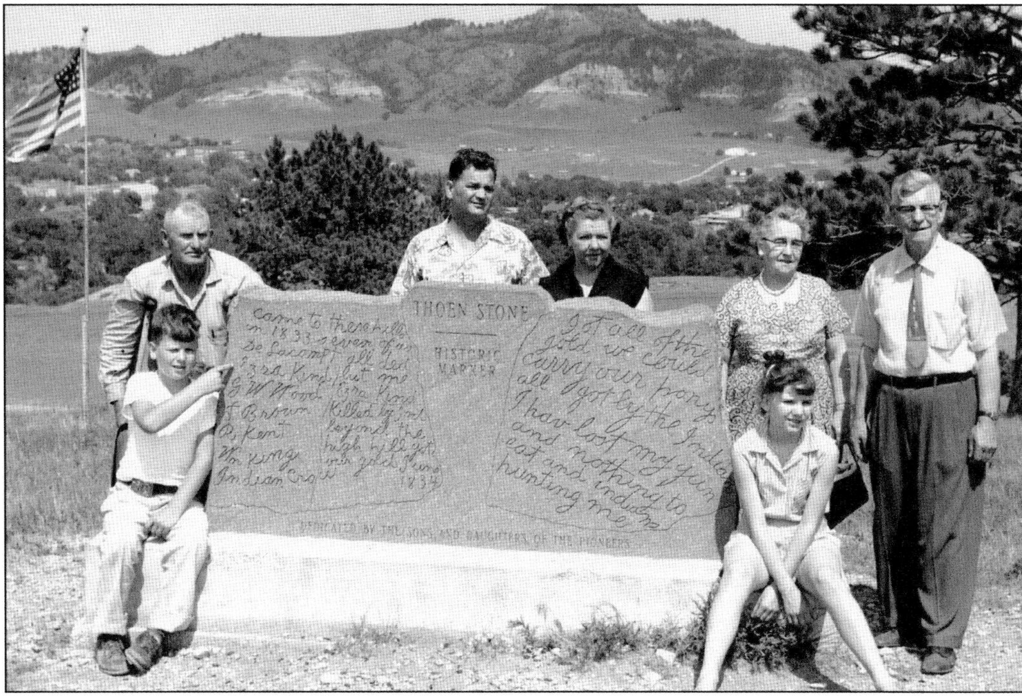

Frank Thomson stands to the left while Mr. Lown, a Spearfish merchant and committee member, stands to the extreme right. All others in the photograph are unidentified.

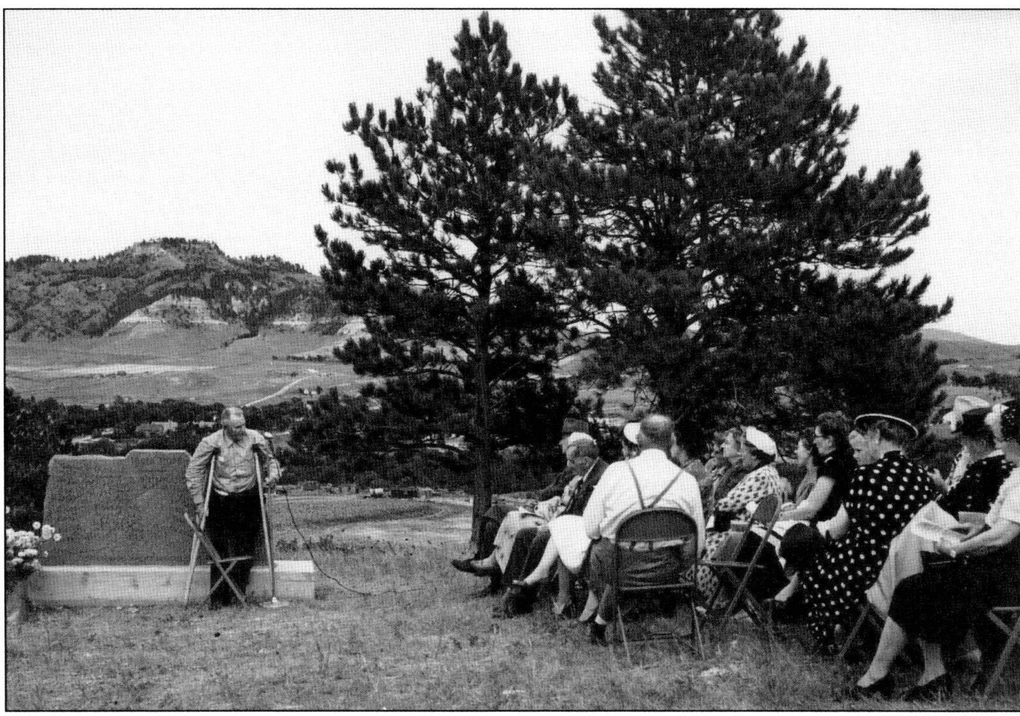

Frank Thomson speaks at the Thoen Stone Marker dedication, August 14, 1953. About 200 people were present.

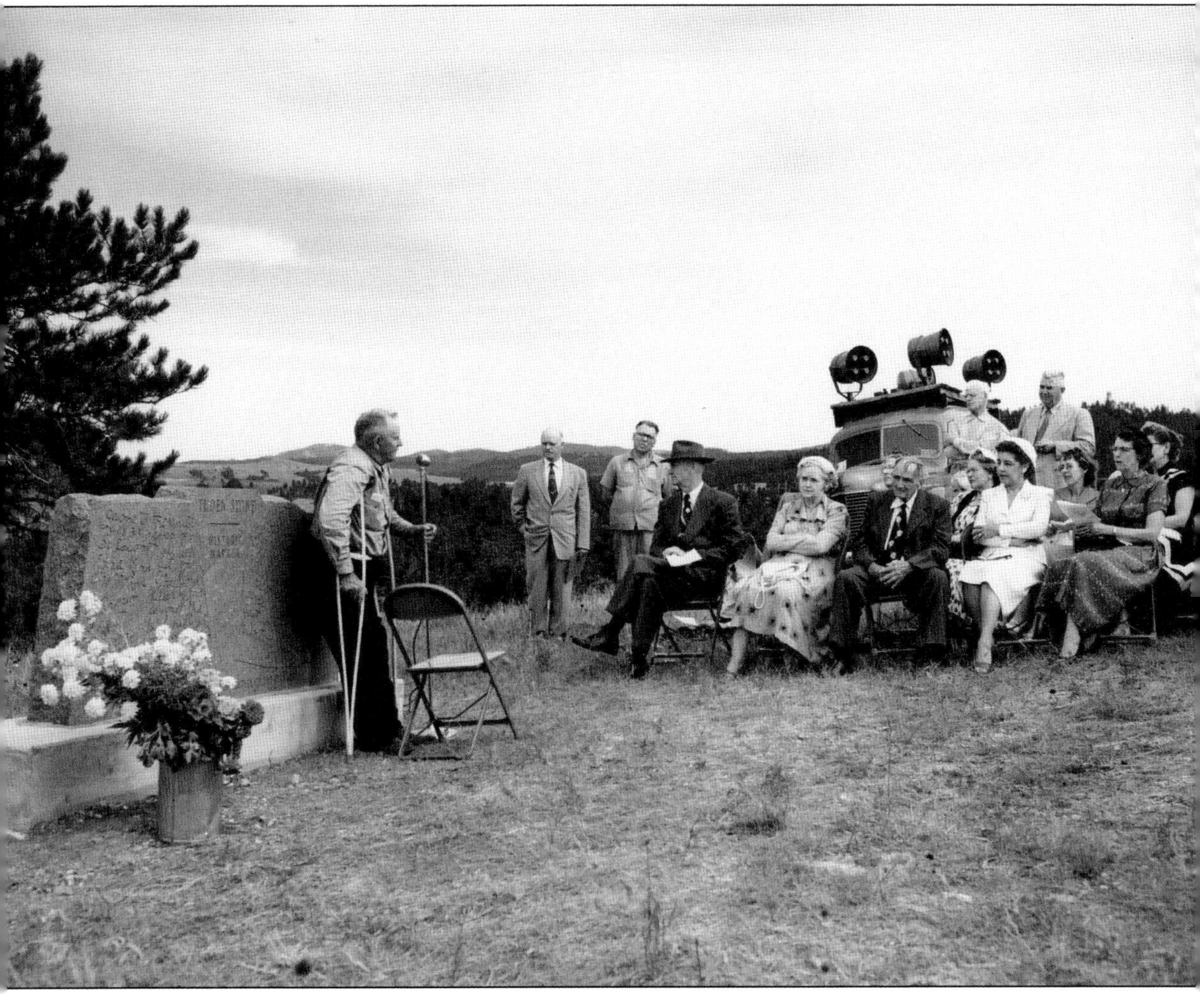

Pictured, from left to right, at the Thoen Stone Marker's dedication are Frank Thomson, speaking; Russell Jonas, president of Black Hills Teachers College; unidentified; Andrew Hanson, son-in-law to Louis Thoen; Anna Thoen Hanson, youngest of the three Thoen daughters; Andrew Brown, grandson of Thompson Brown; Linda Gale, great-granddaughter of Thompson Brown; and Gertrude Banes, great-granddaughter of Thompson Brown. Will Robinson, South Dakota historian, is standing close to the sound system.

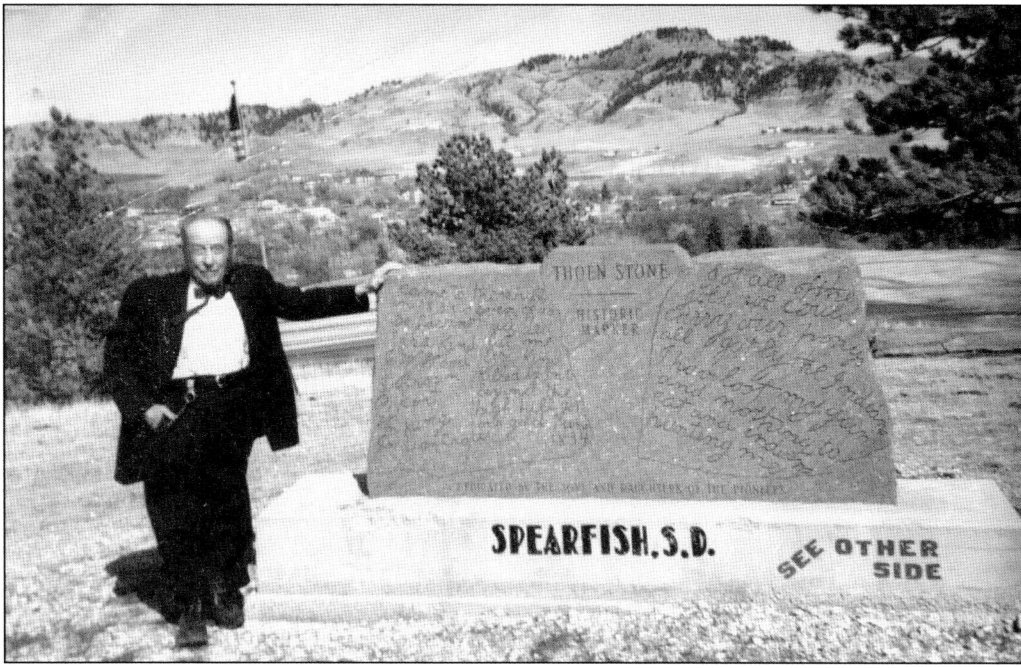

Frank Thomson photographed Thomas Odell at the Thoen Stone Marker. Both were historians and photographers and have left an enduring legacy to the region. Odell also researched the Thoen Stone.

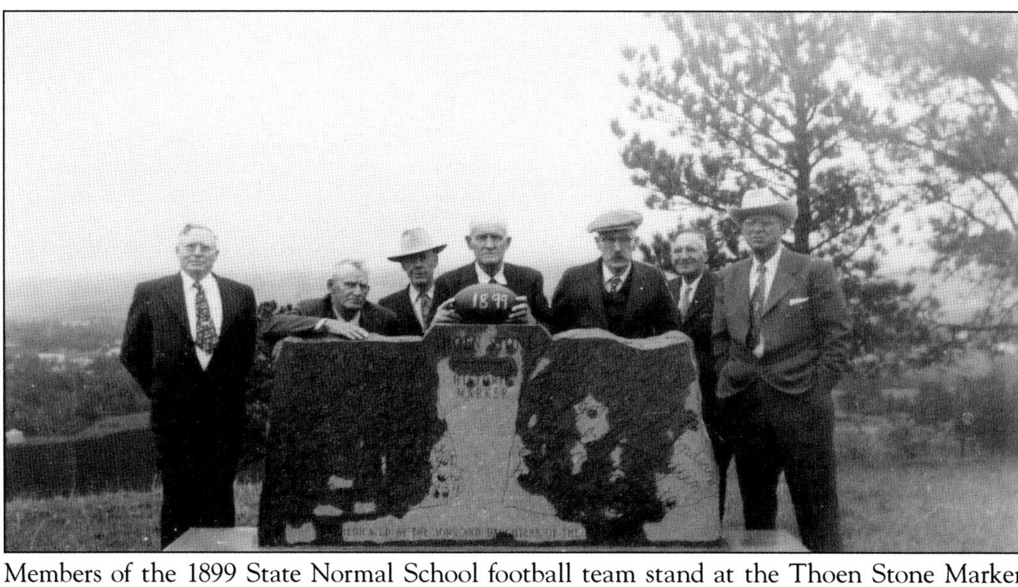

Members of the 1899 State Normal School football team stand at the Thoen Stone Marker. Pictured, from left to right, are James McDermott, Frank Thomson, Jess Driskill, Chris Thybo, Dan Hilton, George Abott, and Arthur Henry.

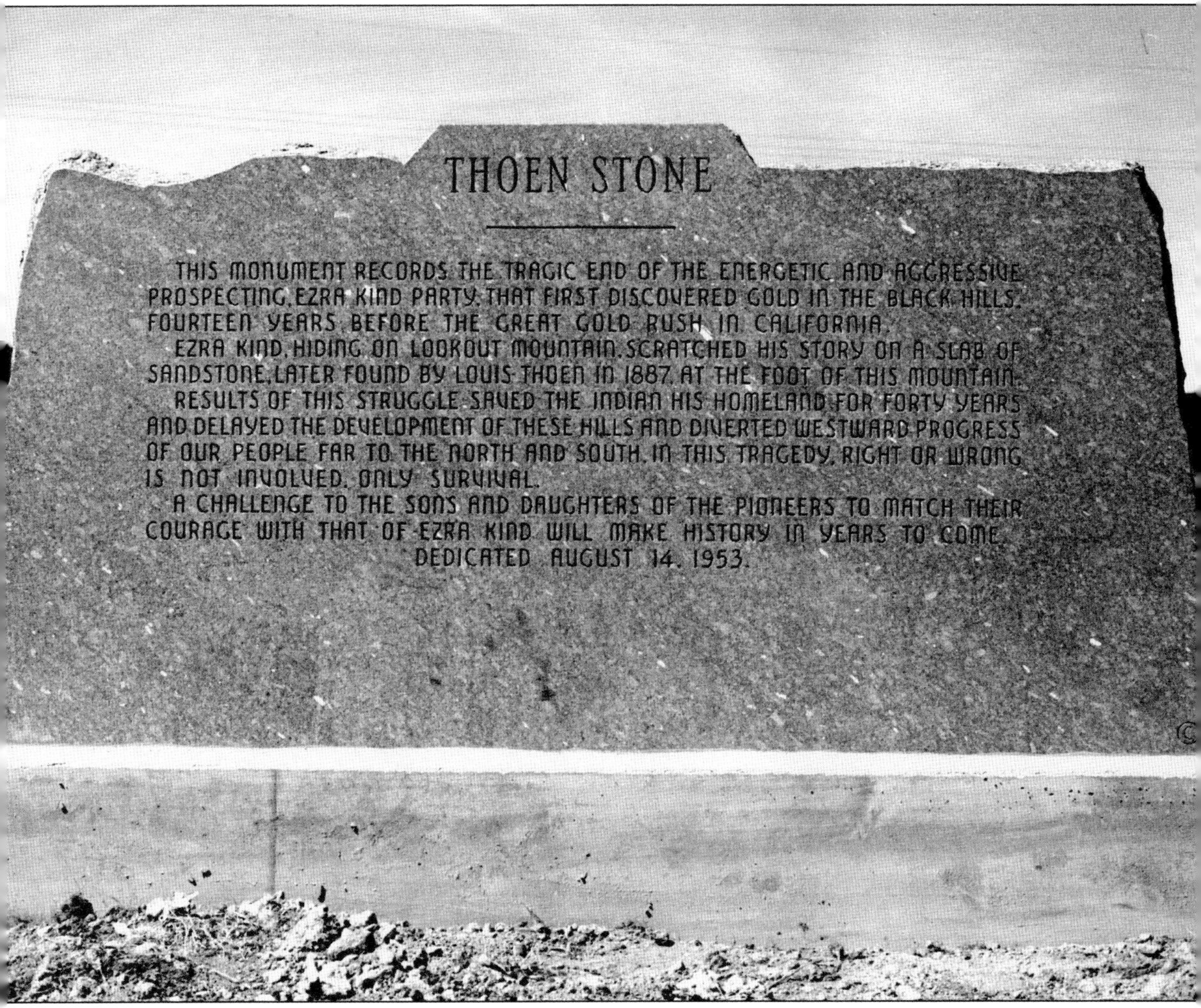

The reverse side of the marker gives tribute to the Ezra Kind party and explains how their discovery would have changed history. On a placard near the marker these words are written: "This is a place of solitude and meditation—that we who live should learn the cost and sacrifice of our pioneers, that we may live here in perfect peace and safety. Each year thousands of people stand here and read this Ezra Kind letter in silence and awe. Peace to Ezra and his companions. May the Stars and stripes float here forever—in honor of these men."

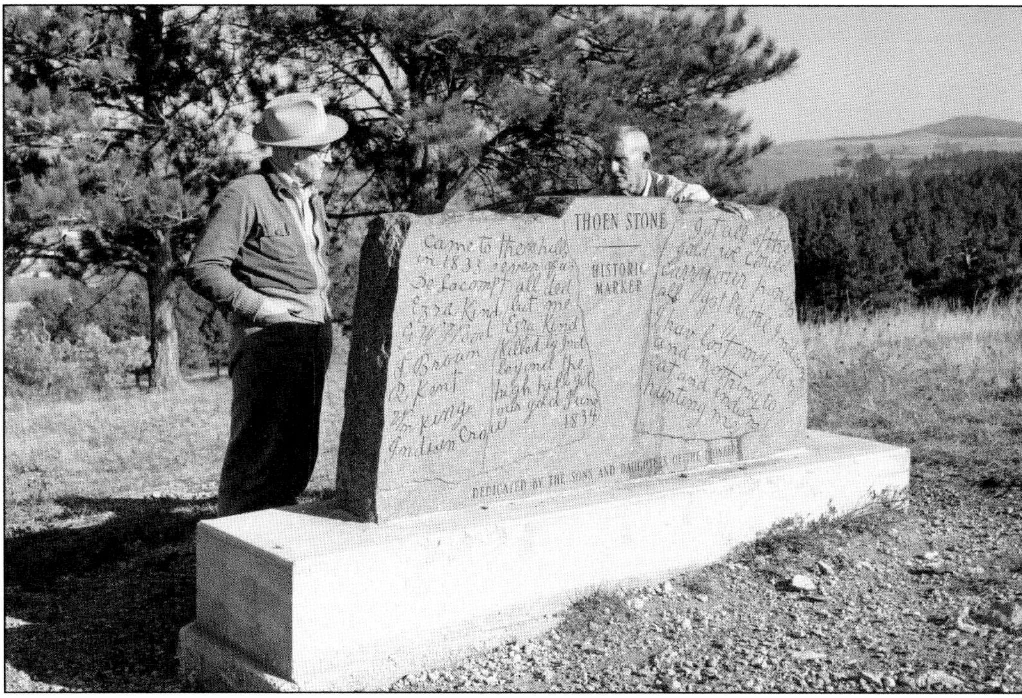

Sen. Francis Case and Frank Thomson are pictured at the marker. Senator Case was a supporter of the marker and visited it several times.

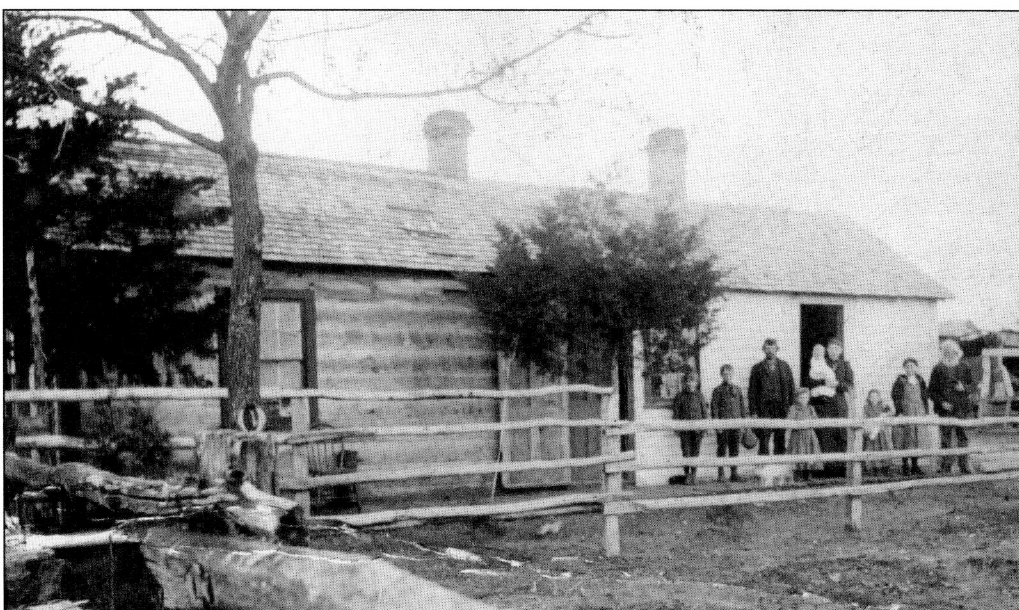

Frank Thomson searched to prove the authenticity of the stone and felt reasonably certain that he had found the family members. According to Thomson, Ezra Kind's family is pictured here at Melrose, Minnesota. Pictured, from left to right, are Edwin H., Charles G., Charles T., Elizabeth, Margaret, Veronica, Florence, Lucy, and Charles. Charles was Ezra's brother and told his grandson Edwin that Ezra went west to search for gold and was never heard from again.

Frank Thomson's search for family members of the ill-fated party of seven led him to Emma Kuhnert of Power, Montana, on April 30, 1958. She was the granddaughter of Dr. George Kind, Ezra's father, the daughter of Ezra's brother George Kind, and the only niece of Ezra Kind living in the United States. She had no knowledge of Ezra but provided Thomson with valuable family genealogy.

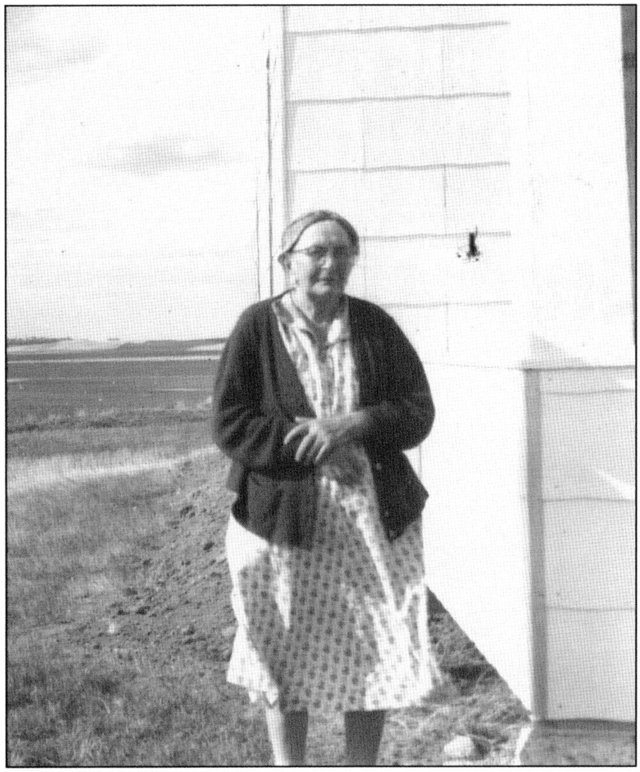

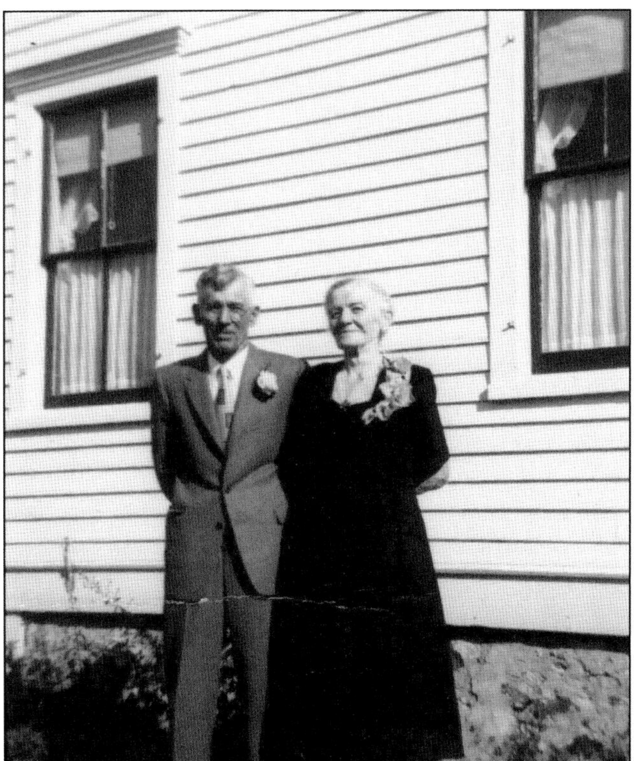

Ed Kind, a great-nephew of Ezra, and his wife, Anna, are pictured here. Ed would have been Charles Kind's great-grandson. Ed said he could remember "Grandpa Charles Kind" talking about Ezra.

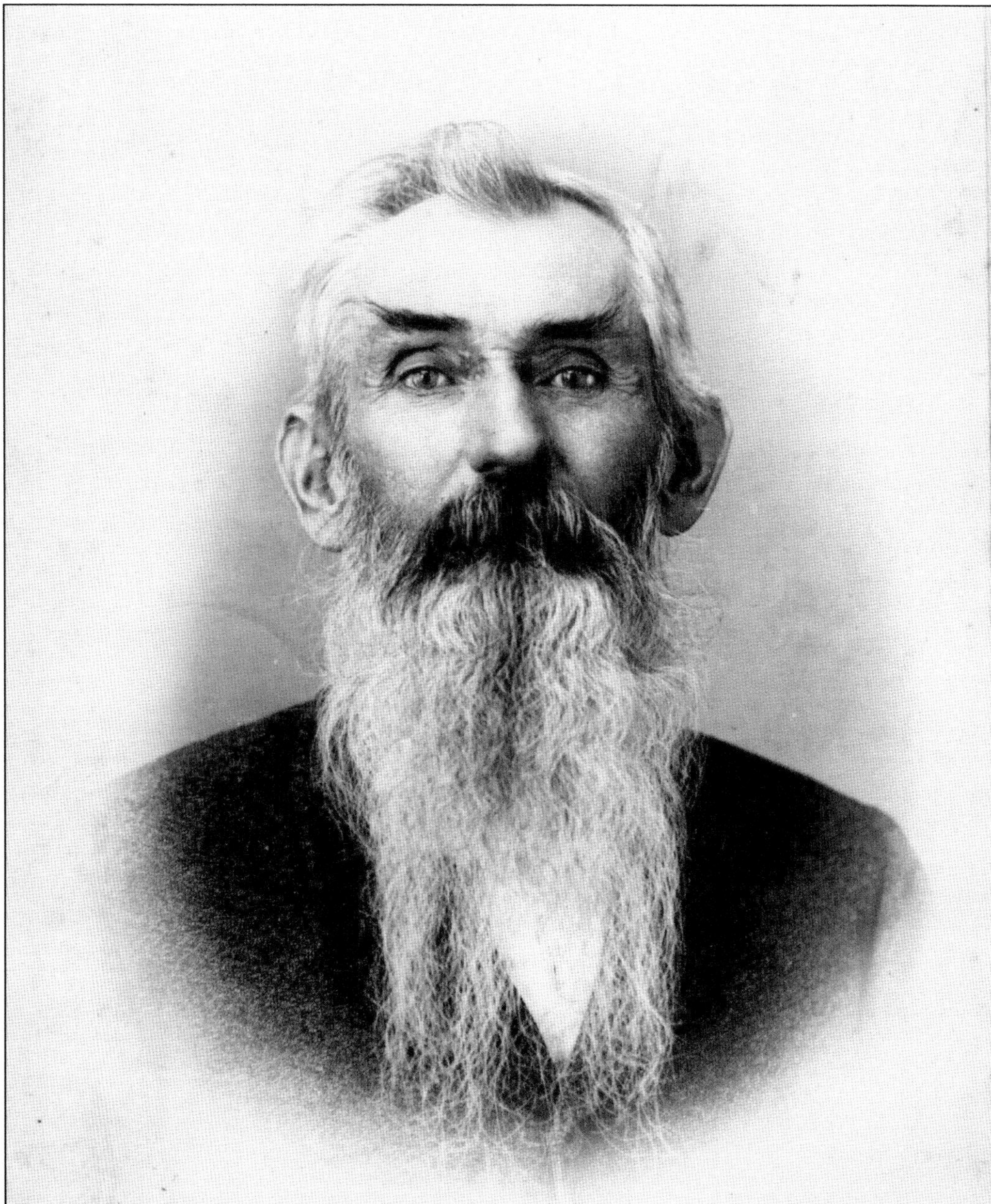

Pictured here is Robert Brown, who, according to Frank Thomson, was the son of Thompson Brown (T. Brown) of Thoen Stone fame. Andrew Brown, Thompson Brown's grandson, claims that his grandfather went west from Troy, Missouri, with a man named Kent in 1832 and never returned. Robert Brown remembered following behind his father while he paced the floor the night before he left on his journey west.

Two

GOLD IN THE BLACK HILLS

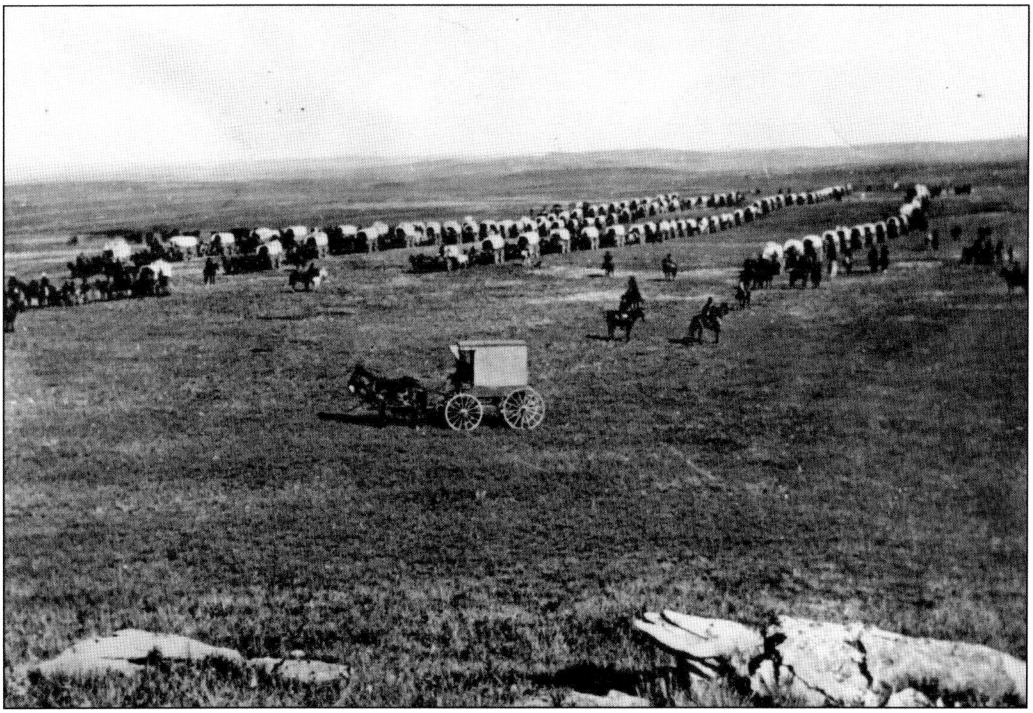

The Custer Expedition, originating from Fort Lincoln to the Black Hills of South Dakota in 1874, verified the rumors of gold and unleashed the gold rush to the Black Hills.

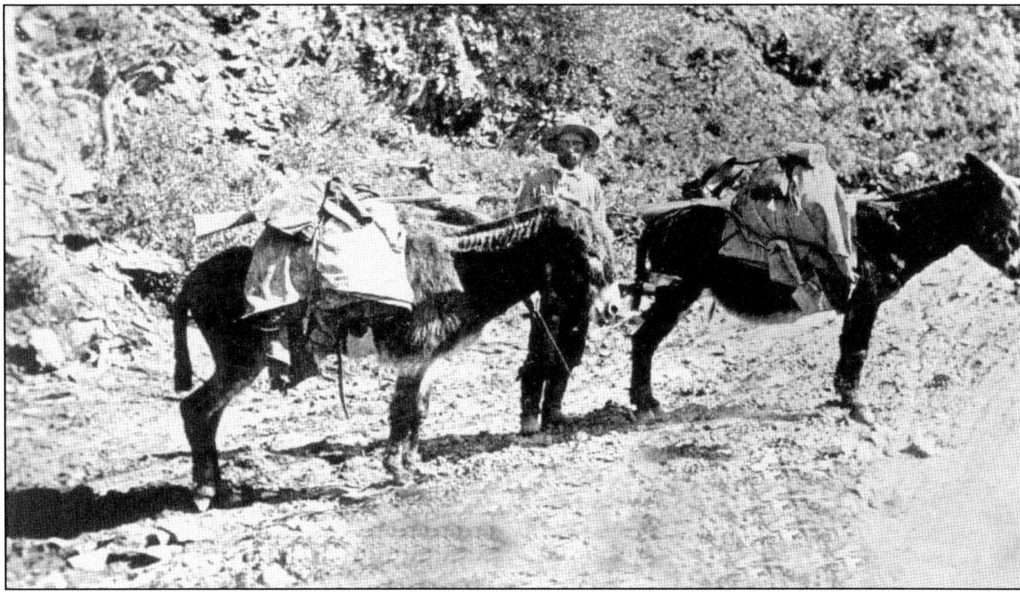

The discovery of gold in 1874 lured gold seekers to the Black Hills even though the region belonged to the Sioux. Many mining towns were founded up and down the gulches. Spearfish organized in 1876 as a result of the gold rush. The Sioux Agreement of 1877 legally opened the area up to prospectors, settlers, and town builders. Angered with the white intrusion, the Lakota Sioux attacked the early settlers causing Spearfish residents to construct a stockade to protect the several dozen citizens.

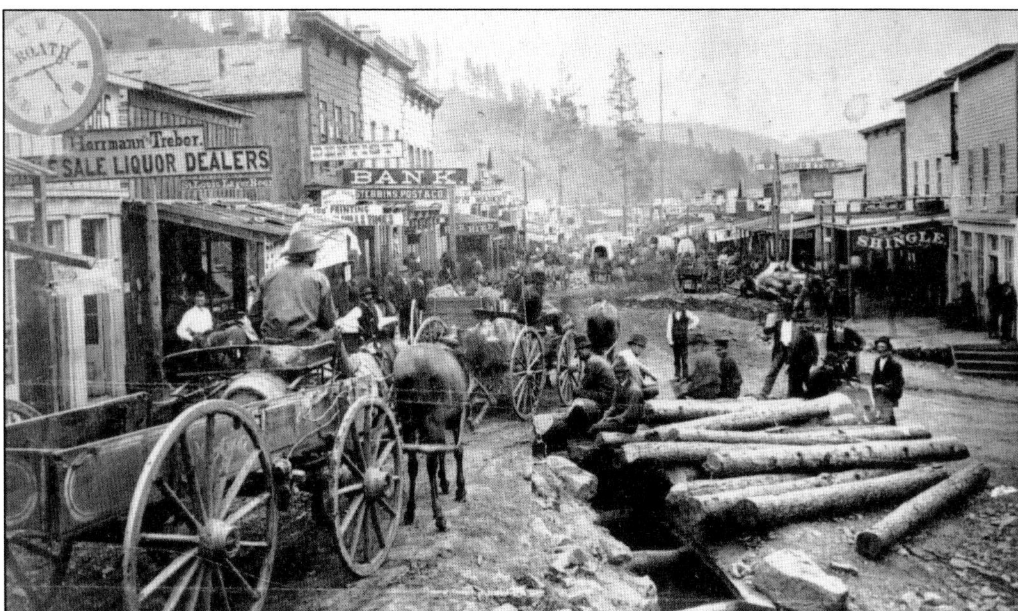

Deadwood became the center of the gold rush and its population soared. The most profitable gold mining operations were concentrated in the Deadwood-Lead area, where the mother lode was located. The Homestake mine, discovered in 1876, would become the richest gold mine in North America. However, prospectors explored the northern Black Hills too, discovering gold that initiated several mining operations in the area.

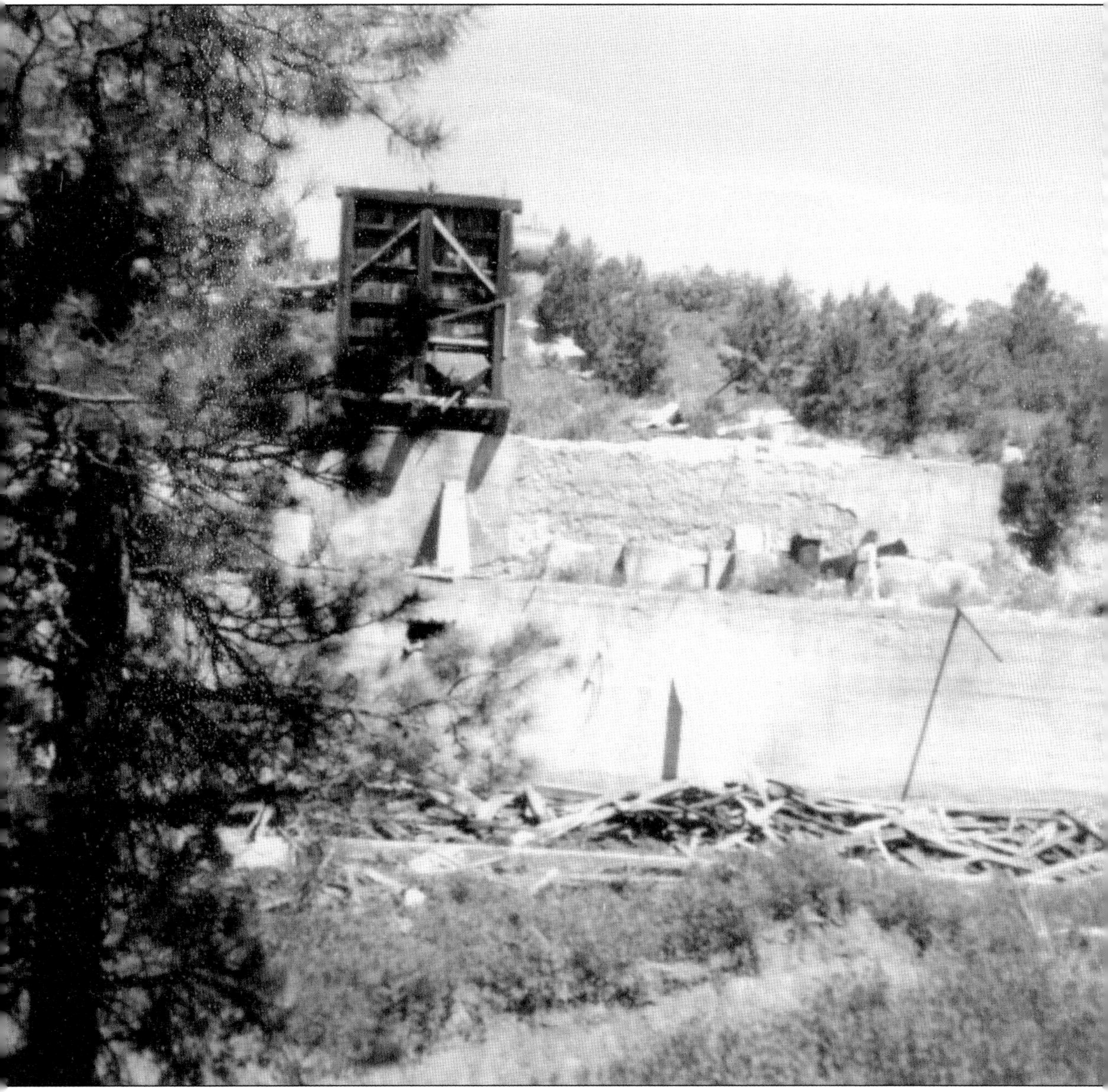

Hundreds of mining towns sprang up and flourished for a time then dissolved into ghost towns. One such town was Tinton, located about six miles from Iron Creek Lake, southwest of Spearfish. In 1879, Deadwood miners sent a group of freed slaves, unwanted in Deadwood, to the hills east of Tinton to look for nuggets, which lay as thick as pinecones. Although the recommendation was intended to be a spoof, the black miners found gold near what would become known as Tinton. They reportedly mined half a million dollars in gold and left for Cheyenne, Wyoming, without squandering a single nugget. Pictured is a building that was once a part of the later mining operations. (Courtesy of Jan Cerney.)

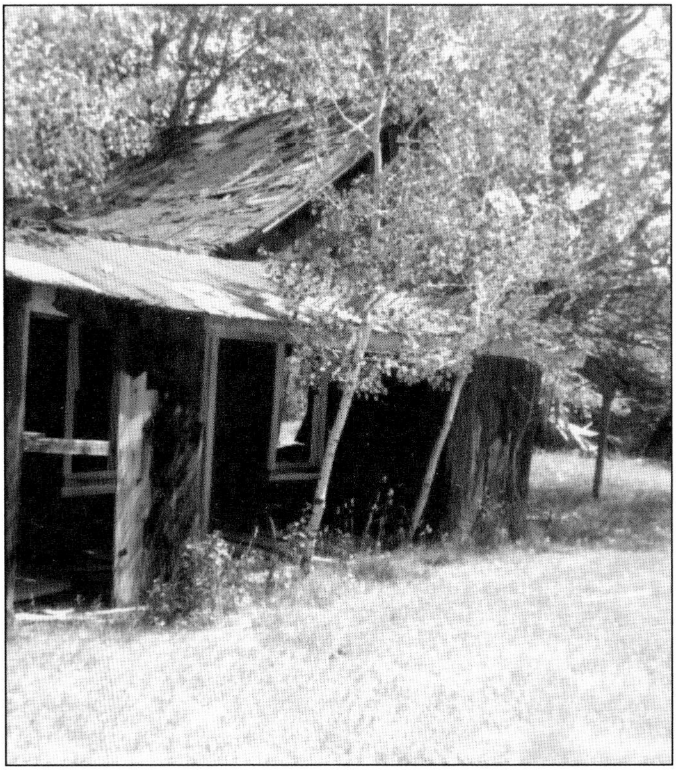

Pictured here is another shack in Tinton, a remnant of a once bustling town. Edgar Saint John arrived in the area in 1876, and by 1877, about 500 miners had joined him. A shortage of water in the 1880s halted gold production. It has been said that miners took out over a million dollars in gold. Cornish miners discovered tin in 1882. Tin, which required less water to crush and refine was mined from the 1880s through the 1920s and 1930s. (Courtesy of Jan Cerney.)

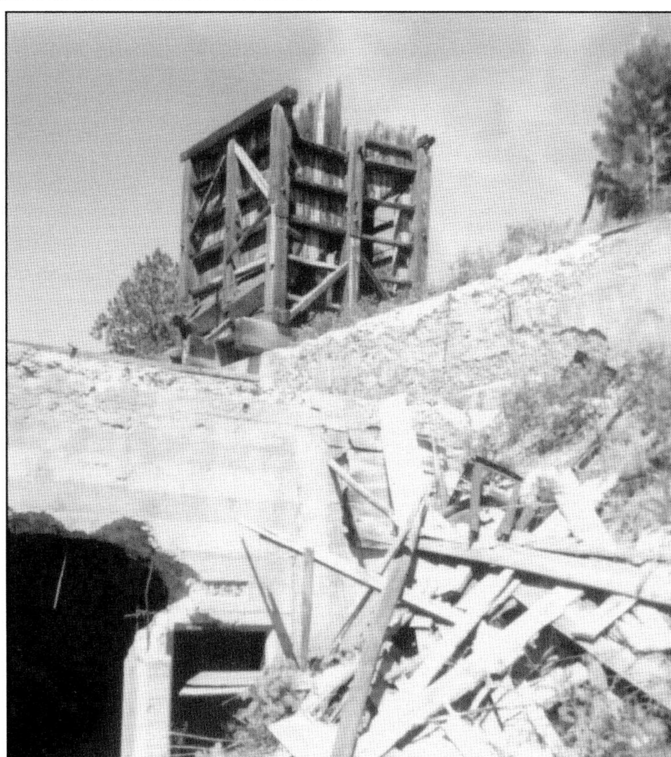

Another view of the abandoned mining operation is pictured here. Frank Thomson, a Thoen Stone researcher, speculated that the Ezra Kind party might have found their gold in the Tinton area. Iron, Potato, Beaver, and Bear Creeks all drain from the area and were all worked by prospectors. (Courtesy of Jan Cerney.)

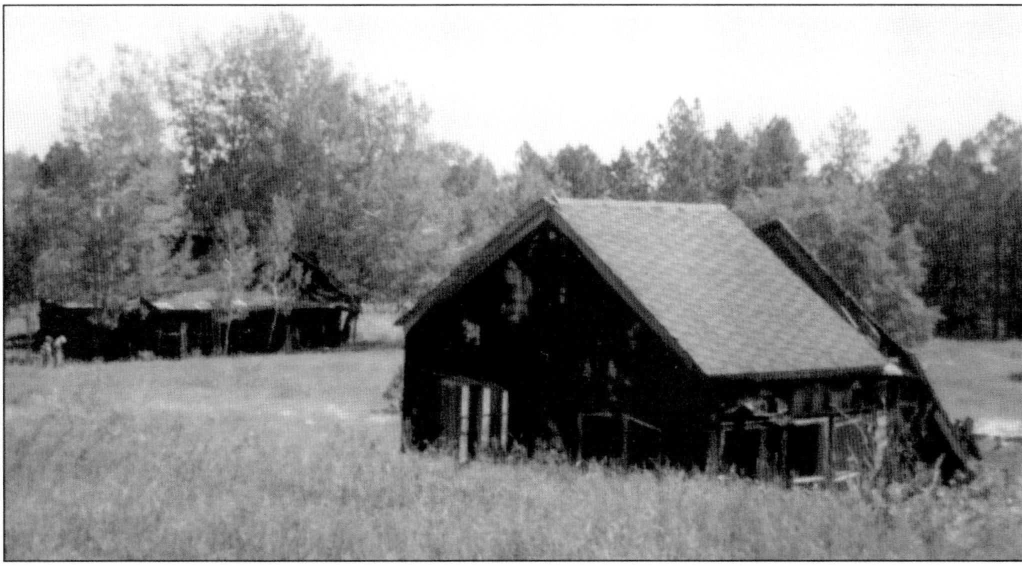

The Tinton Company built the town of Tinton in 1904. Red tar paper covered nearly all the buildings. During World War II, the mine produced lithium and other spodumene minerals. When the war ended, the town was abandoned. Like other mining towns, Tinton contained businesses and public facilities such as a hotel, rooming house, bunkhouse, miners' assembly hall, post office, bank, newspaper, school, and homes all built in a circle around Roosevelt Park. Roosevelt Park was named after Kermit Roosevelt, Pres. Theodore Roosevelt's son who had visited there. (Courtesy of Jan Cerney.)

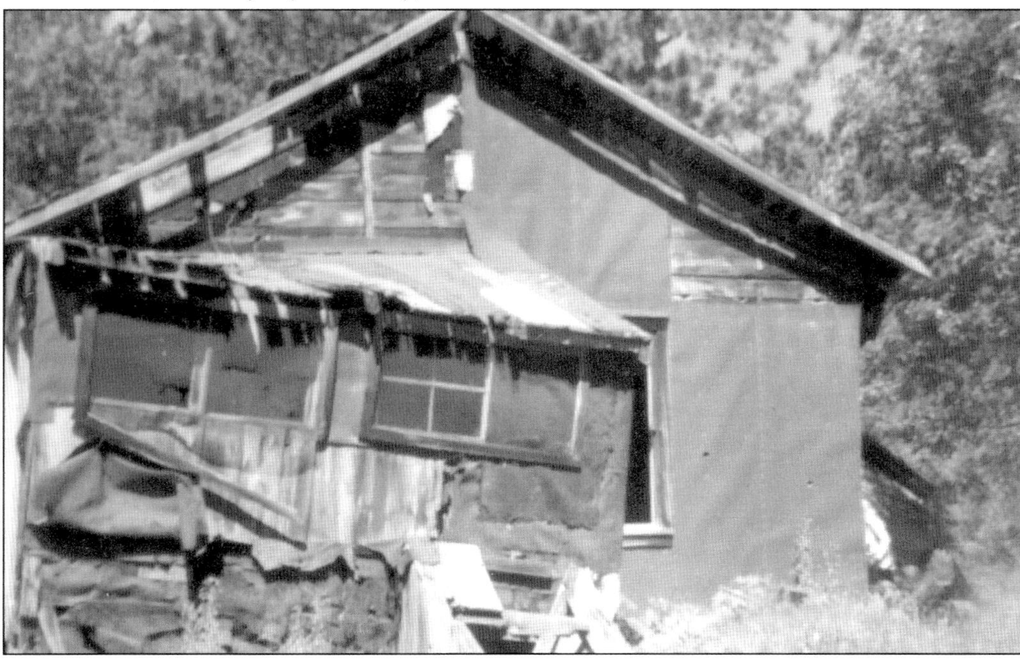

Before the tar papered houses were built, the placer miners lived in log cabins. Often all that was left behind in the tar papered homes when mining shut down were the cook stoves in the kitchens, abandoned vehicles, and unique fireplaces decorated with colorful minerals of varying hues. (Courtesy of Jan Cerney.)

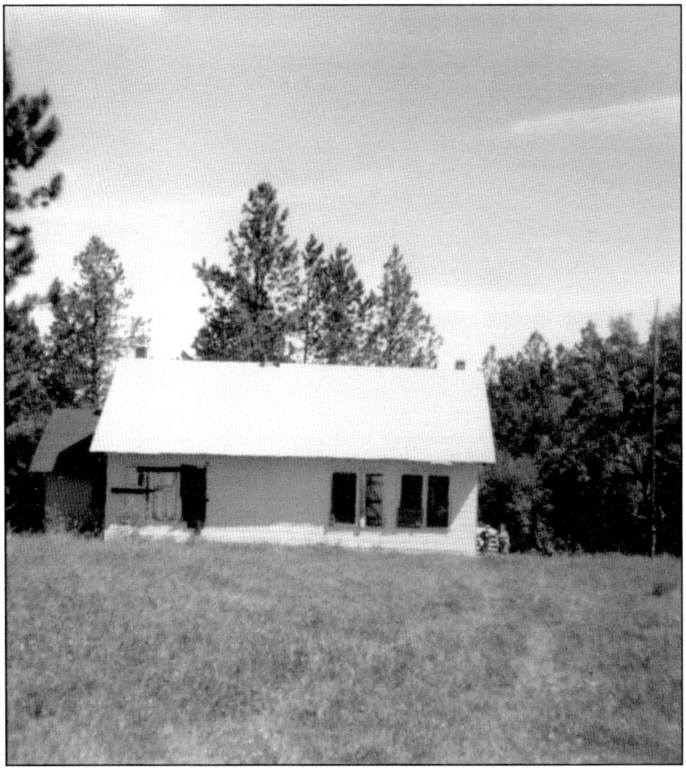

The town of Tinton was large enough to support a school. The Tinton School contained two big rooms and several smaller ones. The school also provided a meeting place for social functions. (Courtesy of Jan Cerney.)

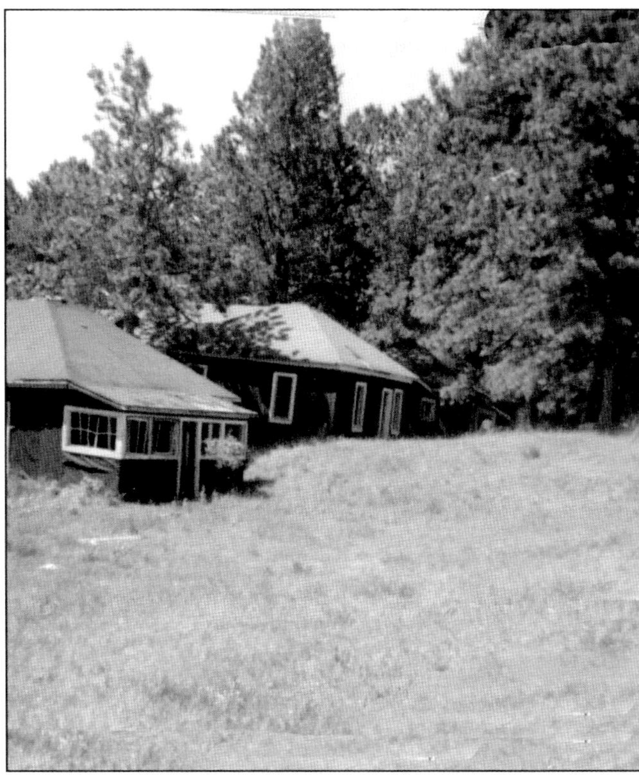

Tinton has been considered to be the best preserved ghost town in the Black Hills, however vandals have damaged the site. Many mining companies, including the American Tin Company, Black Hills Tin Company, and others, controlled the future of the town. In some years the mine made a profit and in others it did not. (Courtesy of Jan Cerney.)

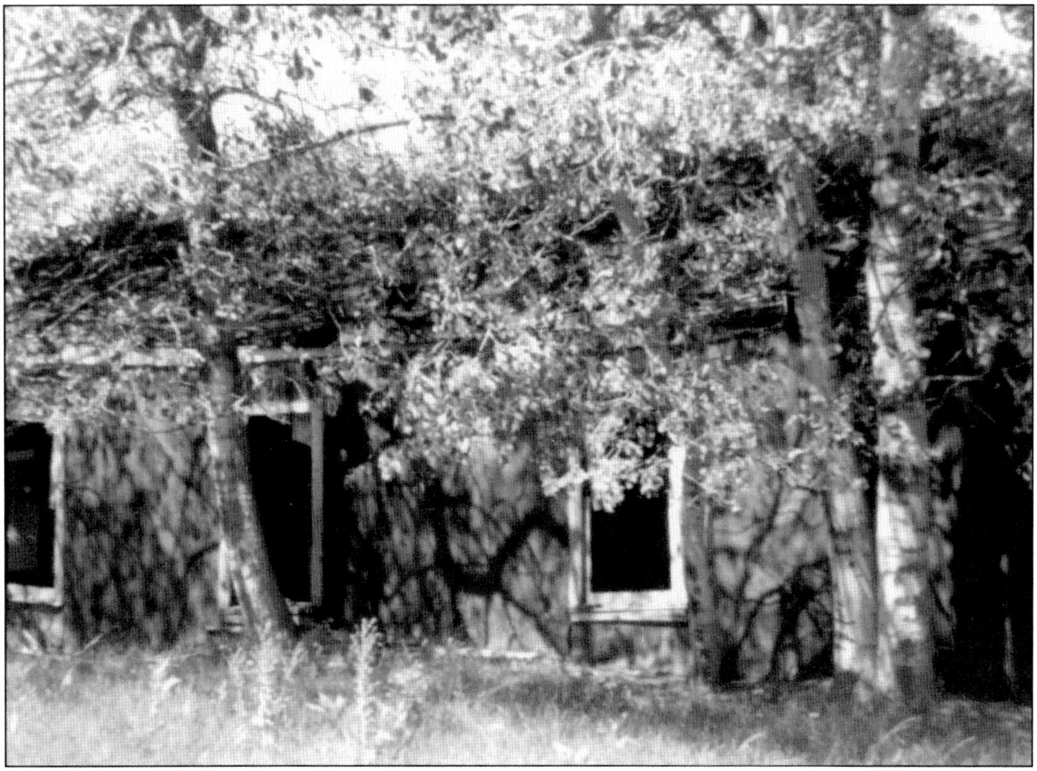

Trees nearly obliterate a dwelling in the ghost town of Tinton. Doors have been left open as if inviting closer inspection. Eventually all evidence of a once thriving mining town faded from the landscape. (Courtesy of Jan Cerney.)

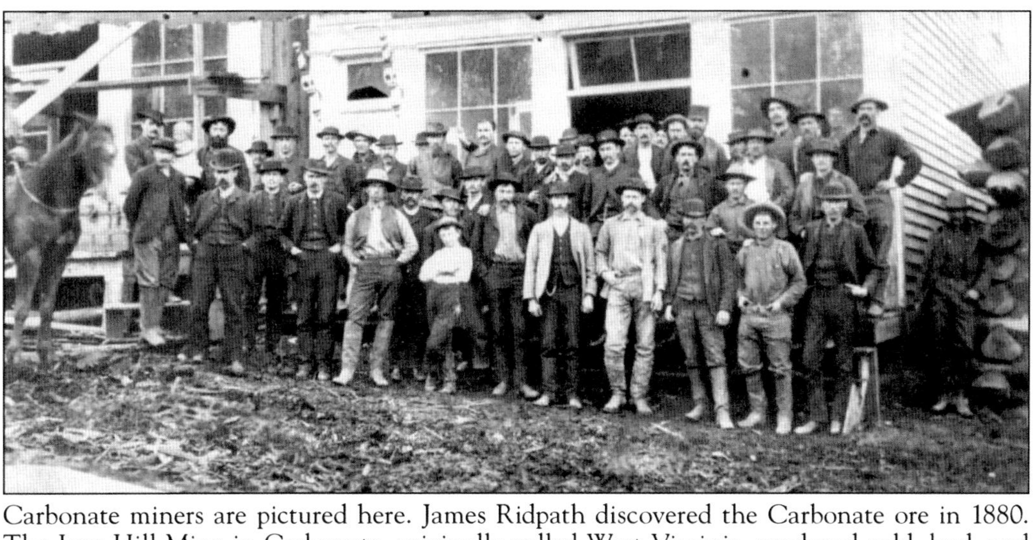

Carbonate miners are pictured here. James Ridpath discovered the Carbonate ore in 1880. The Iron Hill Mine in Carbonate, originally called West Virginia, produced gold, lead, and primarily silver between 1885 and 1891. The mine yielded $667,000 in its productive years. The Seabury-Calkins, Pocahontas, Spanish R., Union Hill, Richmond Hills, and other mining companies also mined for silver and gold in the area. The nearby smelter spewed arsenic fumes, which killed cats and caused sore throats and lung trouble in humans.

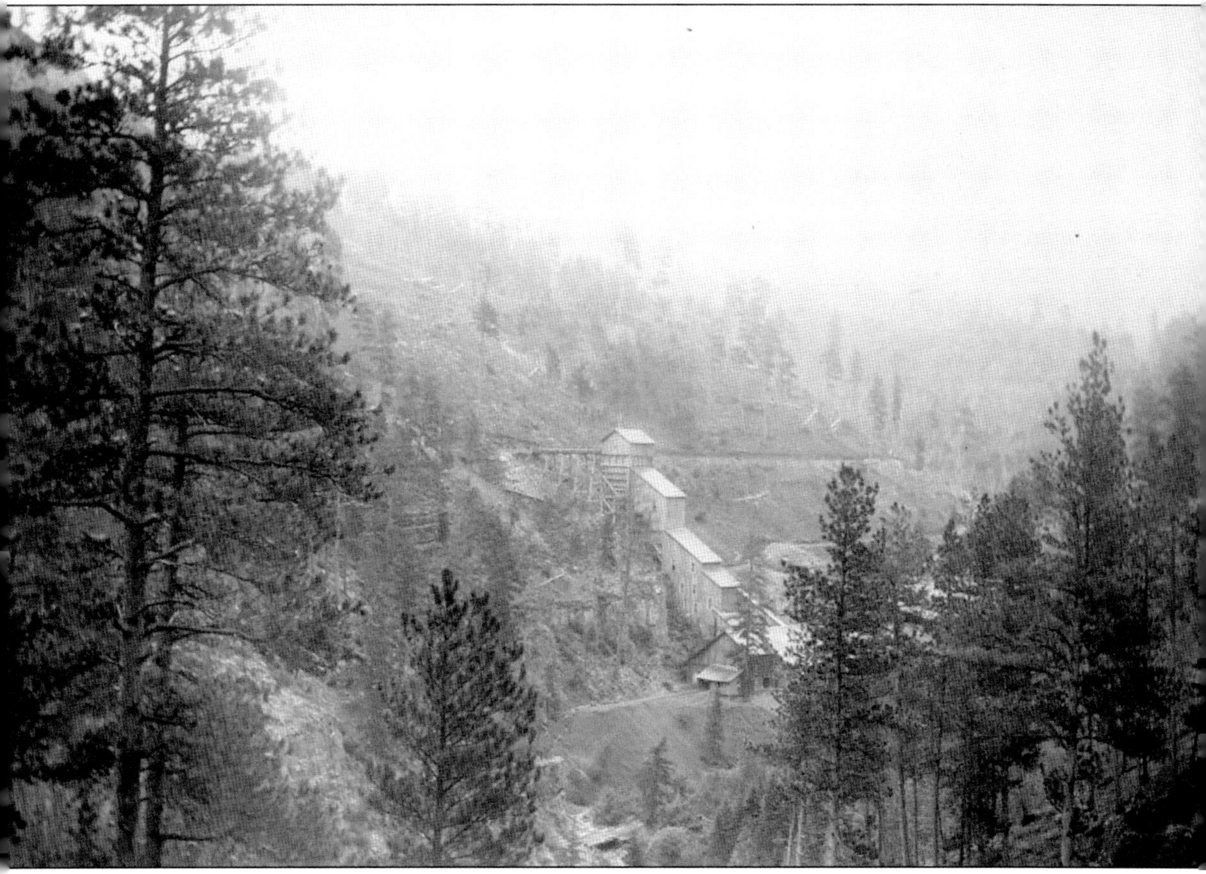

The Cleopatra Mine on Squaw Creek west of Carbonate may have been discovered as early as 1886, but it was newspaperman Richard Hughes, acting as secretary, and J. M. Lawson, as superintendent, with Eastern investors that built the mill on a steep mountainside sometime in the early 1900s. A million shares were sold at one dollar each. This picturesque cyanide mill only operated for 15 months until it shut down with a production sum of $200,000, which was considered a good return on the investment. Thousands of feet of tunnels were built to reach the ore veins. The deepest shaft was 100 feet. (Courtesy of the Minnilusa Historical Association.)

Roubaix, located near Nemo Road in Lawrence County, was named for Pierre Wilbeaux's hometown in France. Roubaix had a population of 500 in 1899. A post office, churches, newspaper, school, boarding house, and hospital completed the town. It was first known as Perry but when it was confused with the town of Terry, it was renamed. (Courtesy of Jan Cerney.)

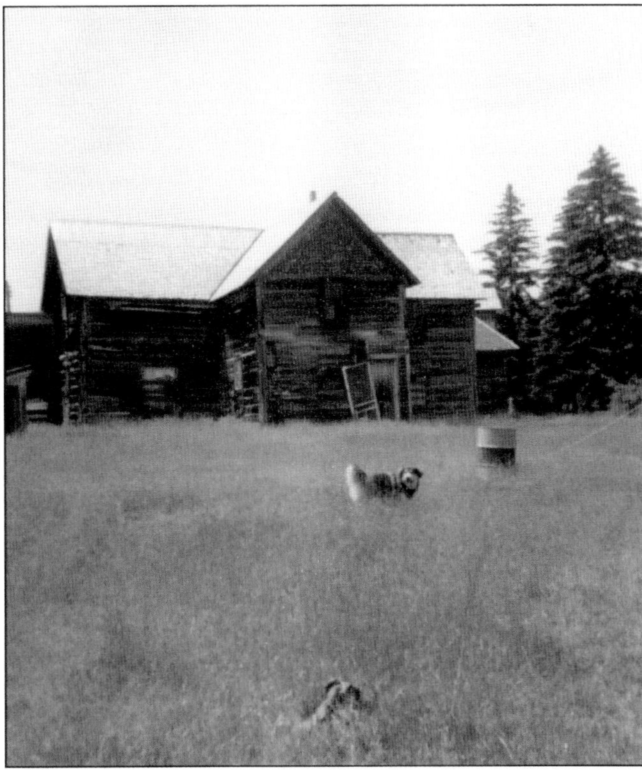

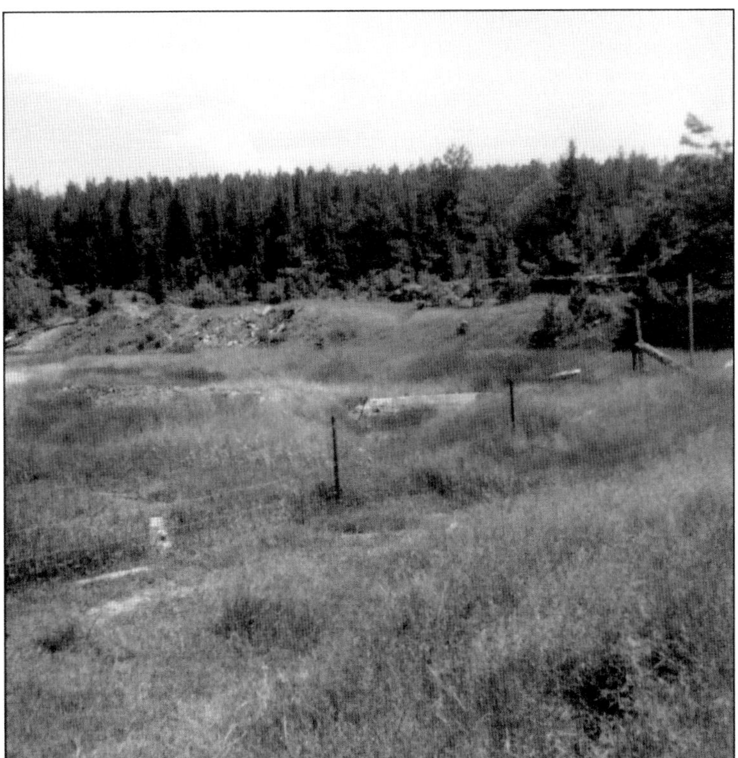

This is the site of the Uncle Sam mine, established in 1878 near Roubaix. Wilbeaux bought it in 1889 and took out $900,000 worth of gold by 1905. The mine was flooded in 1905. Excessive water caused problems and the mine was finally closed in 1937. (Courtesy of Jan Cerney.)

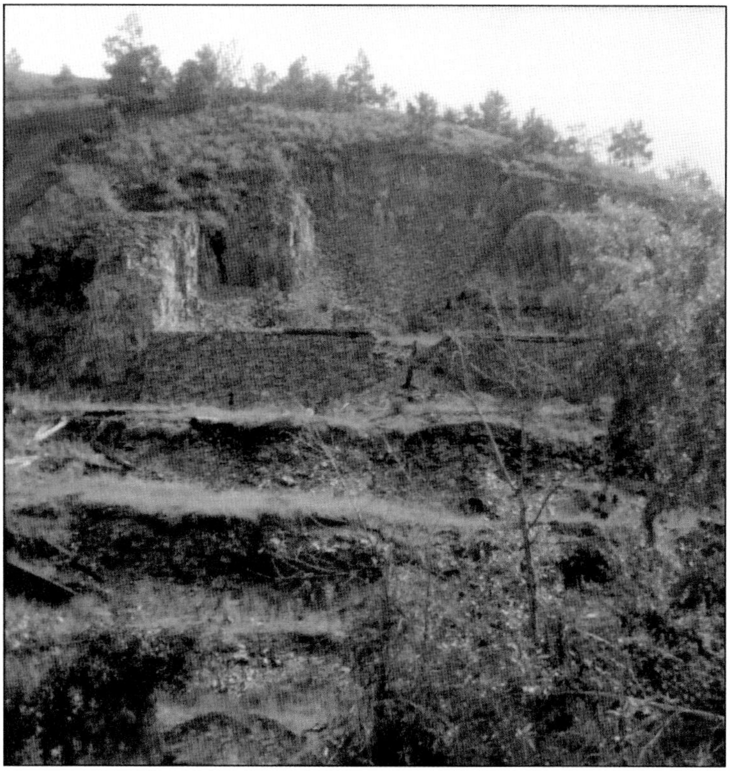

The mill at Maitland was located at this spot. At one time Maitland ranked third in gold production in the Black Hills. Miners staked claims in 1876, and in 1902, the claims were joined together to form the Penobscot Group. Alexander Maitland of Michigan and his sons acquired the group and operated a block of mines. Homestake mine eventually took them over for a while until the Canyon Corporation reactivated the mine. The mine ceased production in 1942 and burned to the ground in 1959. (Courtesy of Jan Cerney.)

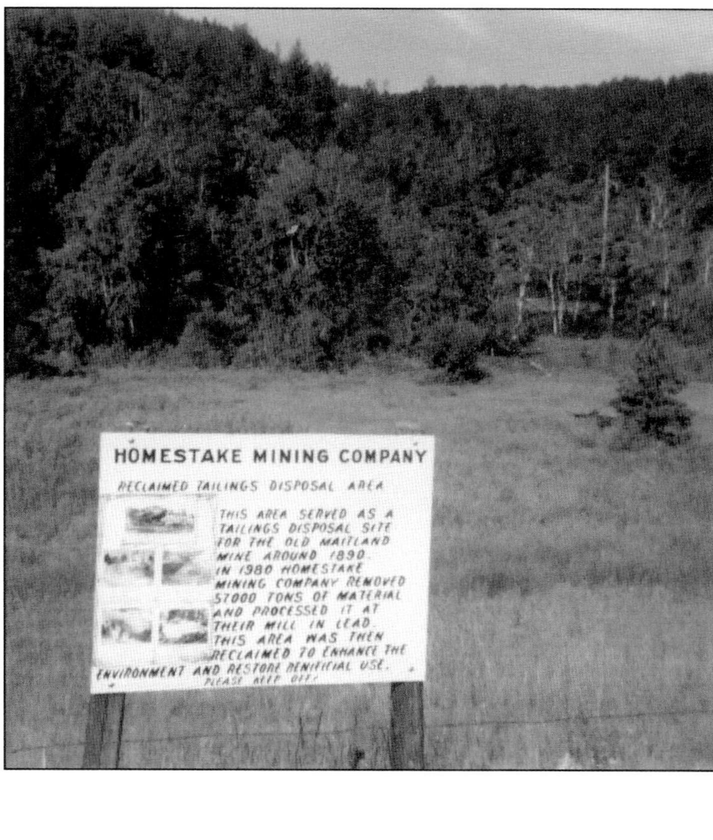

A sign identifies this area as "Homestake Mining Company Reclaimed Tailings Disposal Area. This area served as a tailings disposal site for the old Maitland Mine around 1890. In 1980, Homestake Mining Company removed 57,000 tons of material and processed it at their mill in Lead. This area was then reclaimed to enhance the environment and restore beneficial use. Please Keep off." (Courtesy of Jan Cerney.)

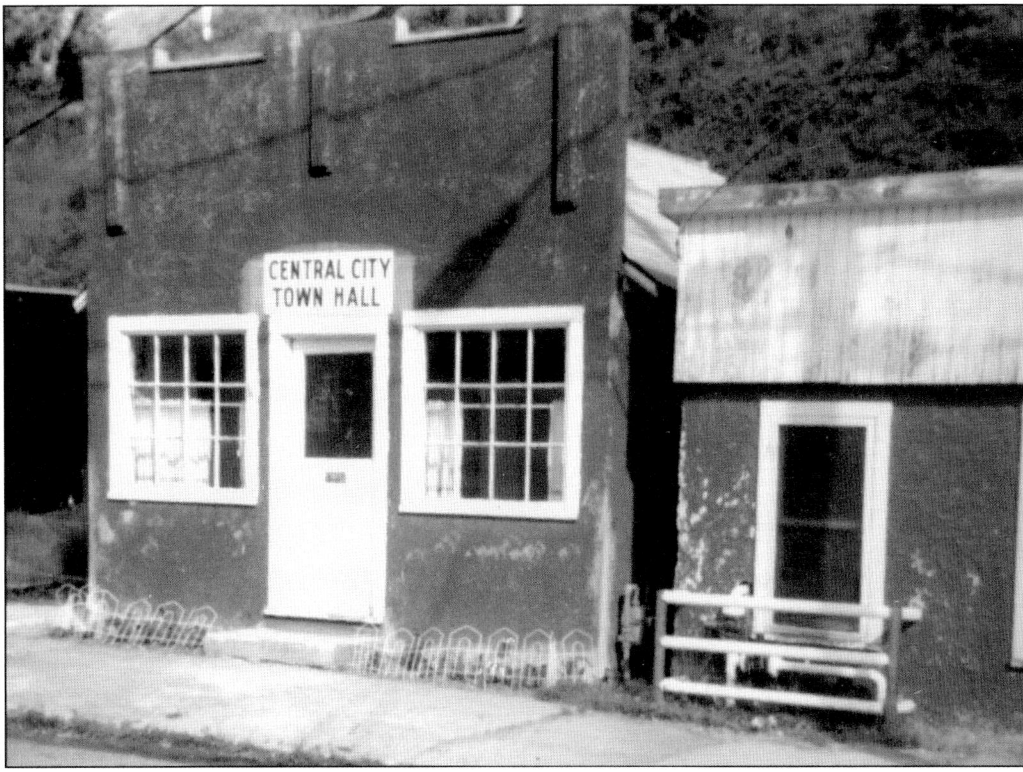

Nearly 3,000 people inhabited the newly formed town of Central City located between Lead and Deadwood. Stores, saloons, and hotels were established. A fire in 1888 destroyed most of the town, but it was rebuilt. (Courtesy of Jan Cerney.)

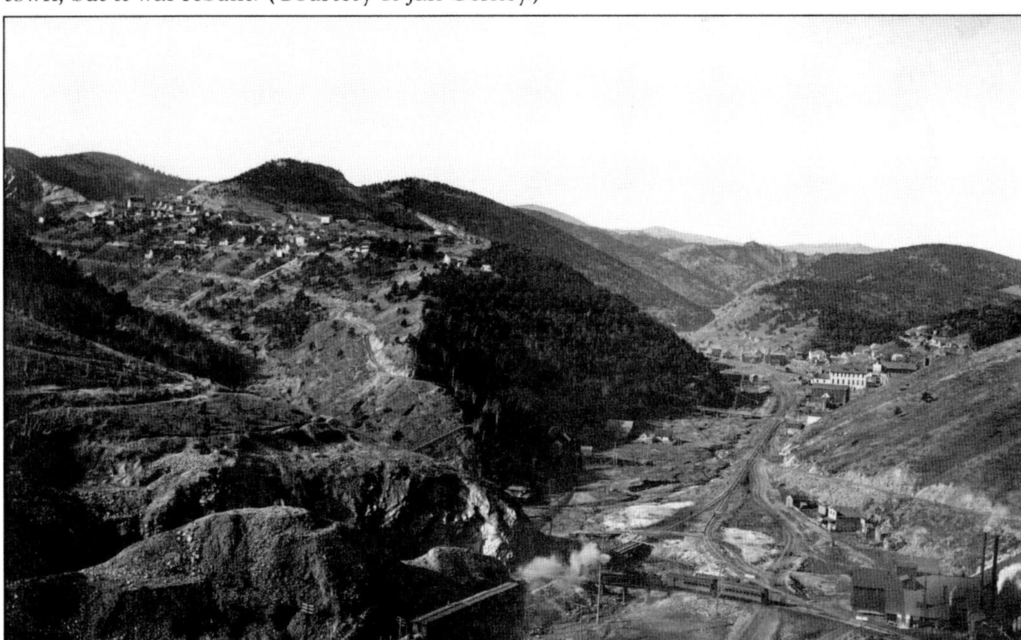

Towns were built all along the gulches. Pictured here are Terraville, Central City, and Black Tail.

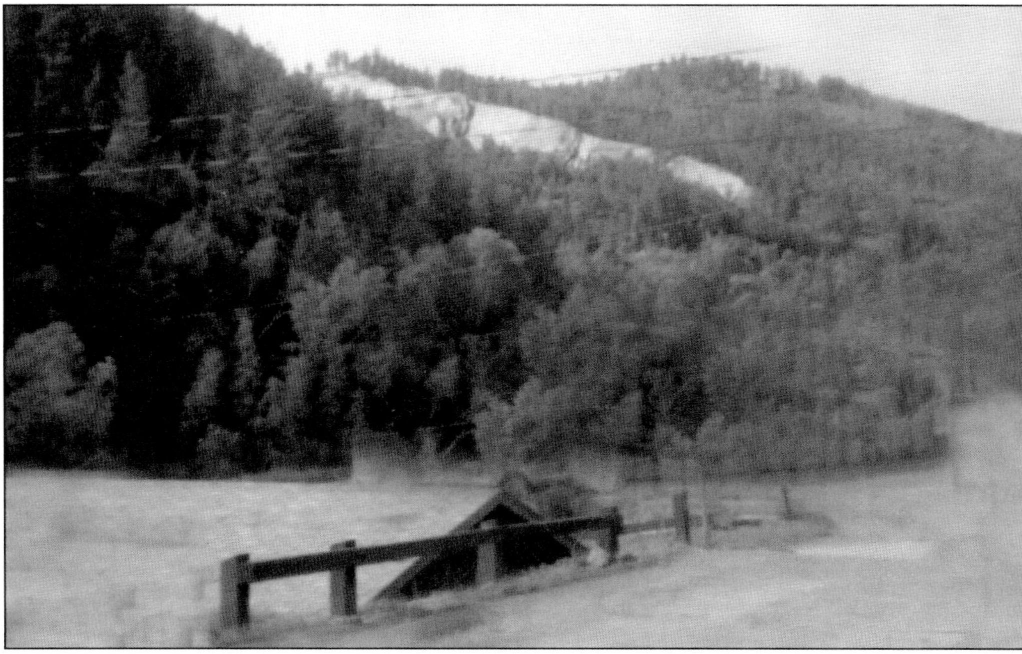

The most famous open-cut mine near Central City was the Father DeSmet Mine, founded around 1876. It became part of the Homestake's ledge, the mother lode. The conglomerates found there and the hard-rock lodes from Central City through Terraville on to Lead were the origin of the placer gold found in the surrounding creeks. (Courtesy of Jan Cerney.)

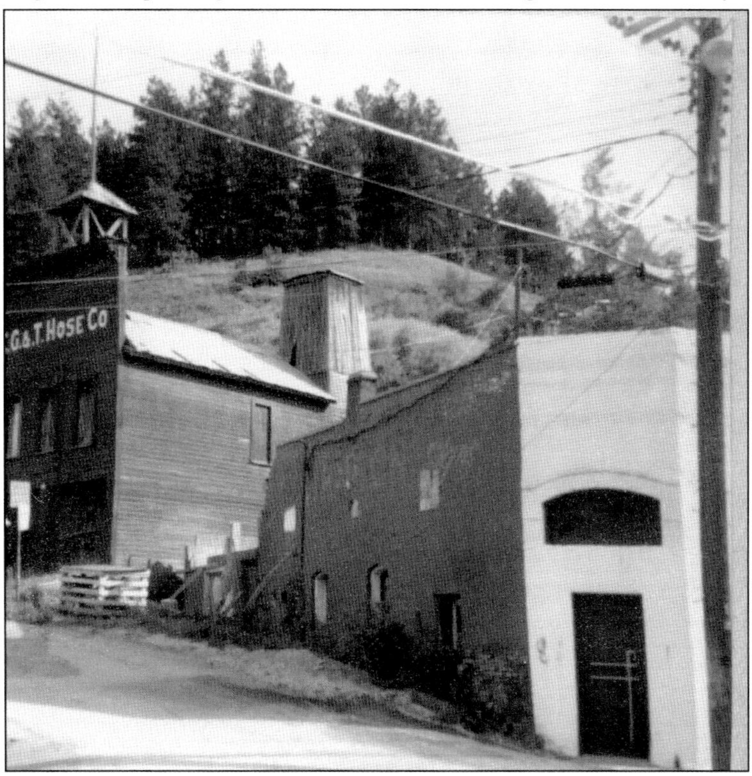

The CG&T Hose Company was organized after the 1888 fire. Terraville, Golden Gate, and Central City organized a hose company, which won the state championship in the 200-yard hub-and-hub race. Two teams, timed by a watch, would run 600 feet and lay out 250 feet of hose. They then spun on the nozzle and started a stream of water. The team with the fastest time won. (Courtesy of Jan Cerney.)

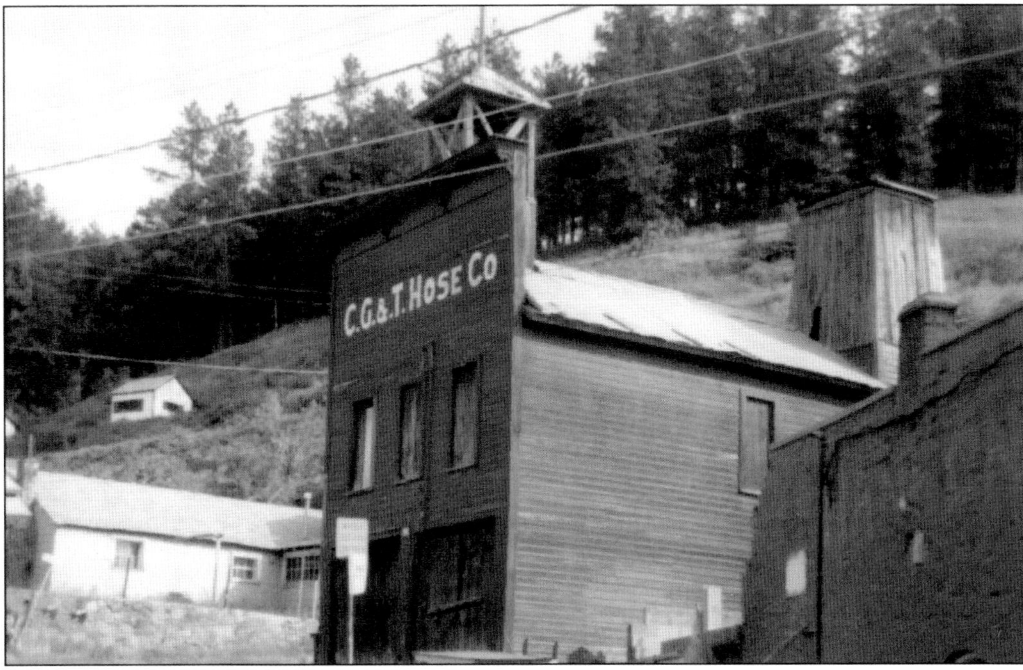

Hose companies organized all over the hills to fight fires that had burned so many towns during the gold rush days. When not combating fires, hose companies participated in competitions and planned social events. (Courtesy of Jan Cerney.)

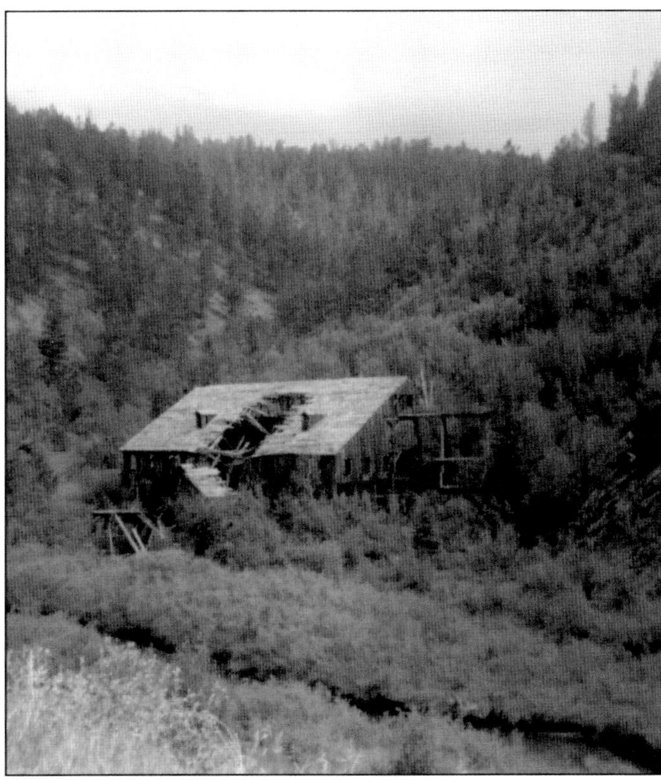

Although not immediately in the Spearfish vicinity, the Standby Mill was a good example of a stamp mill. Dating from the 1880s, the Standby Mill survived into the 1980s. Artists and photographers visited the picturesque Standby often. The heavy snows during the winter of 1982–1983 caused a section of the roof to cave in. Because of its deteriorating and unsafe condition, the mill was demolished in 1987. (Courtesy of Jan Cerney.)

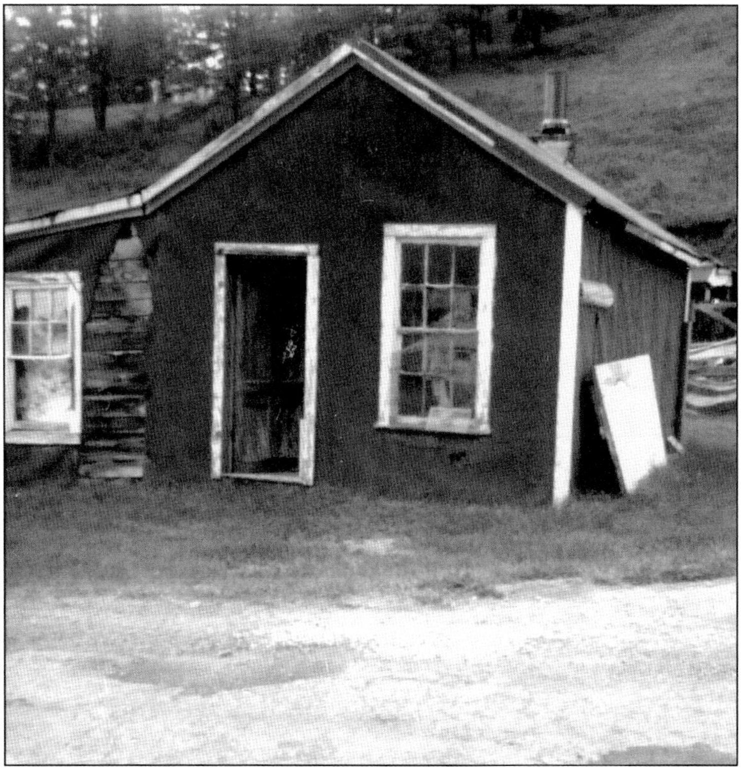

Richard Hughes and M. Rochford founded the mining town of Rochford in 1877 after they discovered gold bearing ore on Montezuma Hill and gold in Rapid Creek. Rochford boomed in 1878 with 500 settlers. The Evangeline and the Minnesota Mines were constructed in 1878, soon followed by the Standby from 1879 to 1880. By 1900, the population of Rochford had decreased rapidly to only 48 residents. (Courtesy of Jan Cerney.)

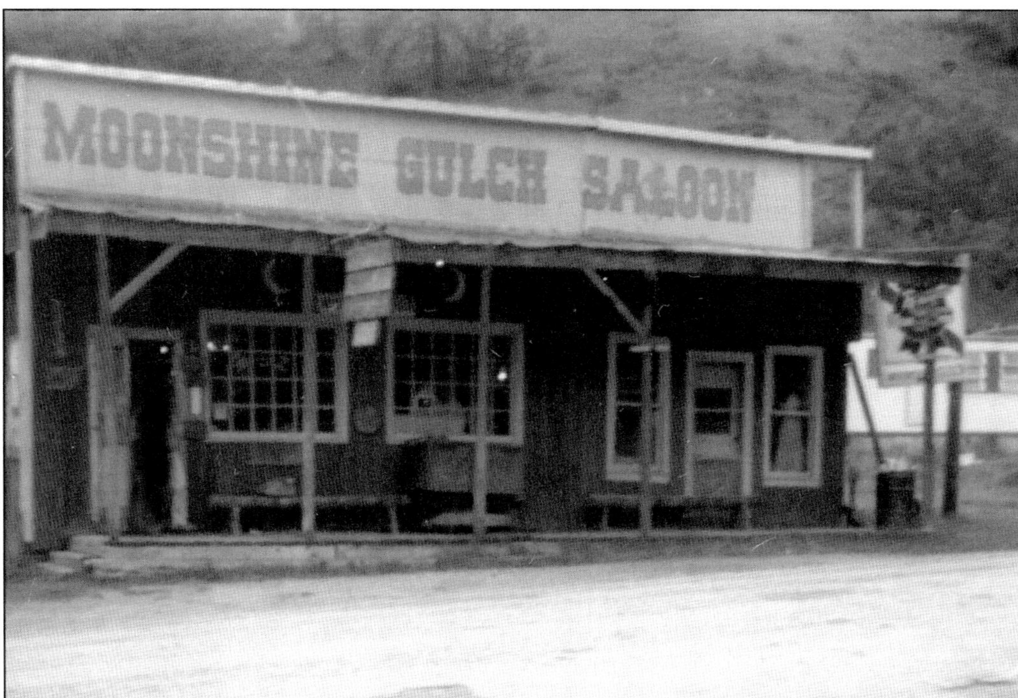

The Moonshine Gulch Saloon in Rochford was typical of the many saloons of the mining area. (Courtesy of Jan Cerney.)

Three

EARLY SPEARFISH

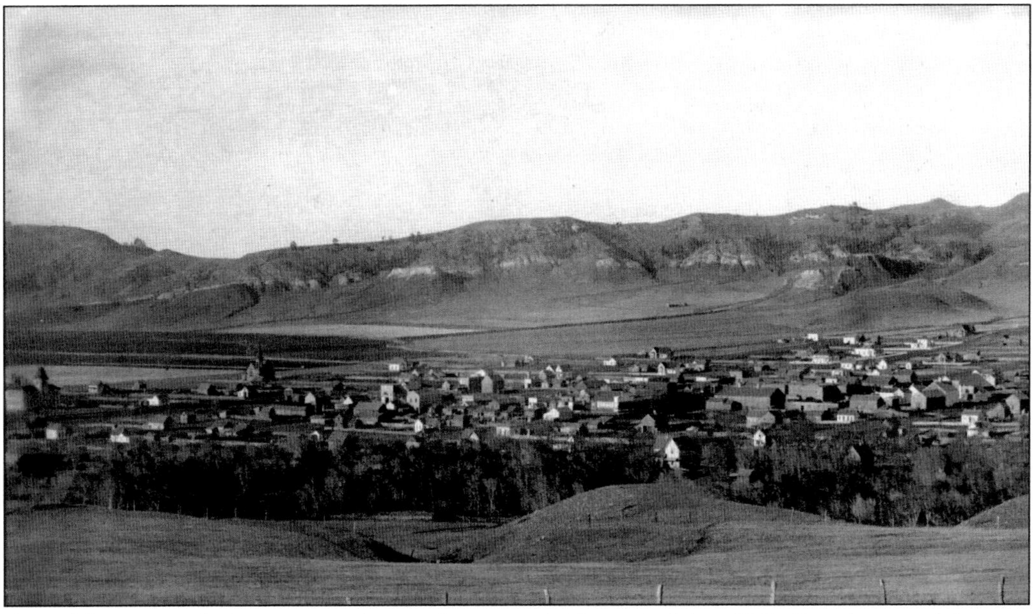

Spearfish, pictured above in territorial days, was laid out in May 1876. Ranchers and farmers relocated to the lush valley. An 1887 issue of the *Black Hills Daily Times* reported that "the 'Queen City' [Spearfish] is preparing for a prosperous era. Buildings are going up by the dozens; awnings are coming down; twelve-foot sidewalks are underway and an air of progress and prosperity is scented everywhere."

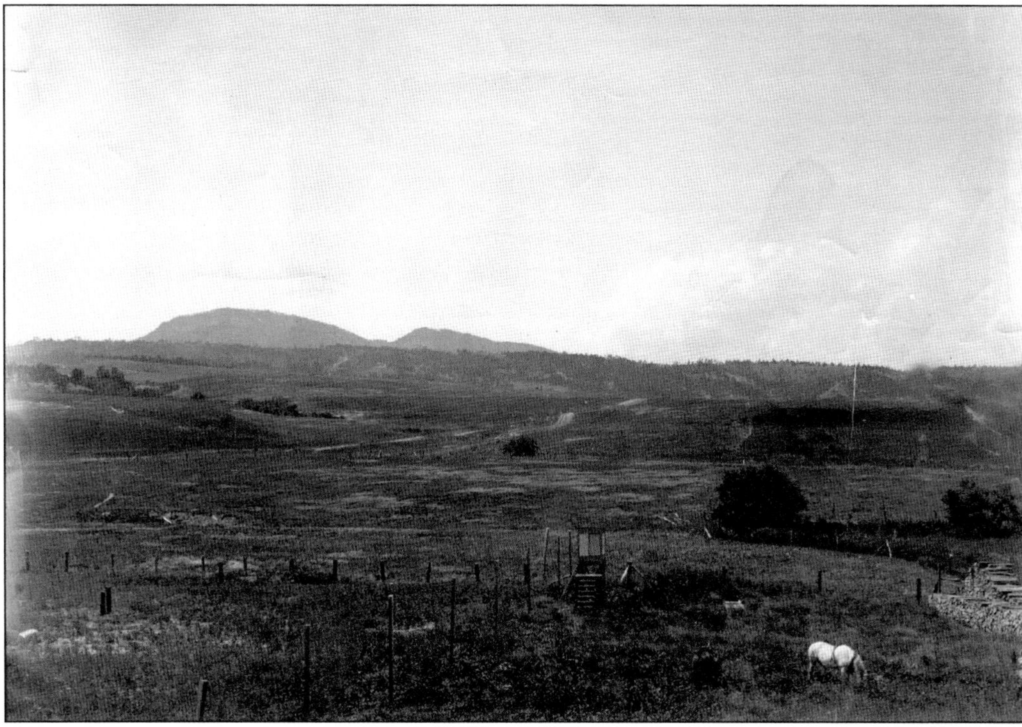

Gardening and farming in Spearfish valley began soon after the town was established. However, farmers and ranchers kept a lookout for Native Americans raiding the countryside. The frequent Native American attacks prompted the town's people to build a stockade that occupied a quarter of a block in the center of town, large enough to accommodate the settlers and their horses and cattle. Farmers and ranchers used the stockade for protection also.

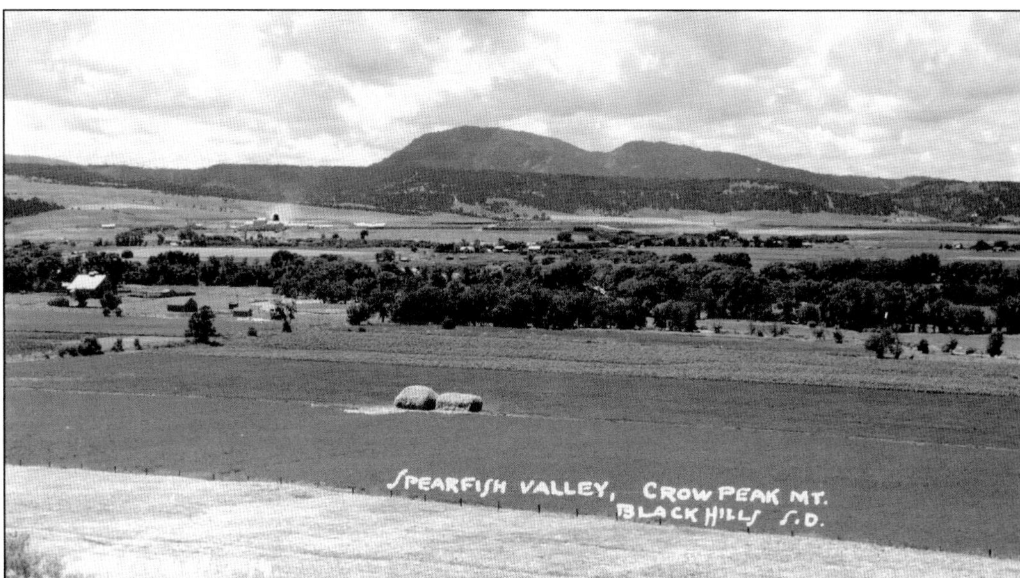

This photograph of Spearfish valley is in the approximate area as the previous photograph, although taken at a much later date by Thomas Odell. Crow Peak can be seen in the background.

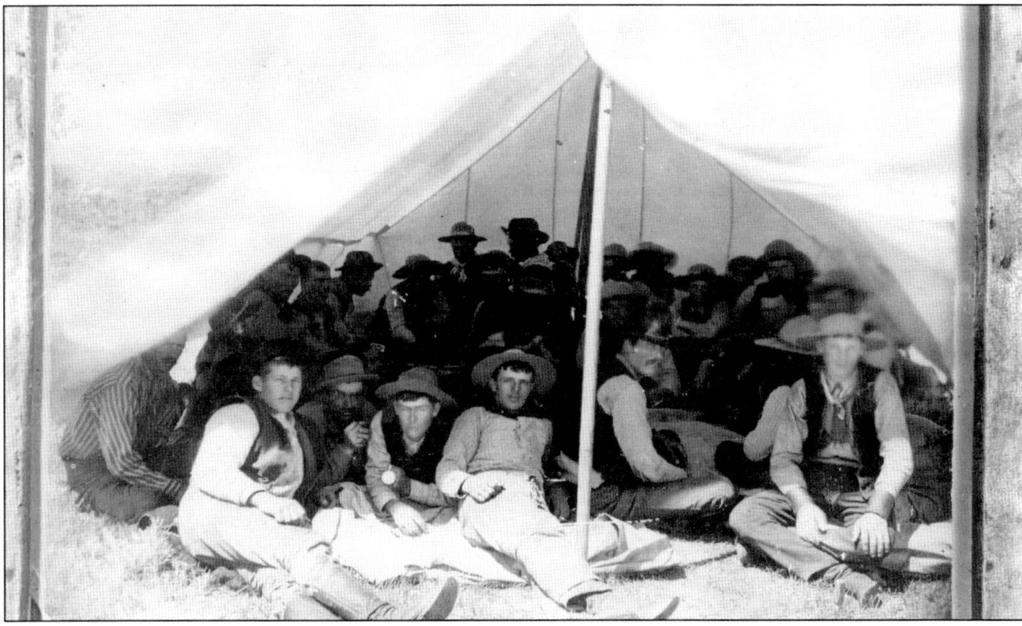

This photograph shows cowboys taking shelter in a tent. Cattlemen such as Frank Moulton, Milton C. Connors, Henry Weare, Jesse Driskill, and others were among the many cattlemen who brought cattle to the Black Hills from 1875 to 1878. More than 100,000 head of cattle populated the Black Hills region by the end of 1879, according to historians. It was men such as these who set the stage for the range cattle industry in the Dakota Territory.

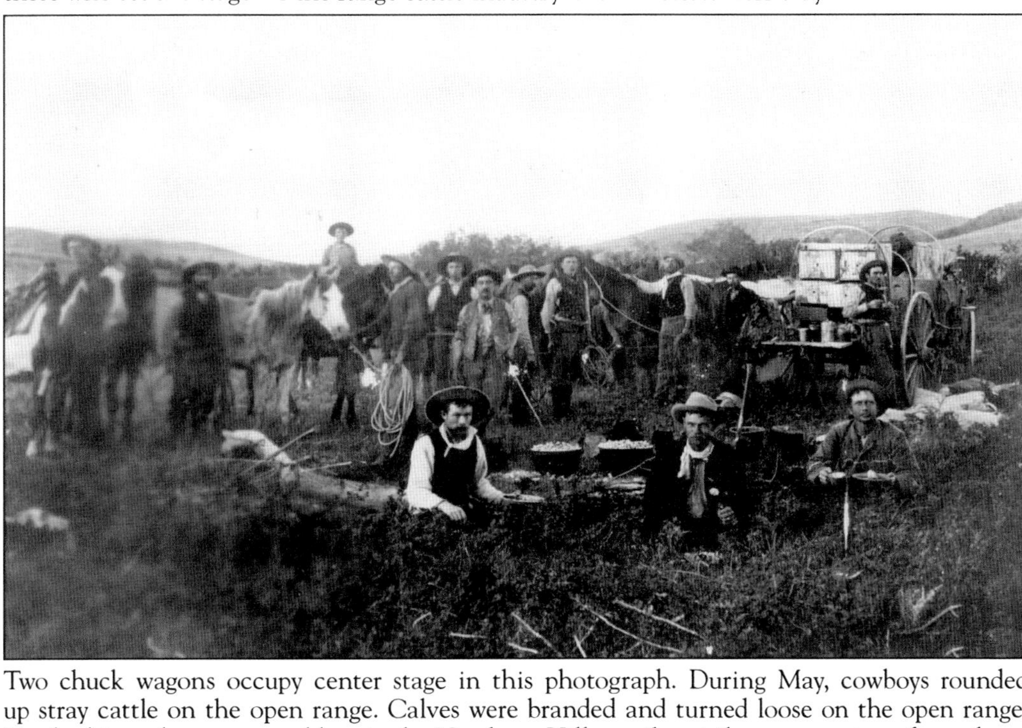

Two chuck wagons occupy center stage in this photograph. During May, cowboys rounded up stray cattle on the open range. Calves were branded and turned loose on the open range. Cattle thieves became a problem in the Northern Hills until a vigilante committee formed and searched out and punished the cattle rustlers.

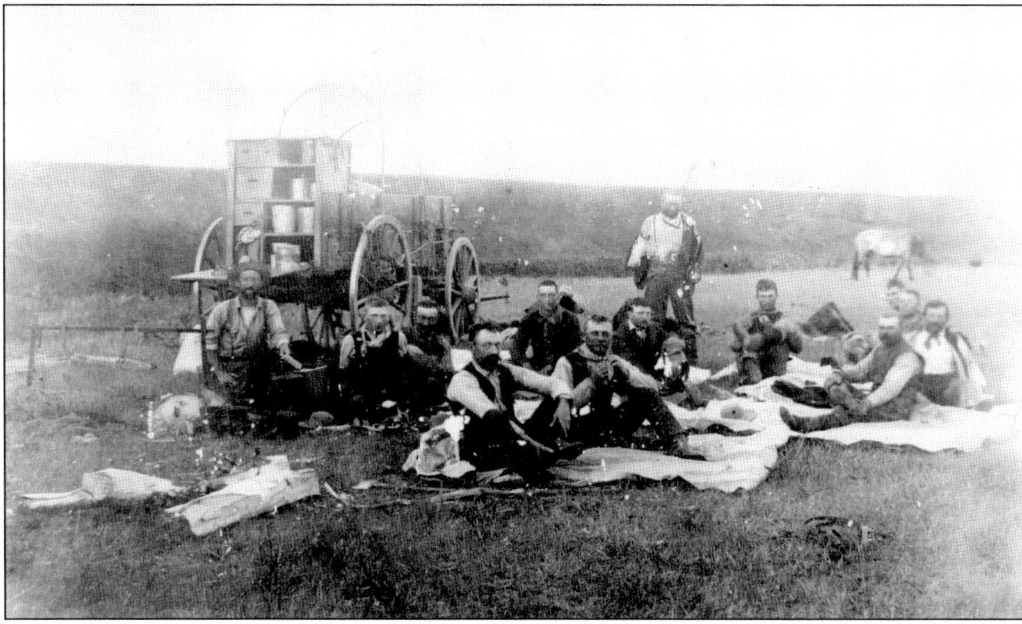

Cowboys bed down for the night in this western scene. During roundup time, cowboys put in 16- to 18-hour days. Tom Sweeny, a successful Rapid City businessman and cattle man had this to say about the roundup cowboys: They "are the jolliest and cleverest class of men . . . they are sometimes compelled to ride all night, their rest is not so well provided for, although an old cowboy will sleep in his saddle if badly worn with fatigue."

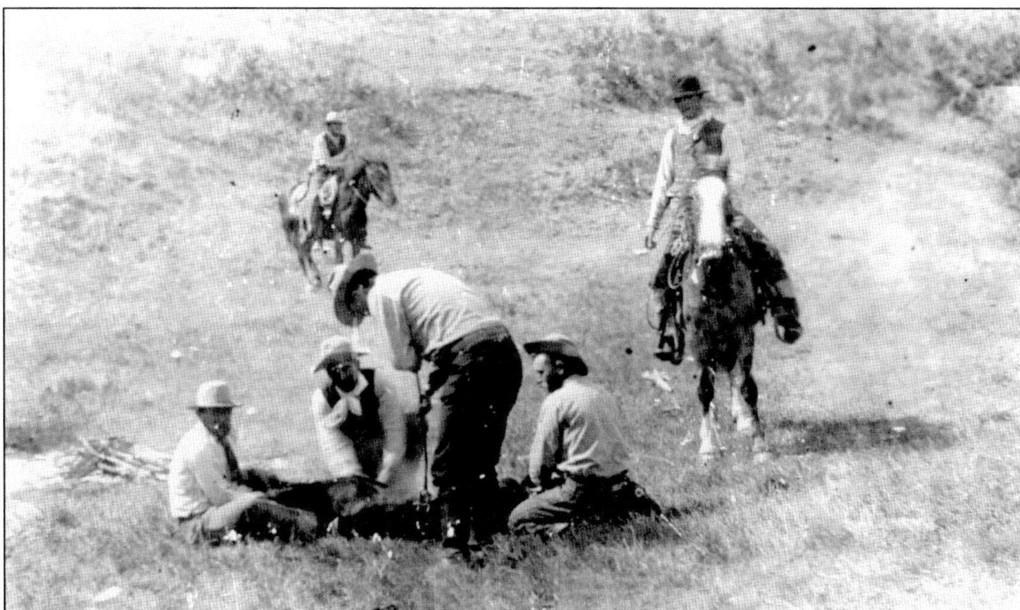

Cowhands brand calves in this photograph. The first brands to appear in a Dakota Territory newspaper, the *Black Hills Journal,* appeared in the November 13, 1880, issue. Cattlemen found the need to organize and form an association. The first Black Hills Stock Association meeting was held November 26, 1880, in Rapid City. Jesse Driskill, Milton C. Connors, and Henry Weare of Spearfish were in attendance.

Jesse Driskill, pictured with his wife, was one of Spearfish's successful cattlemen. The Driskill brothers brought up cattle from Texas and Oklahoma each spring on the Western Cattle Trail. They summered a portion of the lanky longhorns in the Tinton area and rounded up what they wanted and shipped them out by railroad to Chicago from Savoy. Sources say the Driskill brothers had around 30,000 cattle in their herd.

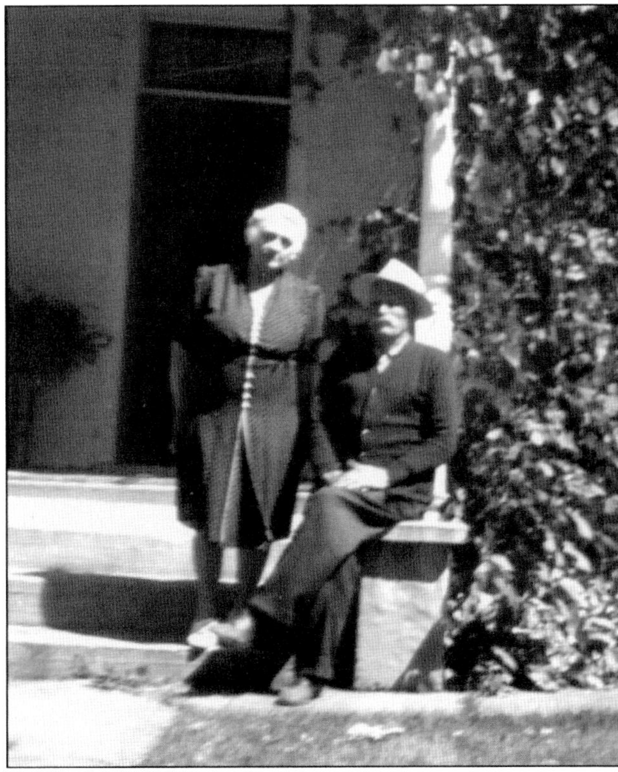

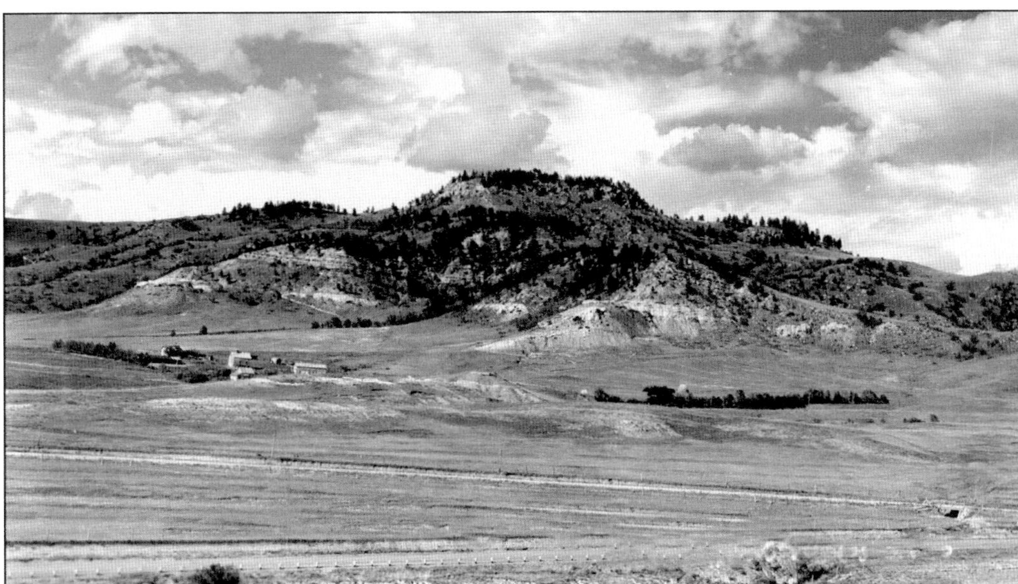

Lookout Mountain has been mentioned often in early historical accounts. The famous Thoen Stone was found here and rustlers were hanged here. Spearfish vigilantes took care of two cattle rustlers, Beans Davis and George Keating, while the two camped at the foot of Lookout Mountain. They earned the distinction of being the first men hanged for cattle stealing in the recorded history of Dakota Territory. (Photograph by Thomas Odell.)

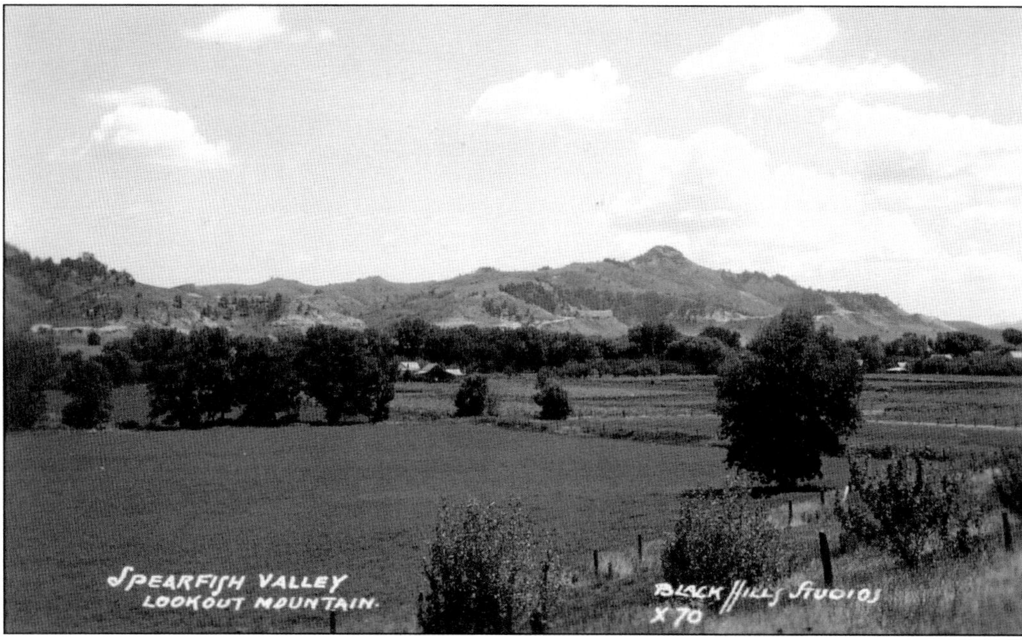

The 10-mile-long and over-one-mile-wide Spearfish valley was irrigated and produced gardens, orchards, vineyards, grain, corn, and lush grass. In the early days, the valley supplied food for the Deadwood-Lead mining communities. (Photograph by Thomas Odell.)

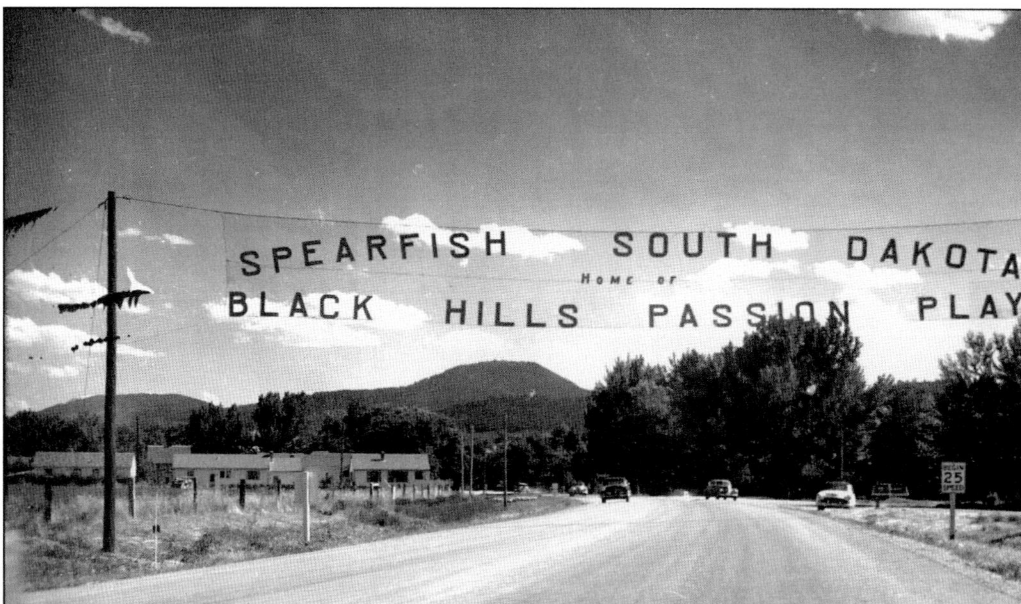

Located in the Northern Hills, Spearfish nestles in a picturesque valley, rimmed by Spearfish Mountain, Crow Peak, and Lookout Mountain. The crowning effect of the mountains has given Spearfish the title the "Queen City." The first use of the title has been attributed to Judge W. W. Bradley, an 1870s Spearfish lawyer. During a Fourth of July speech in 1878, he welcomed the crowd to Spearfish and then added the "Queen City of the Black Hills." From that time on the sobriquet stuck.

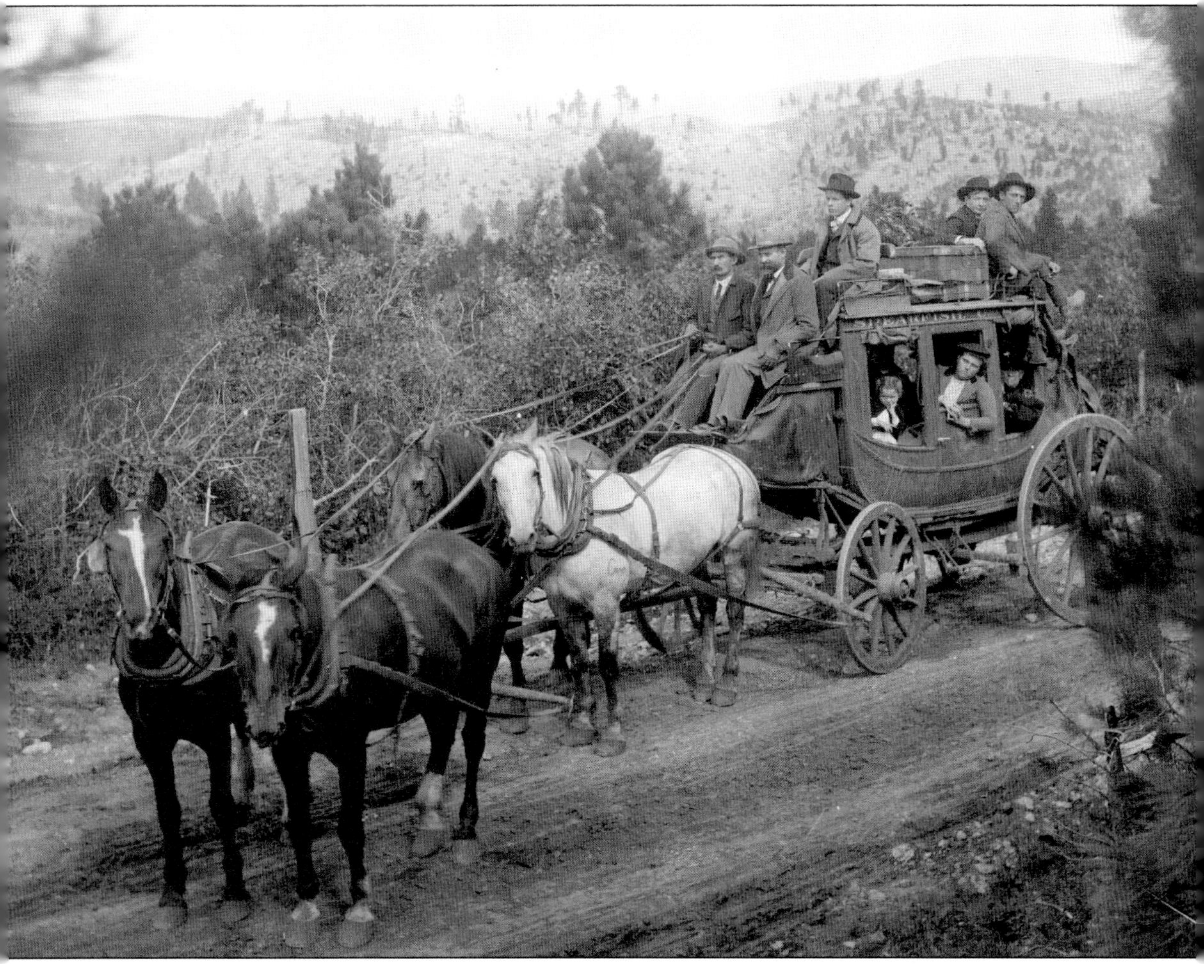

Pictured is the Spearfish–Deadwood stagecoach. Harvey Fellows, pictured here as the stage driver, drove the stage for over 30 years and logged in over 500,000 miles. Hank Monk also drove for the stage line in 1881. The *Black Hills Daily Times* had this to say about him: "His benign countenance adorned the pilot house and hurricane deck of that craft as she appeared in sight this morning. He has an engagement for the season." James Rogers and Spear placed an advertisement in an 1884 newspaper listing themselves as proprietors of the stage line. Rogers started the stage line and then later sold it to John McClintock who took charge of the Spearfish–Deadwood stagecoaches with headquarters in Deadwood. He ran it for 25 years. The stage transported an average of 10 passengers per day, which totaled up to 90,000 passengers when McClintock ran the stage line. The stage carried mail, express, and freight also. No lives were lost, there were few accidents, and no holdups were reported.

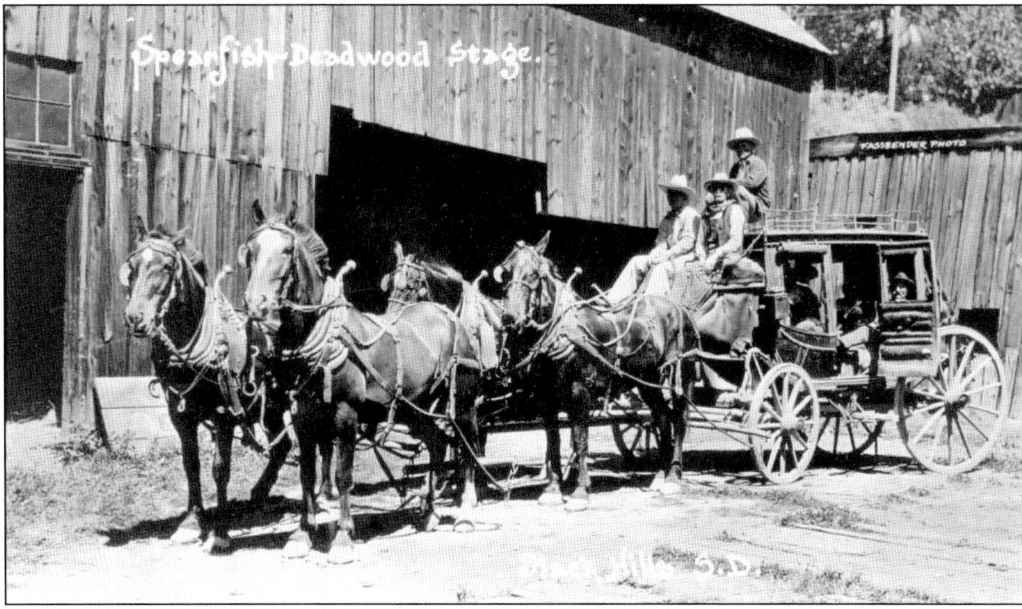

The Spearfish–Deadwood stage comes out of retirement in this 1946–1947 scene. The stage from Spearfish to Deadwood ended its regular runs in 1913. Most stagecoach service to Deadwood ended in 1890 with the arrival of the railroad. The stage took three hours to arrive at its destination over a rugged trail. According to the *Black Hills Daily Times*, "Coaches leave Spearfish daily, Sunday excepted, at 7 o'clock a.m. and 2 p.m. Coaches leave Deadwood daily, Sunday excepted, at 8 o'clock a.m. and 2 p.m. On Sundays a coach leaves Deadwood at 8 o'clock a.m., and leaves Spearfish at 3 p.m. Tickets for sale at the Spearfish Hotel in Spearfish and at the Wentworth Hotel in Deadwood."

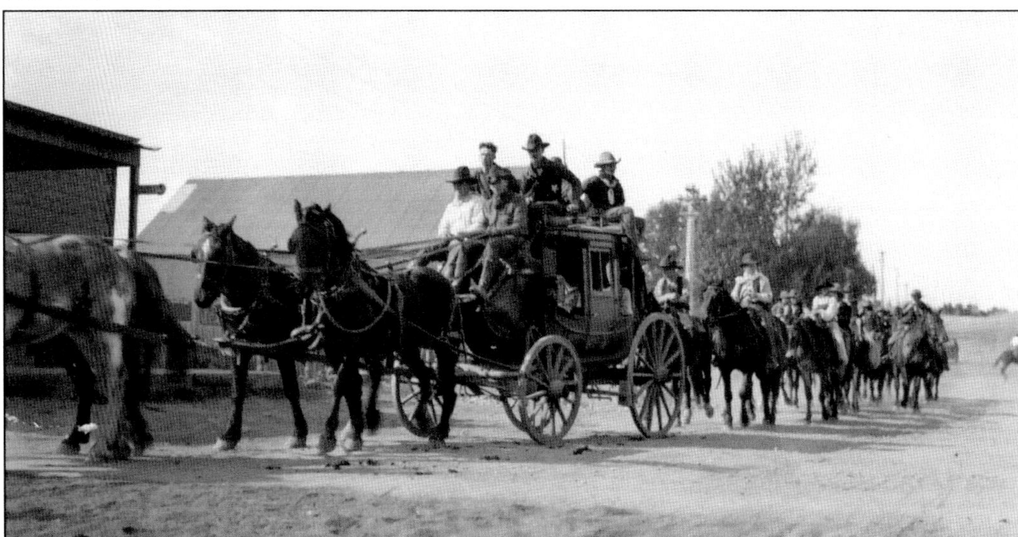

The Spearfish–Deadwood stage appears here in 1948. This Concord coach was built by Abbott-Downing in Concord, New Hampshire, in 1890 and then shipped to the Black Hills Stage Company of Rapid City. For some time the stage was housed in the city park. The Naja Shrine Cowboys restored the coach, and now it is on display at the High Plains Heritage Museum in Spearfish.

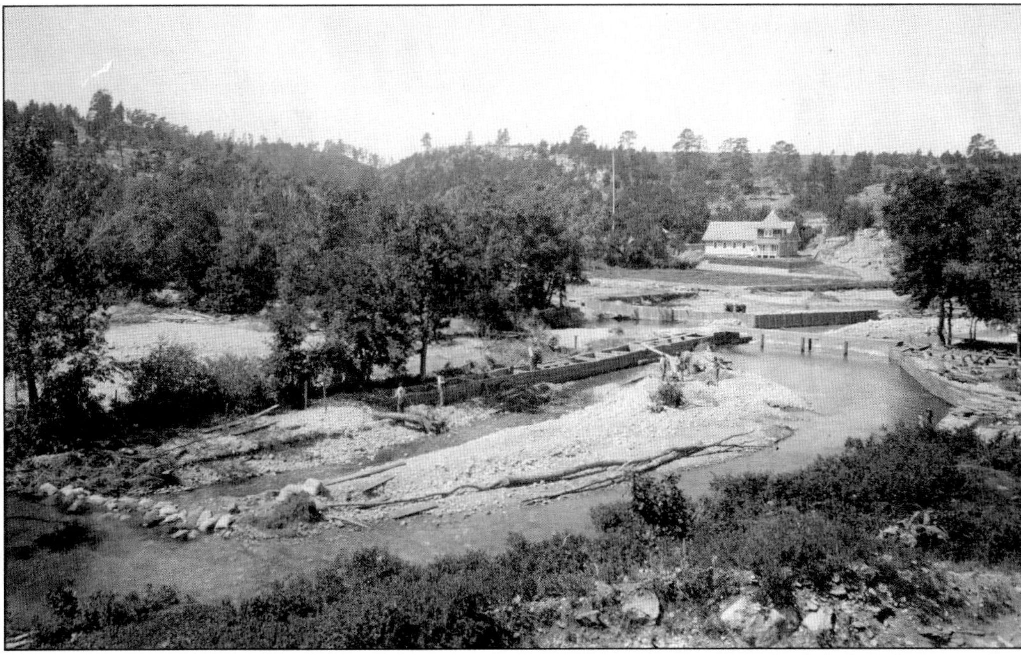

An early 1890 United States congressional bill funded the Spearfish fish hatchery. Dewitt Clinton Booth became the hatchery's first superintendent in 1899 and would remain there for 34 years. Chubs, dace, and suckers were the only fish swimming in Black Hills streams before the first stocking of trout at Cleghorn Springs near Rapid City in 1886.

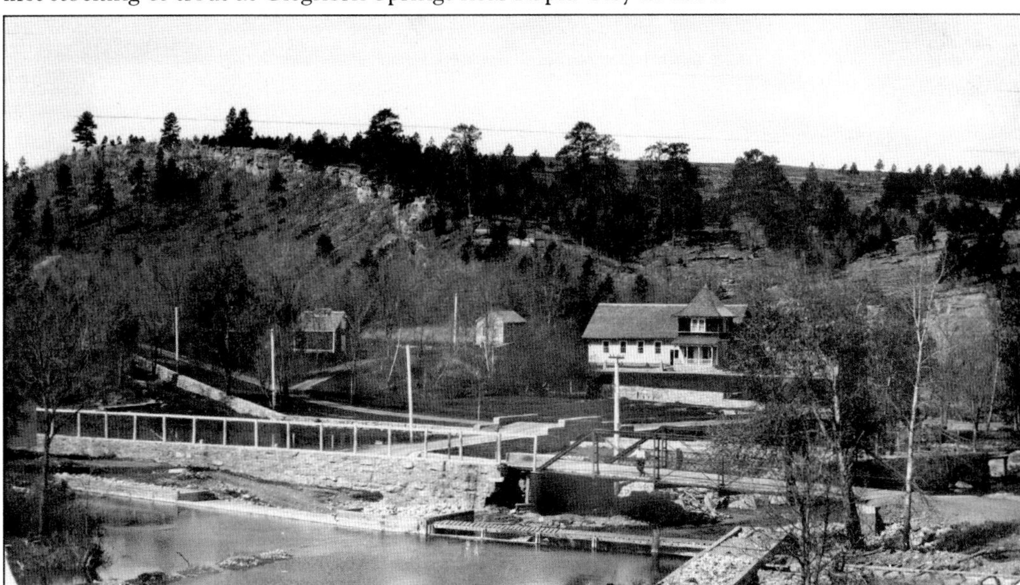

The fish hatchery building was designed in 1899 in Victorian style, common to all fish hatcheries in the United States. Seventeen ponds were constructed to accommodate 100,000 fish eggs. A flash flood, only days after the hatchery opened, swept away the eggs and deposited debris from a former sawmill on the site. It filled the spring reservoir and left sediment in the ponds and hatching troughs. Under the direction of Booth, the hatchery built storm channels, bridges, and bulkheads constructed of limestone rock and cement to combat the periodic flooding.

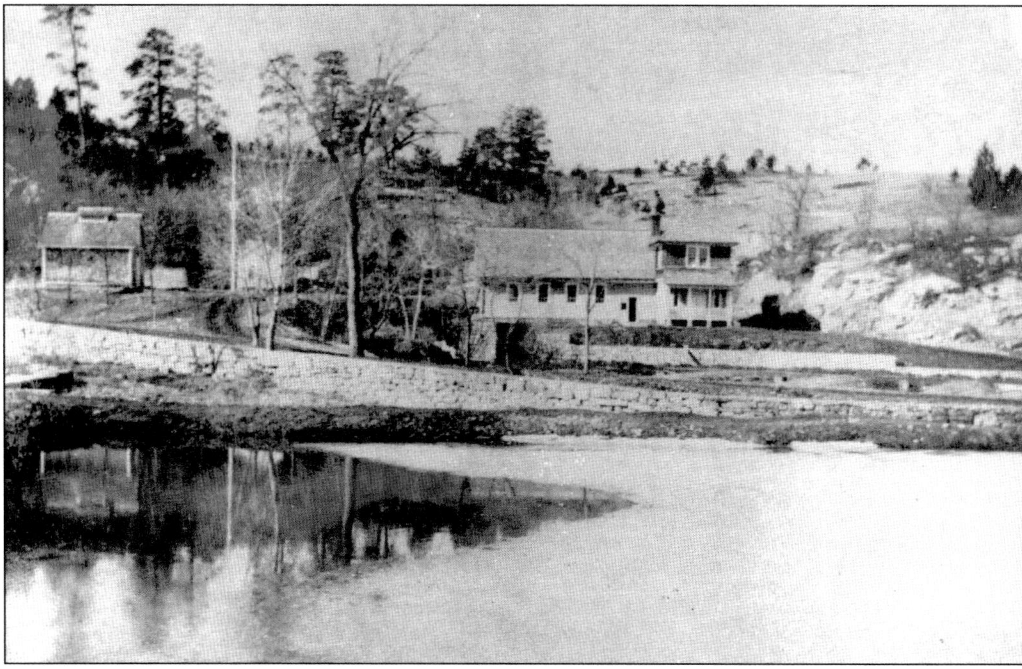

The first hatchery trout were released in April 1900. Three-inch trout, placed in milk cans, were loaded on wagons and transported to Whitewood, Spearfish, and Iron Creek. Later special railroad fish cars would transport fish to farther destinations.

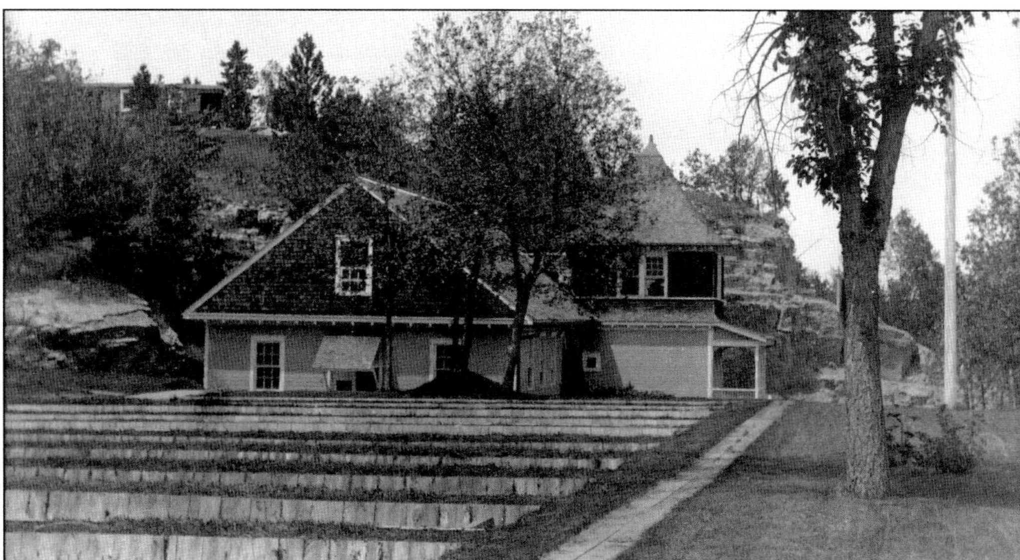

The Victorian-style fish hatchery, now a living fishery museum, was established in 1896 for the purpose of propagating and stocking trout in the Black Hills of South Dakota and Wyoming. The hatchery operated in this capacity until the mid-1980s and now is a museum with the goal of preserving the United States Fish and Wildlife Services historic and cultural heritage and in providing interpretive and educational programs. The hatchery still rears trout for the Black Hills. The museum has the largest collection of fishery history and artifacts in the nation.

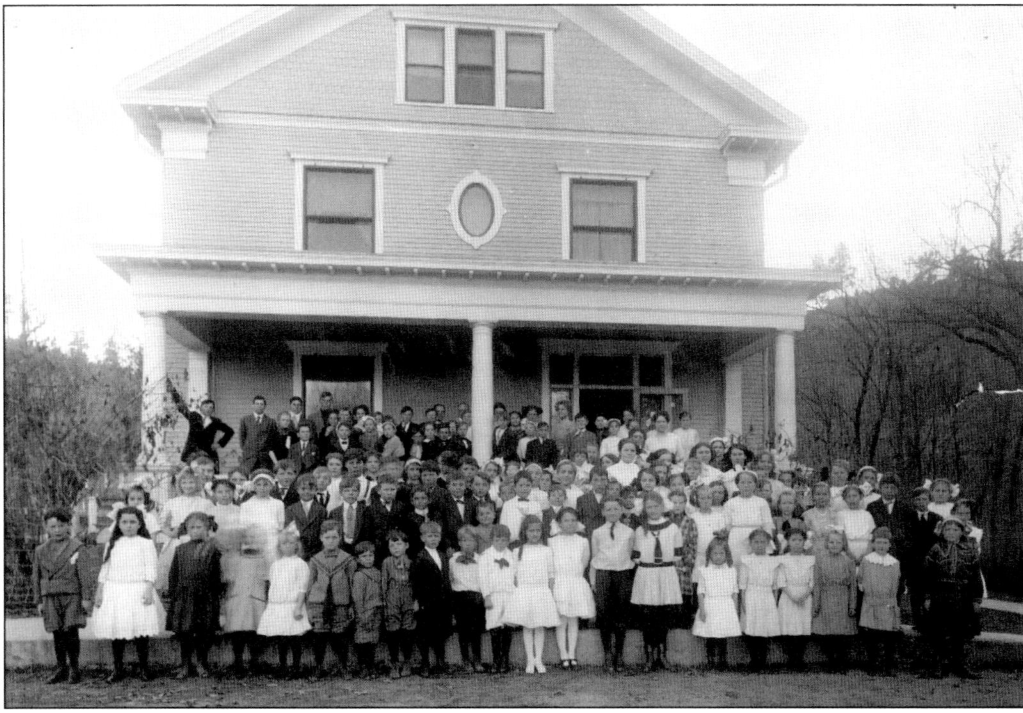

A residence, known as the Booth House was constructed in 1905 with eight rooms and a bath. This 1917 photograph is of a training school party given by Ruby Booth.

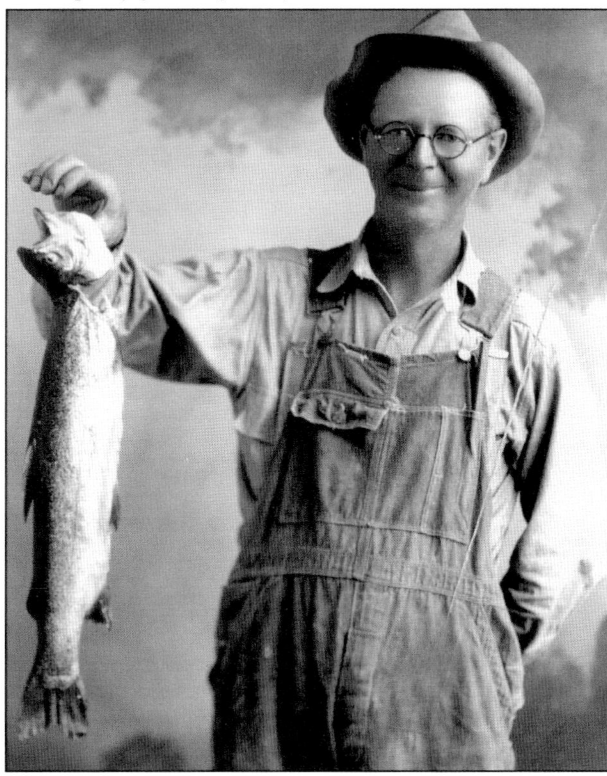

Sandy Waugh appears to be a happy angler with his catch of the day. Four species of trout were introduced in the Black Hills, those being brook trout, brown trout, rainbow trout, and splake, a hybrid speckled brook and lake trout.

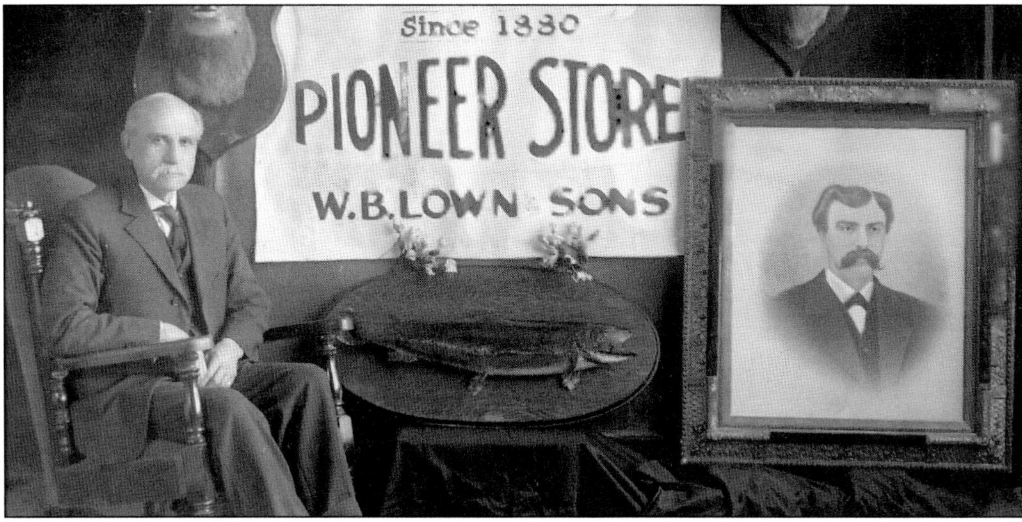

W. B. Lown is pictured here with a poster that reads: "Pioneer Store since 1880." William and Clara Lown opened their first store in 1880 on the northwest corner of Main and Hudson Streets. Later they moved their business farther north and became the major retailers for the Spearfish community, providing general merchandise in demand. The upstairs portion of the building was used for dances.

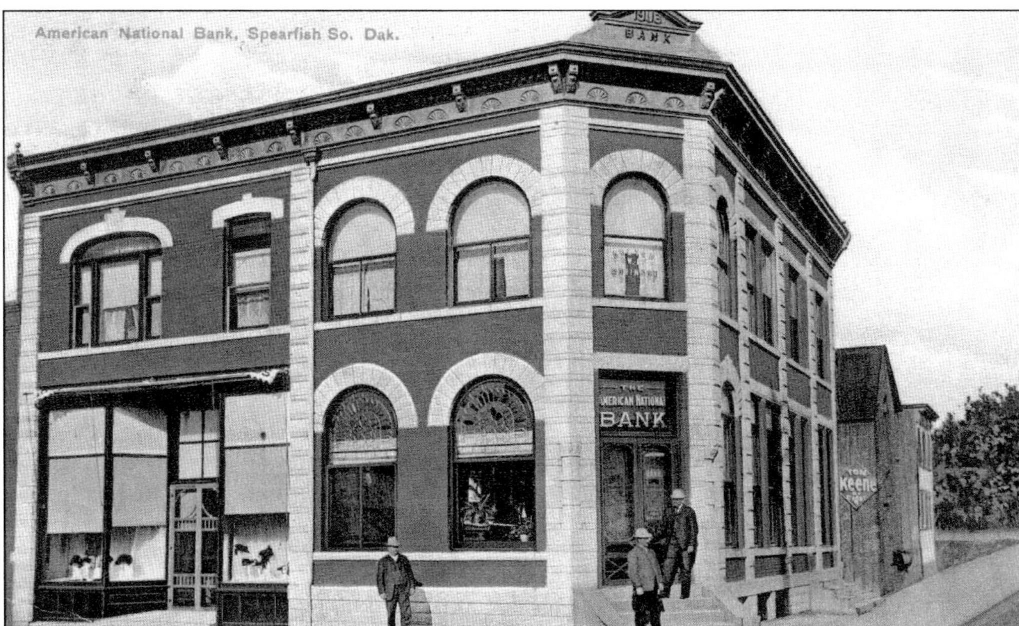

In 1882, Stebbins, Fox and Company established a private bank, the first brick building in Spearfish, which would be later chartered as the Bank of Spearfish. In 1887, it became the First National Bank of Spearfish. Then in 1935, it became a branch of the First National Bank of Lead, and from 1938 it was known as the Spearfish Office of the First National Bank of the Black Hills, Rapid City.

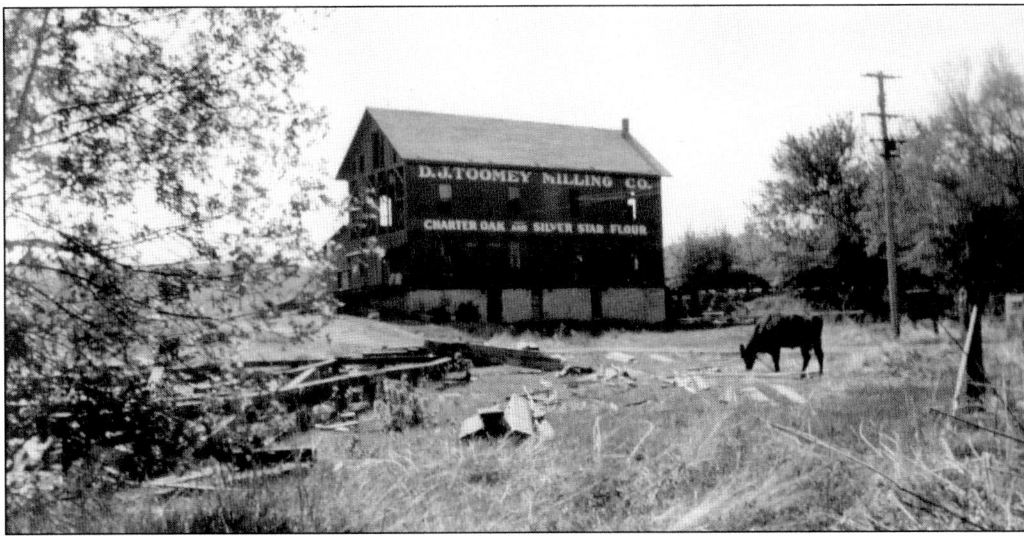

Frank Thomson took this photograph of Toomey mill just before it was torn down on May 12, 1930. C. V. Gardner and Porter Warner opened a gristmill in 1879. The flour was marketed under the name of Charter Oak. "Pride of the Hills" was added in 1920 and when Daniel Toomey took over, the "Silver Star" brand was milled. An 1883 issue of the *Black Hills Daily Times* described Toomey as the "handsome young grainger of Spearfish valley [is] in town."

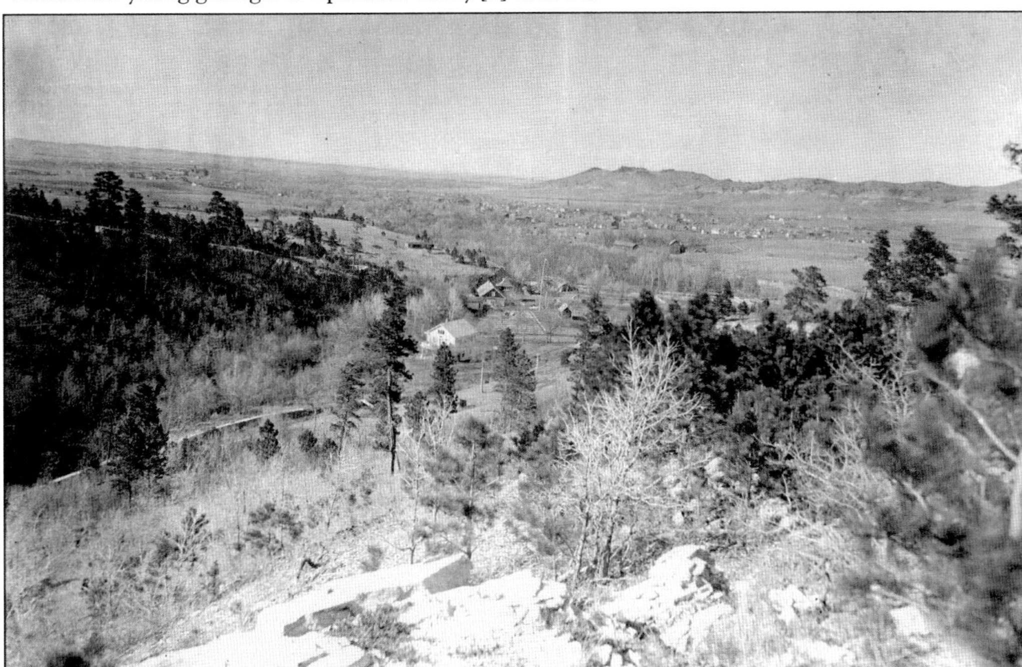

Richard Hughes, a prominent Black Hills journalist, wrote about Spearfish in his book *Pioneer Years in the Black Hills*: "Among the most promising towns established in the first year was Spearfish. Beautiful in its location, with the towering mountain background, and with the broad and fertile valley stretching away to the north and the magnificent scenery of the Spearfish Canyon traversed by the loveliest of mountain streams, it has grown to deserve the appellation bestowed upon it at an early day by the eloquent Judge Bradley, the Queen City."

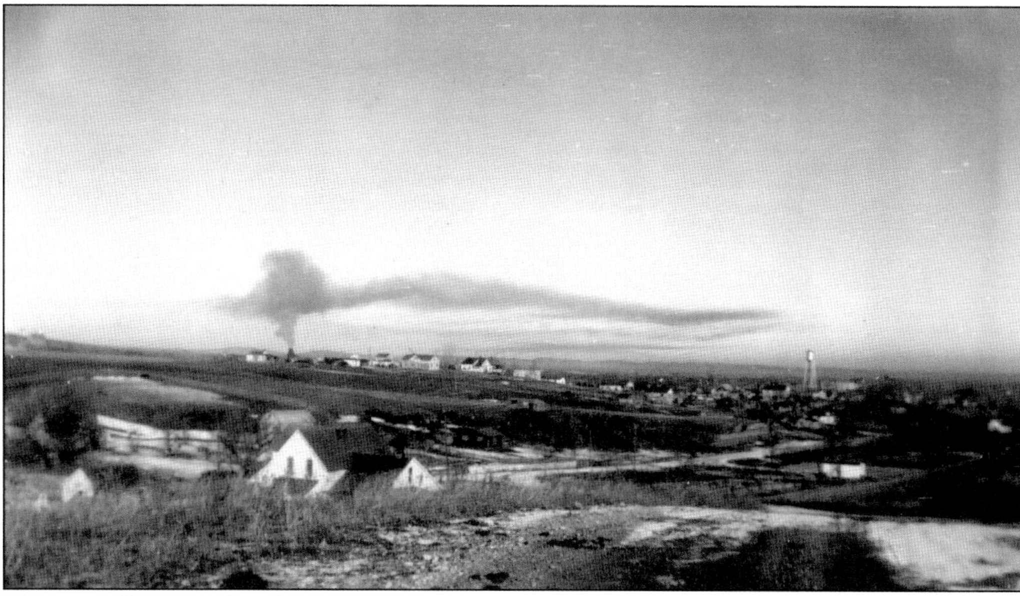

The sawmill pictured in the background processed timber bracing for the gold mine for 40 years until it burned in 1980. The Homestake mine no longer needed the bracing so it did not rebuild the sawmill. A lumber milling plant replaced the old sawmill. The McGrady House is pictured in the foreground, the water tower at the right, and the Black Hills Teachers College is in the center in this 1942 photograph.

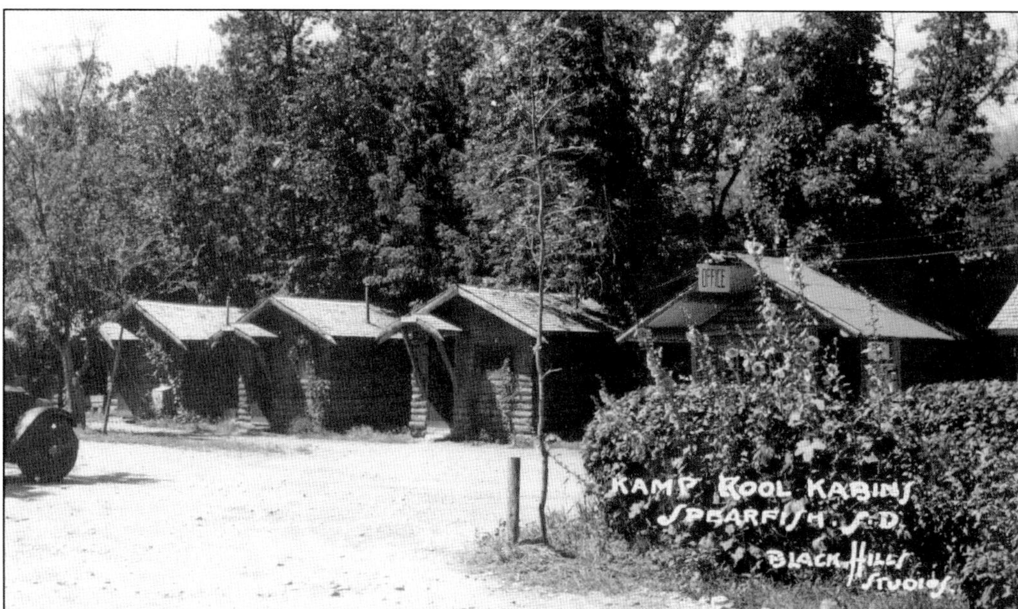

With the advent of the automobile, the tourism industry showed promise in the 1920s and 1930s. Spearfish, as the entrance to Spearfish Canyon, saw its share of tourists. In 1930, the road through Spearfish Canyon was completed. Tourist cabins such as Kamp Kool Kabins, pictured here, accommodated these adventurers. (Courtesy of Roberta Sago.)

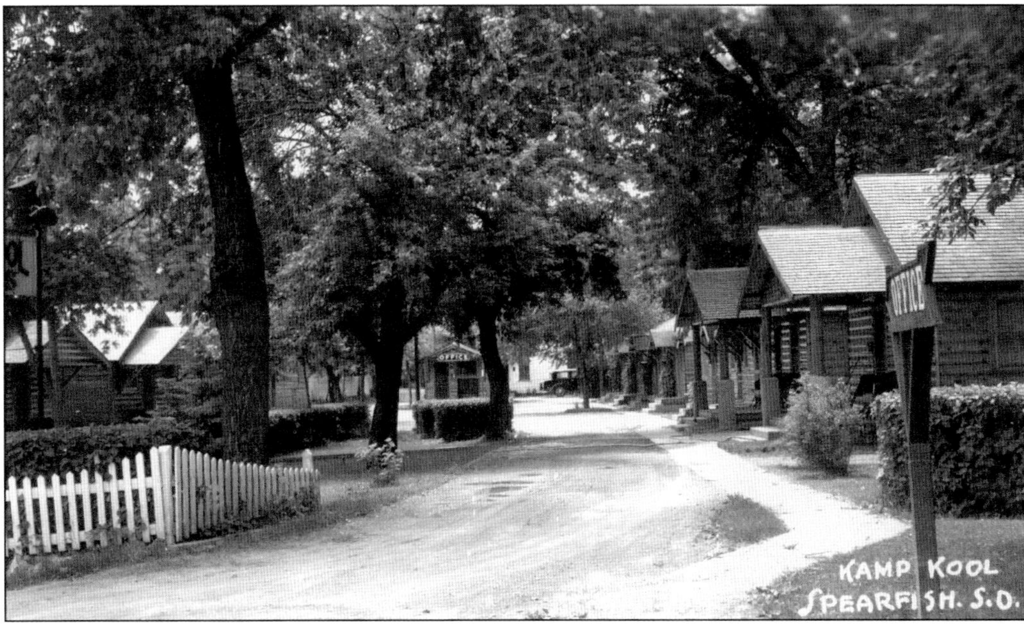

Many motels and cabins, such as Kamp Kool Kabins, were built in the 1950s to provide lodging for the growing tourist industry. (Courtesy of Roberta Sago.)

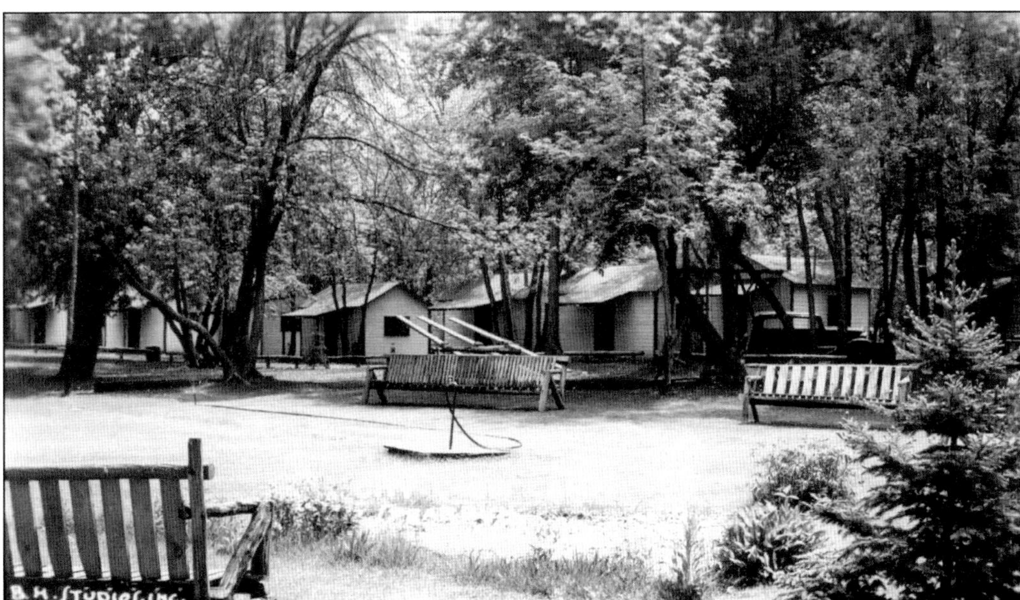

Photographed by Thomas Odell, the quaint city cabin camp offered a quiet respite for the weary traveler.

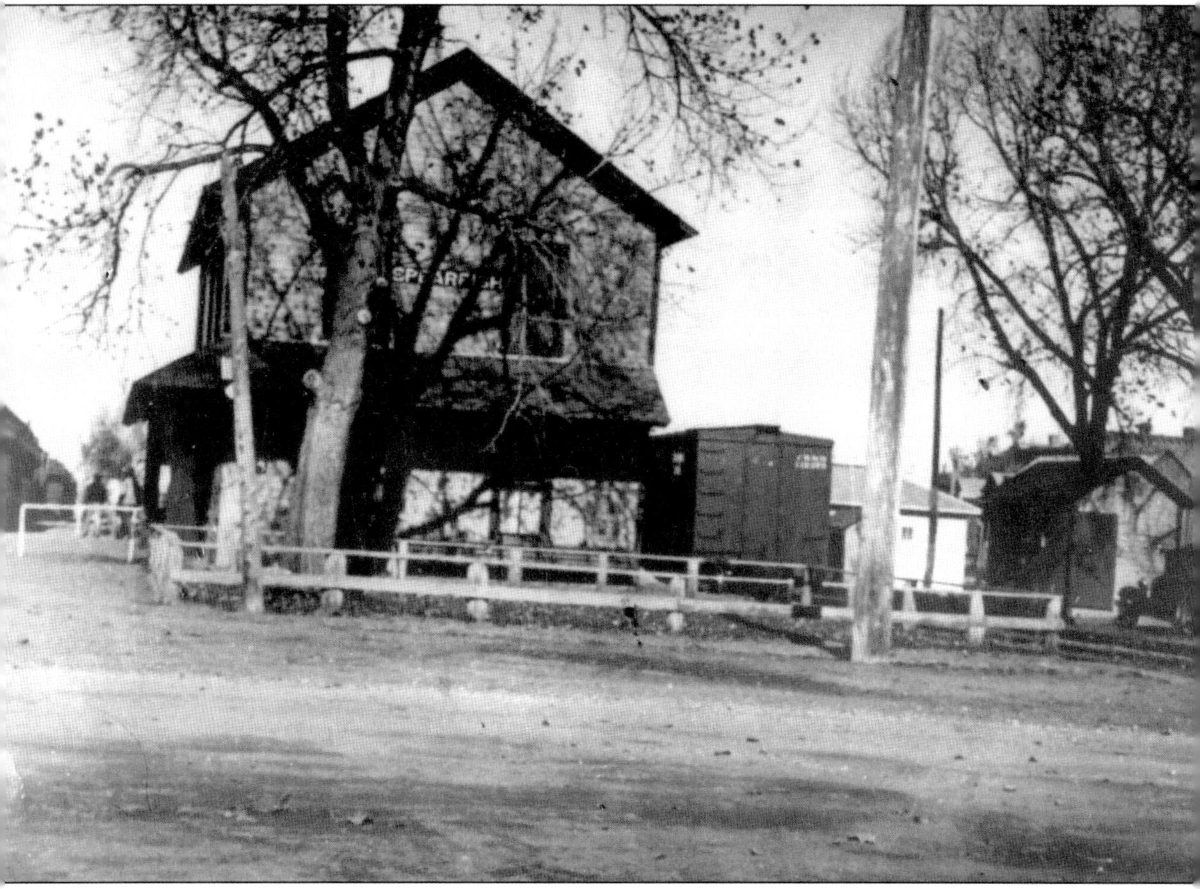

In 1893, an extension of the Burlington Line reached Deadwood through Spearfish Canyon. The original intention of the railroad was to bring ore from the many mines for processing. Investors built a chlorination ore treatment plant, which was destroyed by fire and rebuilt. By the time the railroad was built many of the mines like Carbonate, Tinton, and the Ragged Top area began to close. The railroad was then used for commercial service to farmers and ranchers and also transported local passengers and tourists to Spearfish Canyon. The railroad closed down when the flood of 1933 destroyed miles of track that were never rebuilt.

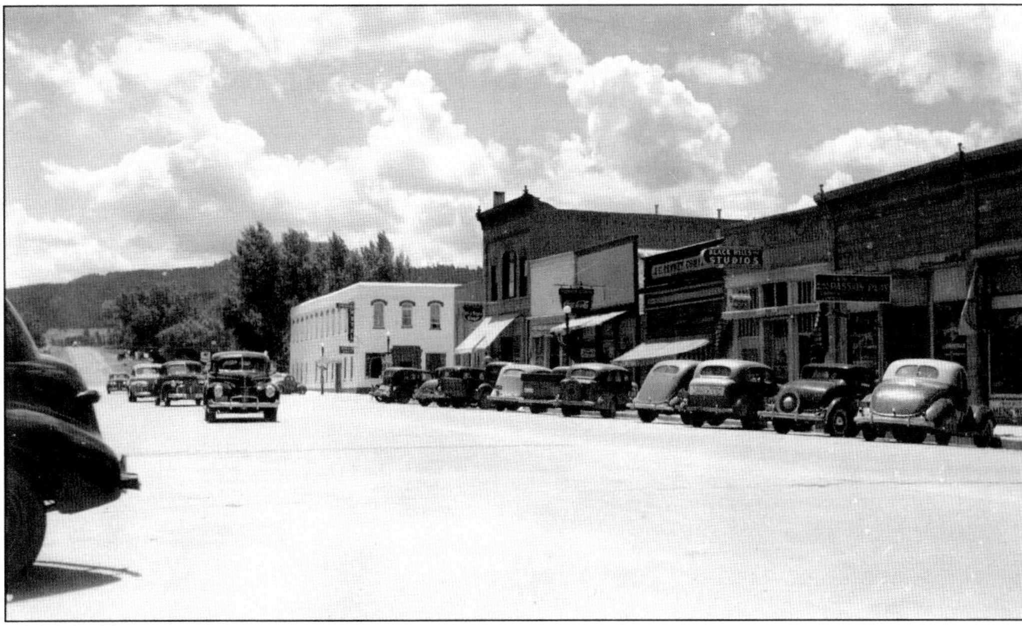

Spearfish grew slowly but steadily through the years. The Spearfish Hotel is the white building in the background. (Courtesy of Roberta Sago.)

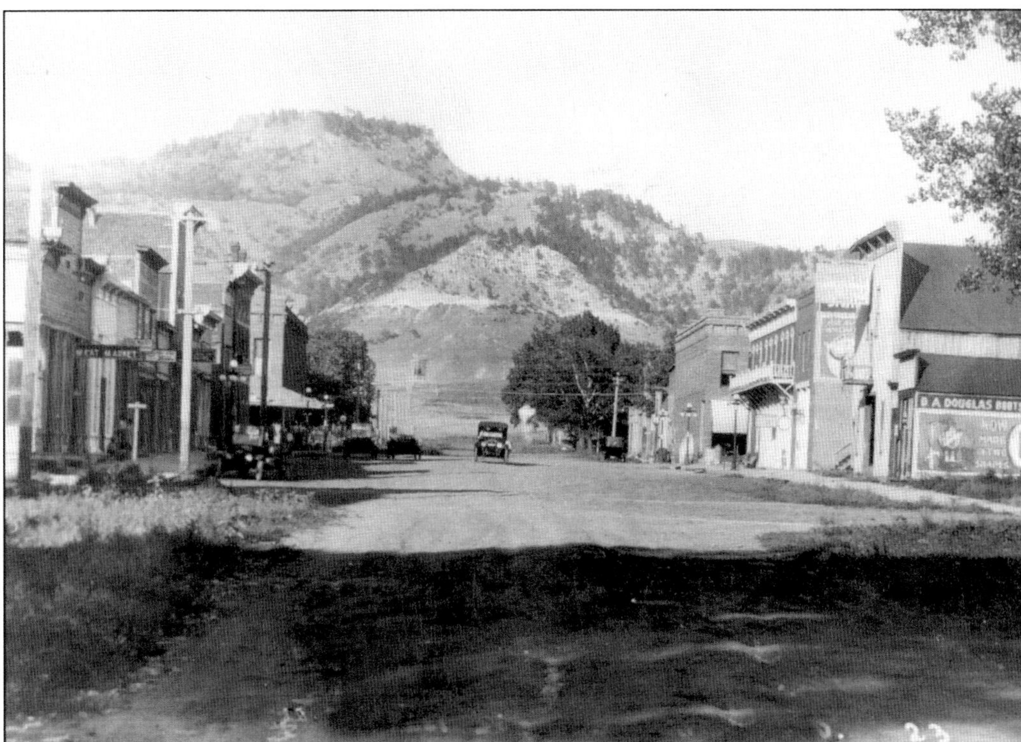

An undated scene of Spearfish looks east on Hudson Street from below Fifth Street. A meat market, stable, and boot shop, with the advertisement, "D. A. Douglas Boots Now Made in Two Shapes," can be seen.

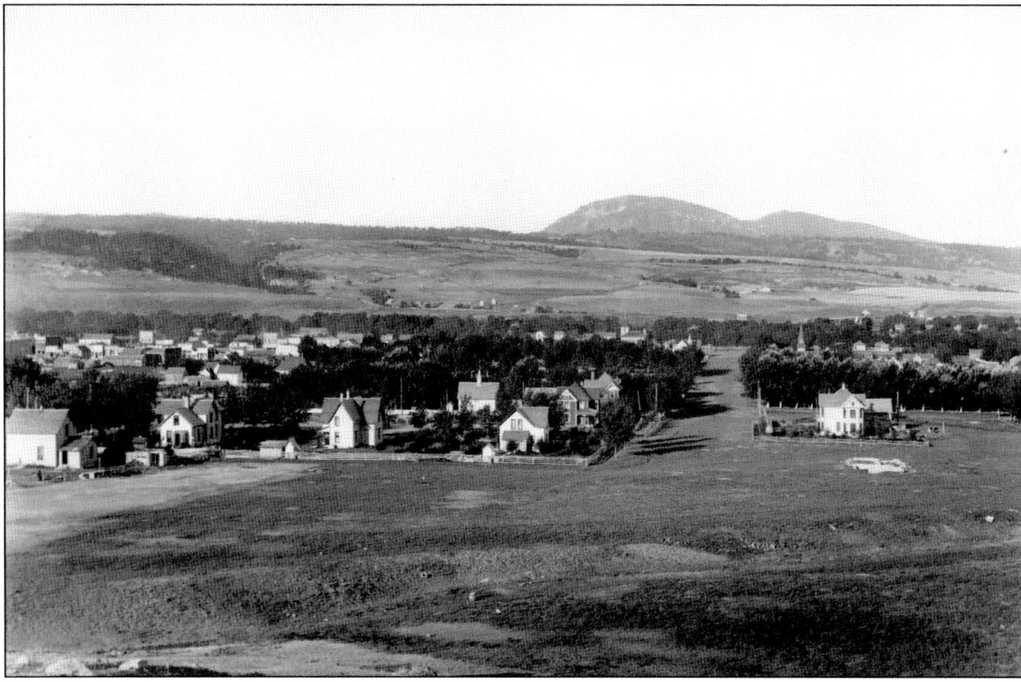

This early 1902 Spearfish scene is of the residential section, before Jackson Boulevard took center stage. Crow Peak is pictured in the background.

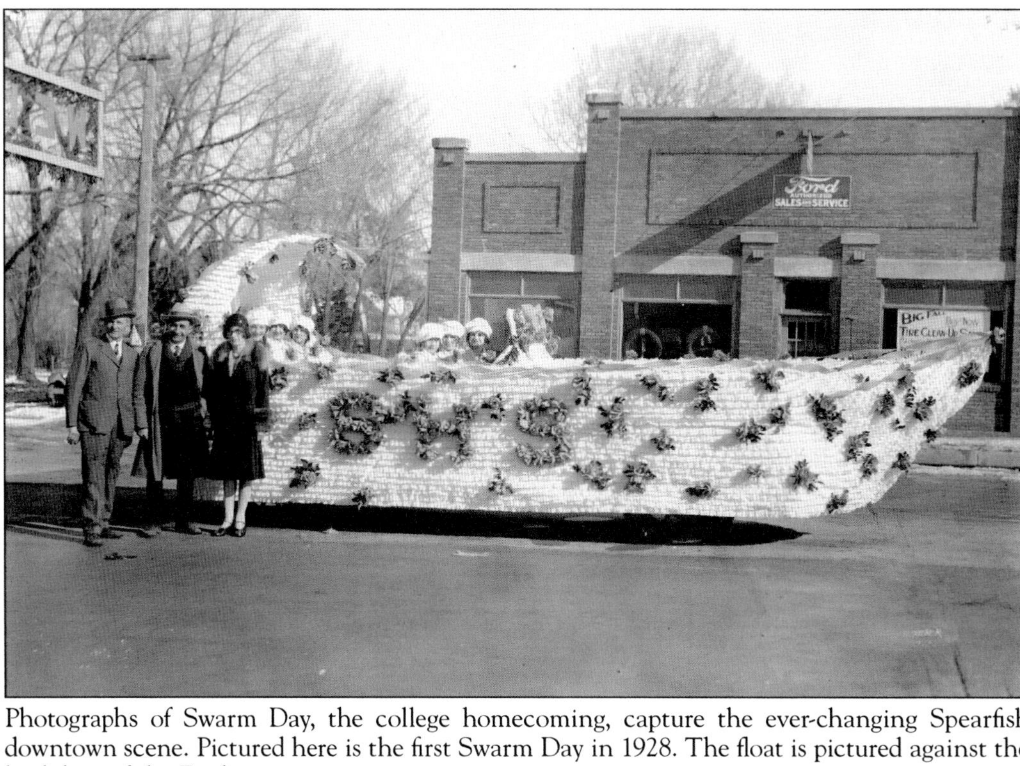

Photographs of Swarm Day, the college homecoming, capture the ever-changing Spearfish downtown scene. Pictured here is the first Swarm Day in 1928. The float is pictured against the backdrop of the Ford garage.

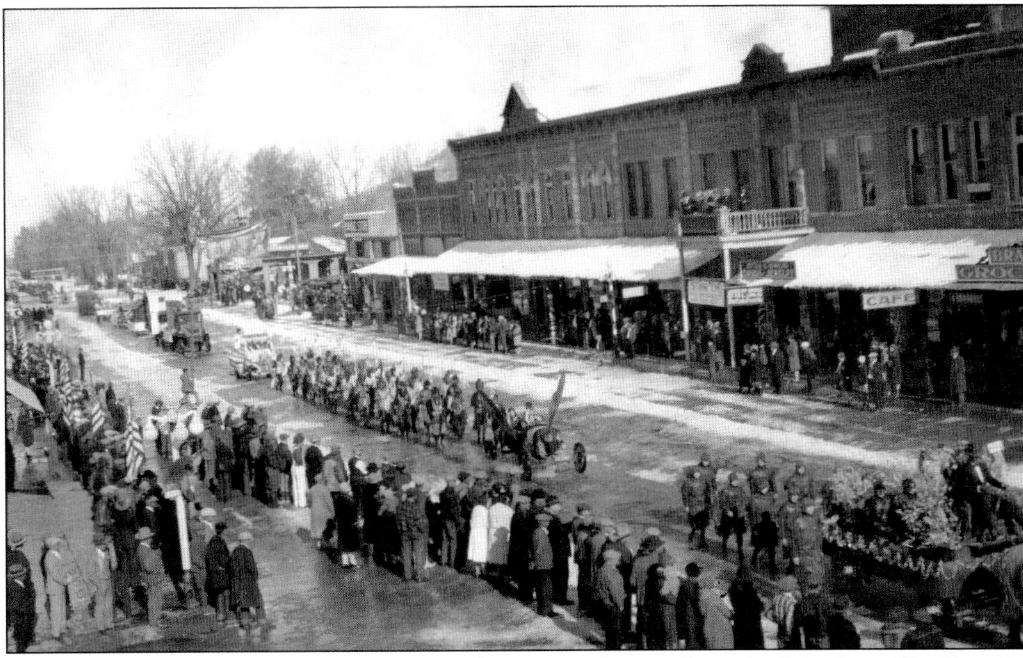

The 1928 Swarm Day parade moves down the center of town along the Matthews Block in this photograph. Pictured are spectators standing on the balcony of the Matthews Opera House, a drug store, jewelry store, café, and grocery.

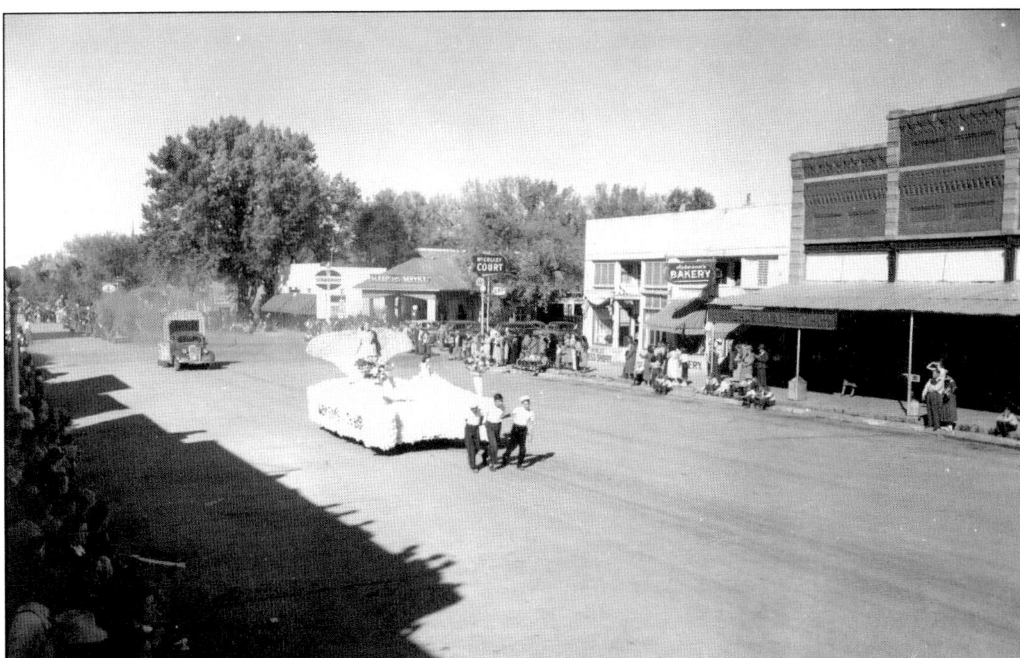

The same Swarm Day parade passes the Standard station, McColley Court, Johnson's Bakery, a variety store, and Myrlee's Dress Shop.

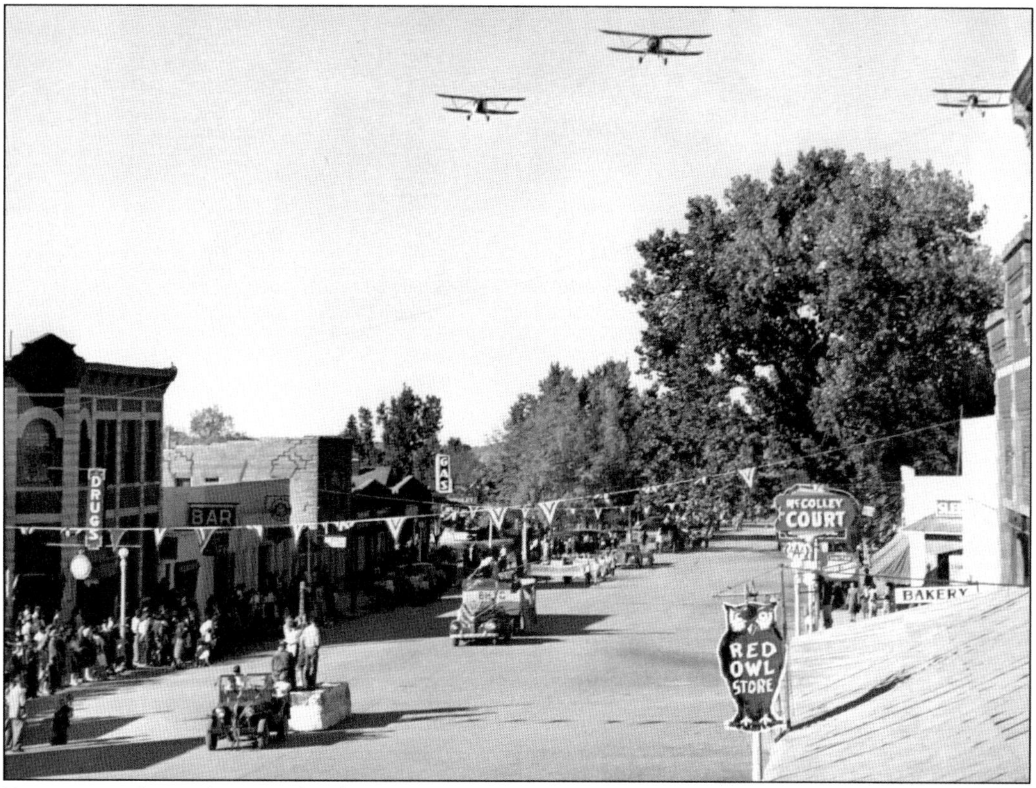

Bi-wing airplanes show up for this 1948 Swarm Day event. The Red Owl Store and McColley Court are featured in this parade scene.

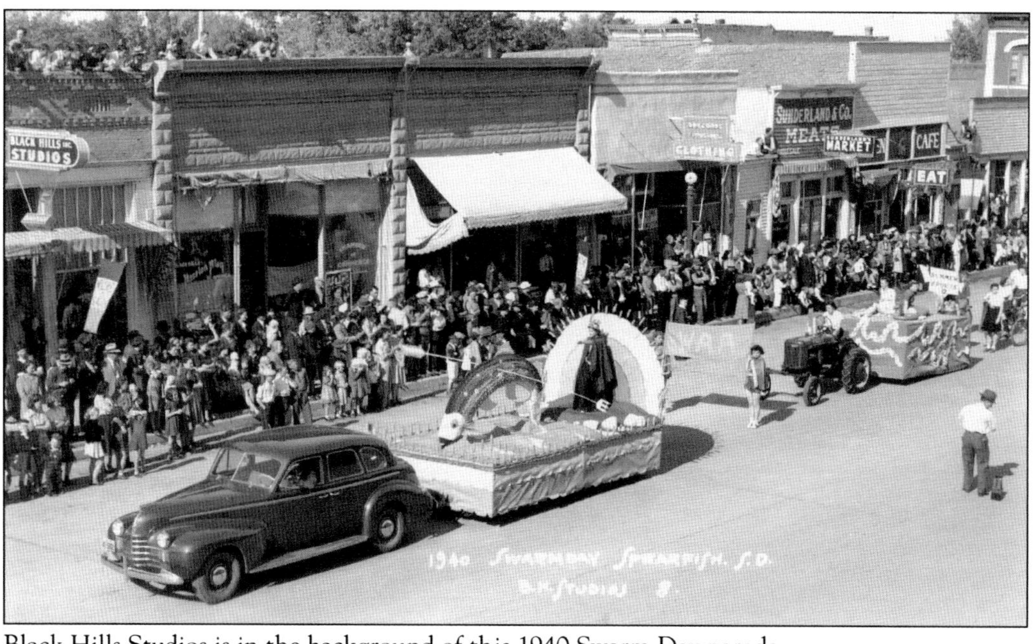

Black Hills Studios is in the background of this 1940 Swarm Day parade.

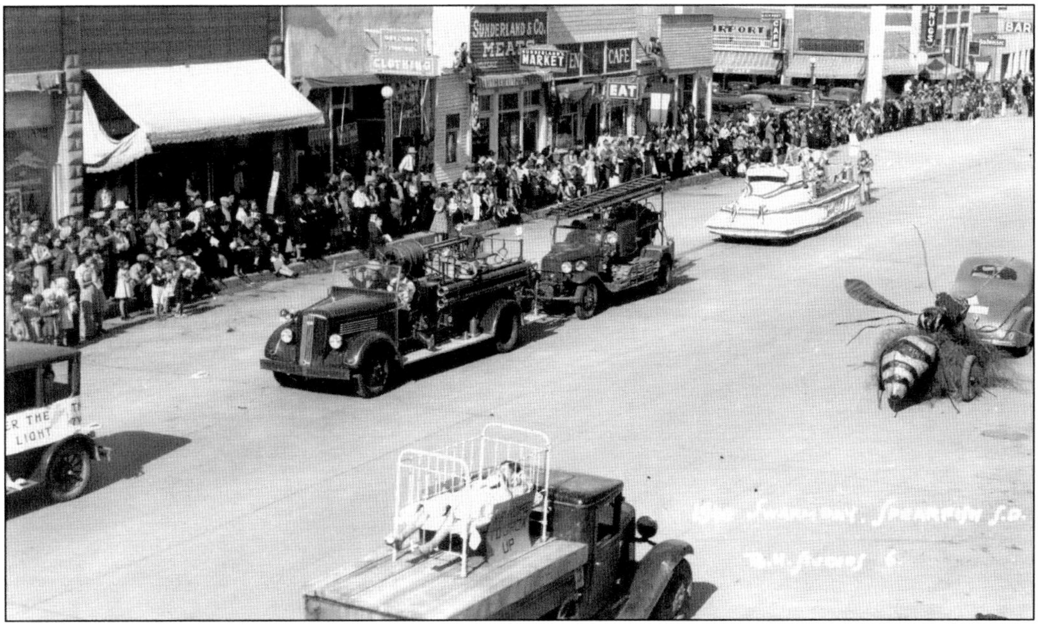

The Yellow Jacket mascot parades down the street in this 1940 Swarm Day event. A clothing store, Sunderland and Company Meat Market, a café, a drug store, and a bar are pictured.

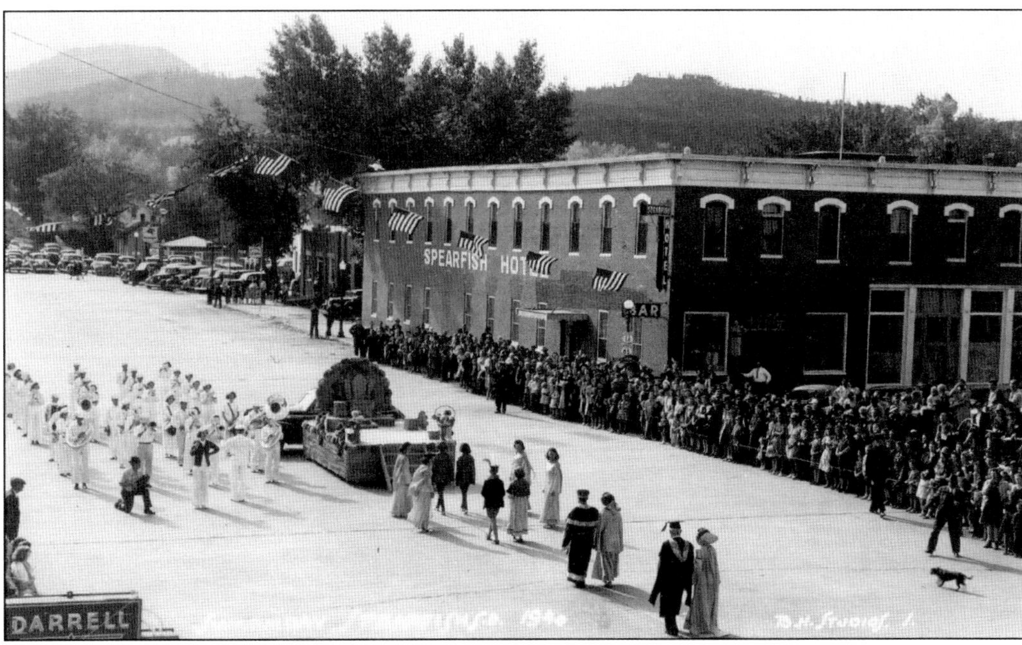

The Swarm Day parade route passes the Spearfish Hotel in this 1940 photograph.

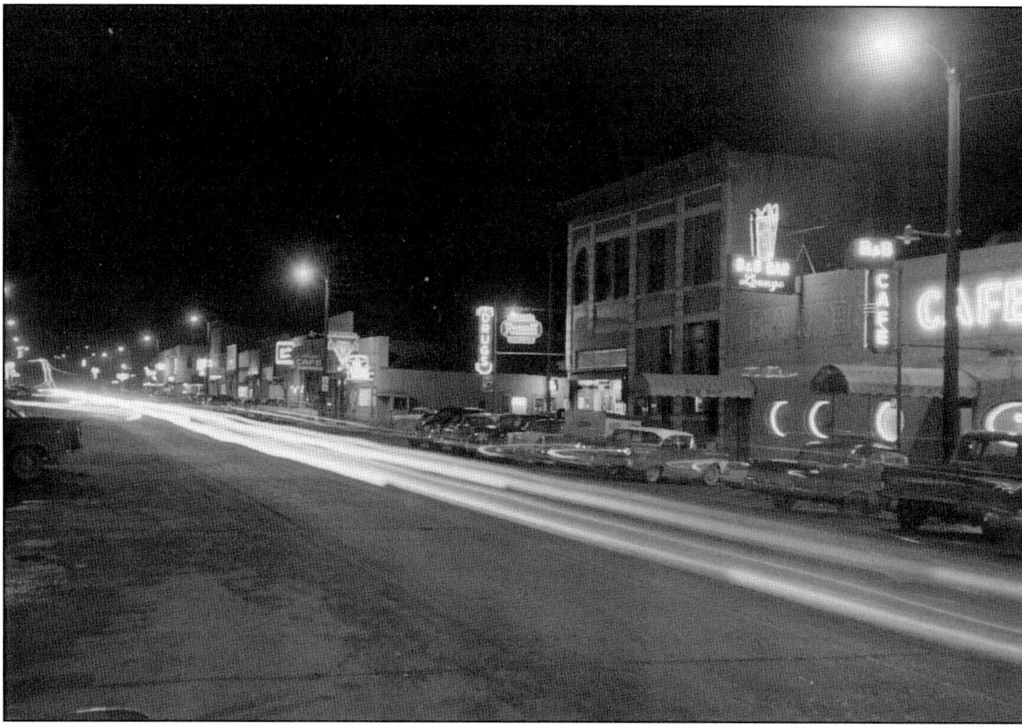

This 1958 nighttime scene pictures the B&B Bar, Rexall Drug, Canyon Café, and Conoco.

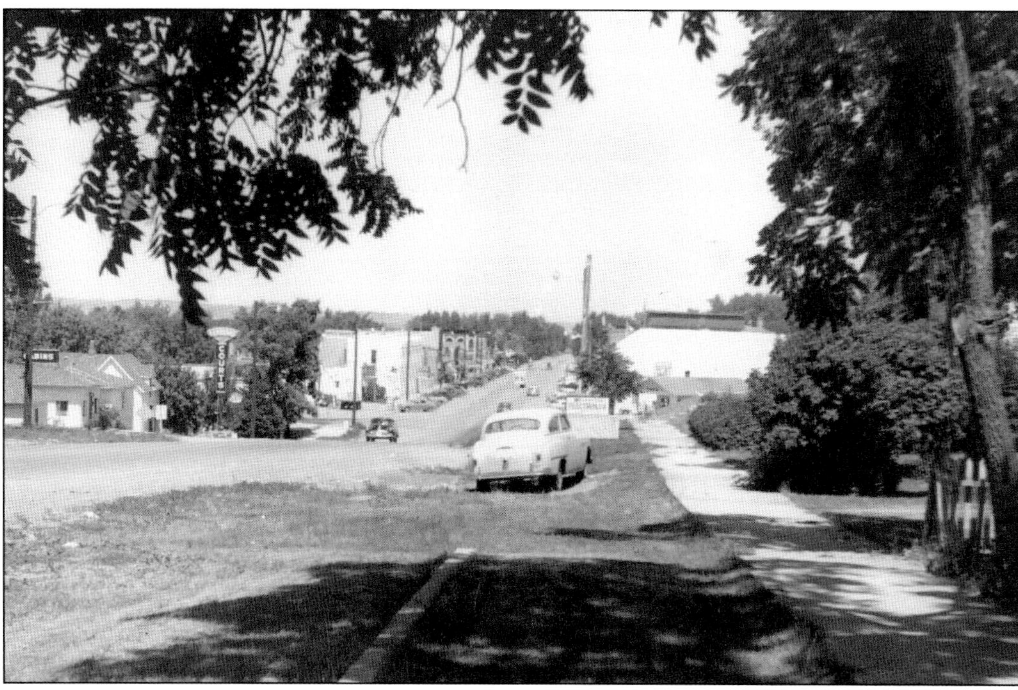

In 1955, Spearfish's Main Street seemed to be peaceful and serene with little traffic. Berhens Gas Station and the roof of the Vita Theatre are seen to the right while the Spearfish Hotel, the white building, appears to the left.

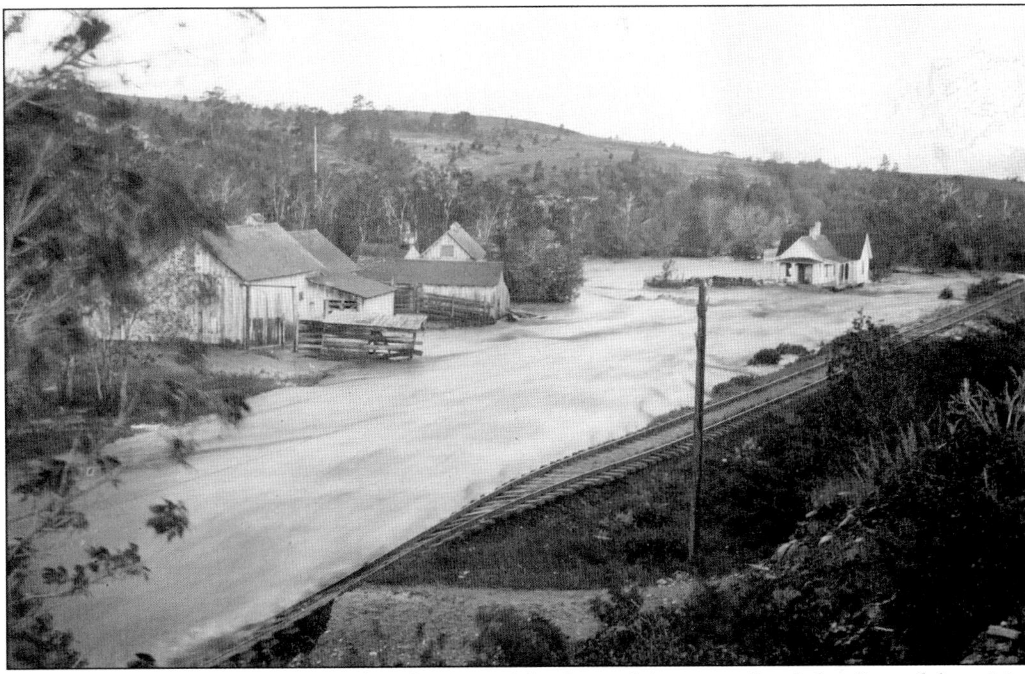

Flooding became a periodic problem for Spearfish. One of the worst floods hit Spearfish in May 1933. The flood washed out railroad tracks on the Burlington route. They were never repaired and brought about the demise of the railroad.

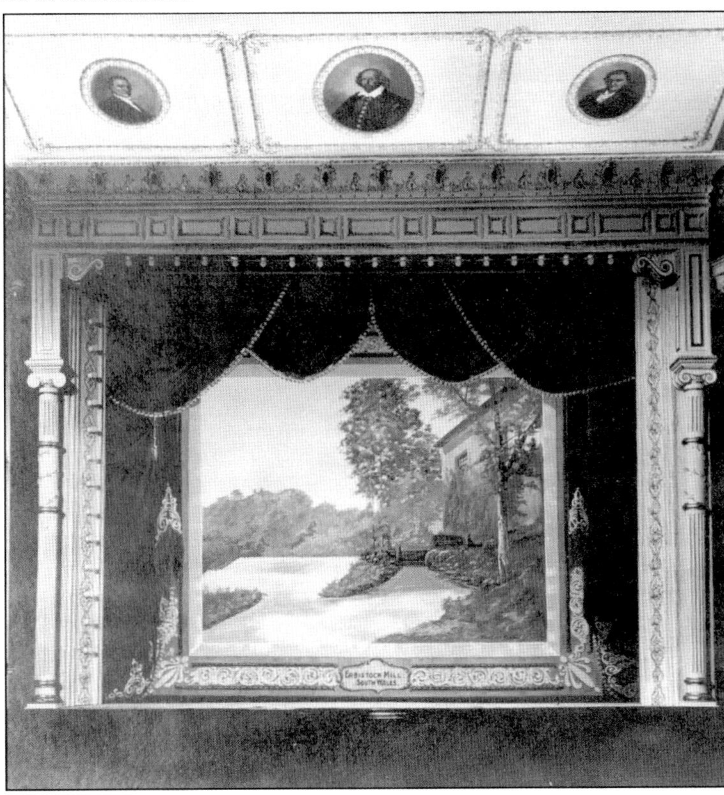

The interior of the Matthews Opera House is pictured here. Wealthy Wyoming cattlemen T. N. and T. W. Matthews financed the building of the Matthews Opera House in 1906 for $50,000. The opera house occupied the second floor of a 100-by-125-foot building. The portraits above the stage area are of Joseph Jefferson, William Shakespeare, and Edwin Booth. Many traveling vaudeville shows performed in the opera house in its first years. The opera house has since been restored to its original grandeur. (Courtesy of Paul Higbee.)

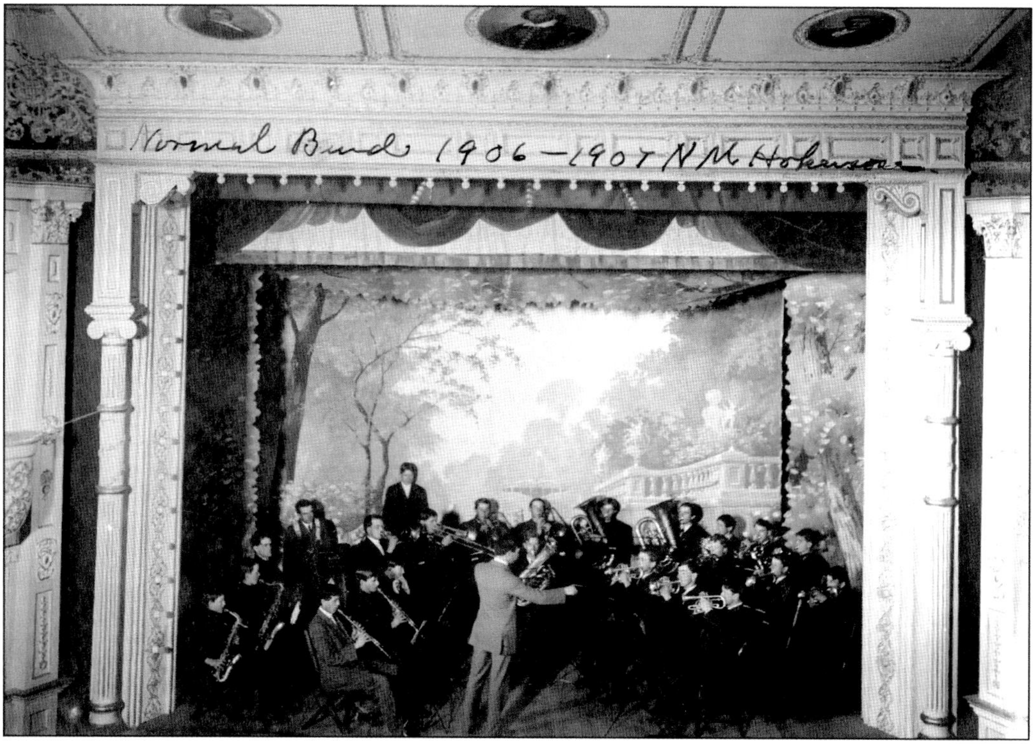

In 1906, the State Normal School's band played at the Matthews Opera House.

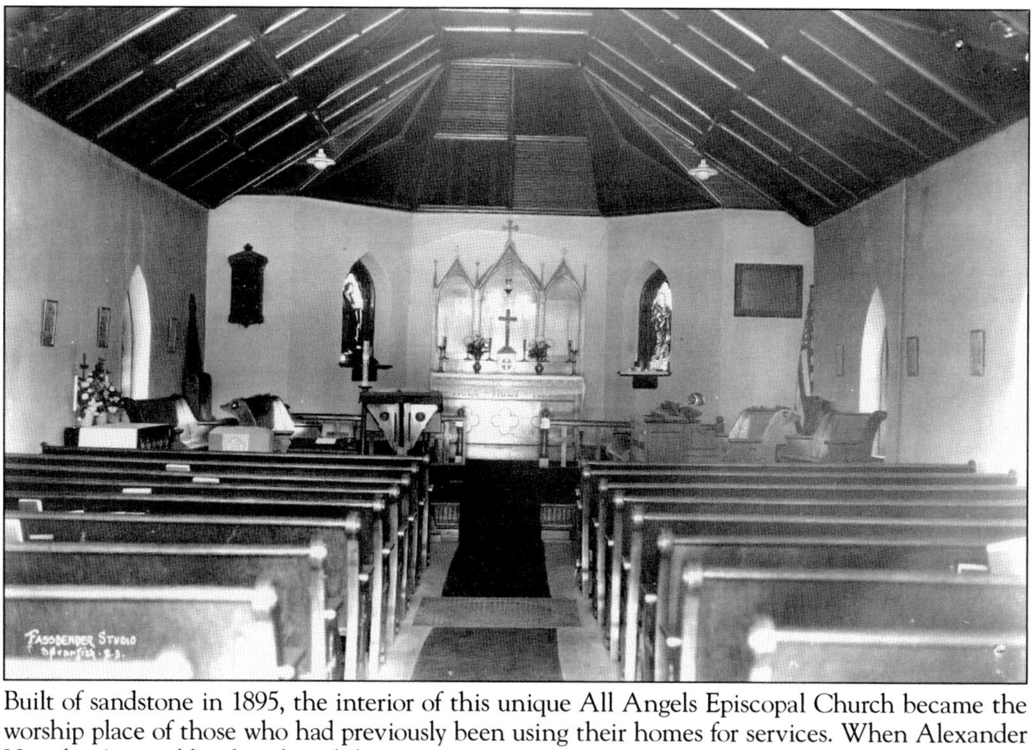

Built of sandstone in 1895, the interior of this unique All Angels Episcopal Church became the worship place of those who had previously been using their homes for services. When Alexander Hamilton's granddaughter heard there was no church, she sent money to Spearfish to build one.

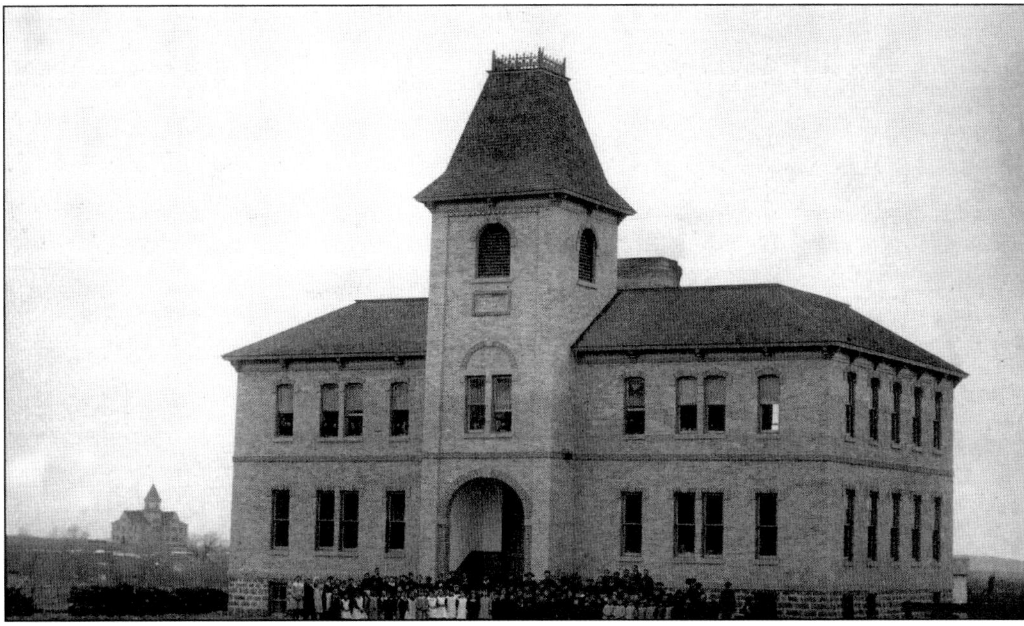

The Spearfish Public Elementary School, commonly known as the "Little Red School", was used for teacher training from the fall of 1887 to the spring of 1895. Central Elementary replaced the red brick school in the 1950s.

A group of unidentified but prominent Spearfish citizens are photographed in front of a real estate business.

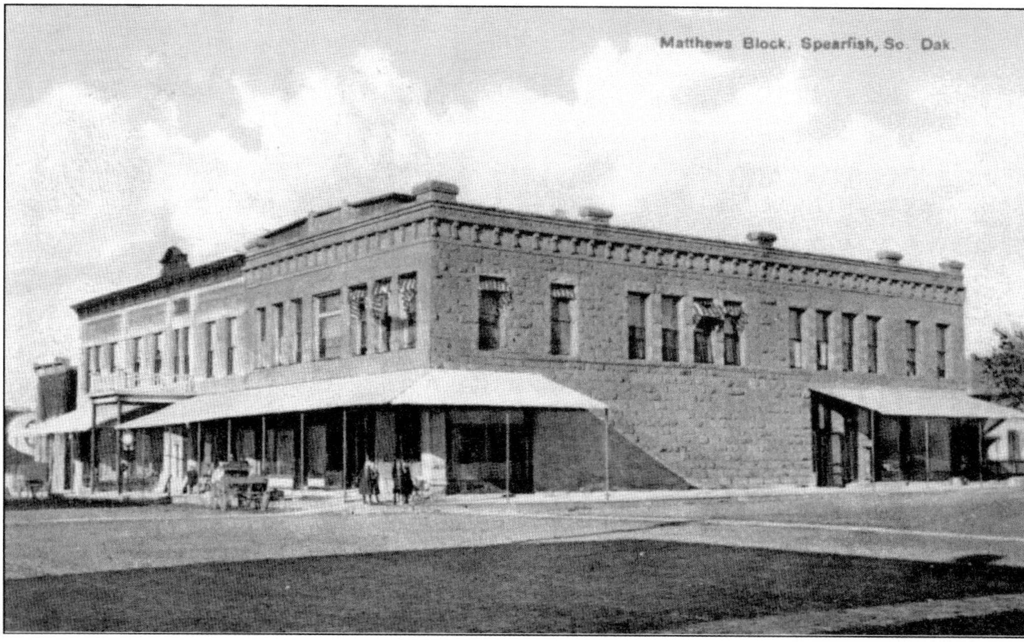

The Matthews Block was built shortly after 1900. The building contained businesses and shops.

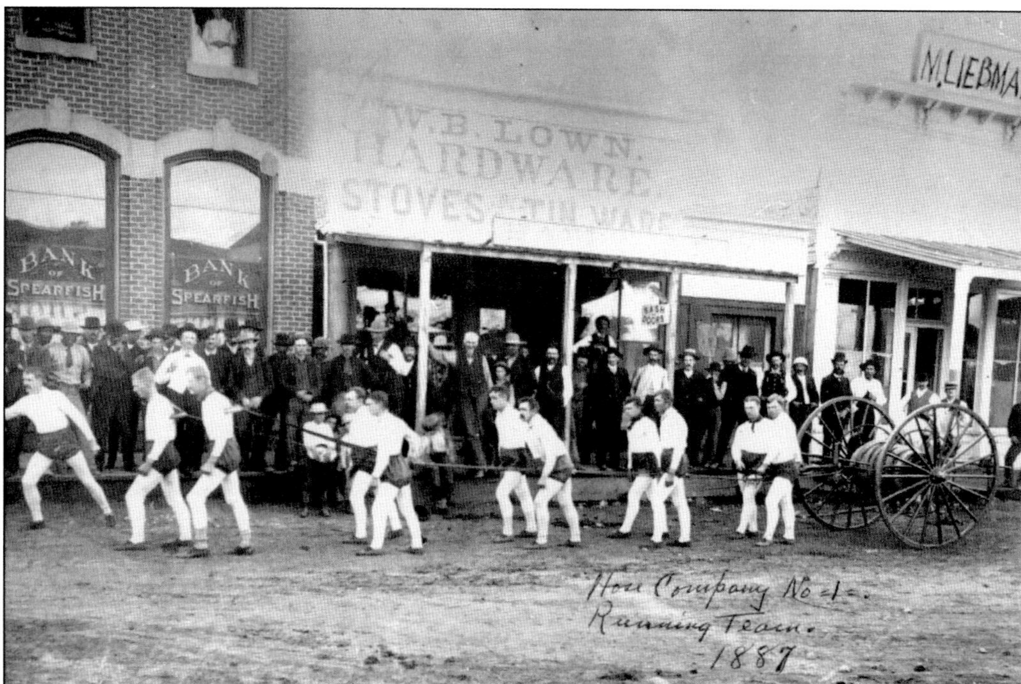

Pictured in front of the Lown hardware store is the Spearfish Hose Company in 1887. Hose cart teams representing various towns participated in parades. Man-powered firefighting equipment required athletic men; therefore contests between fire departments of different towns were commonplace. Hose cart races, tugs-of-war, and hose fight contests entertained the audiences.

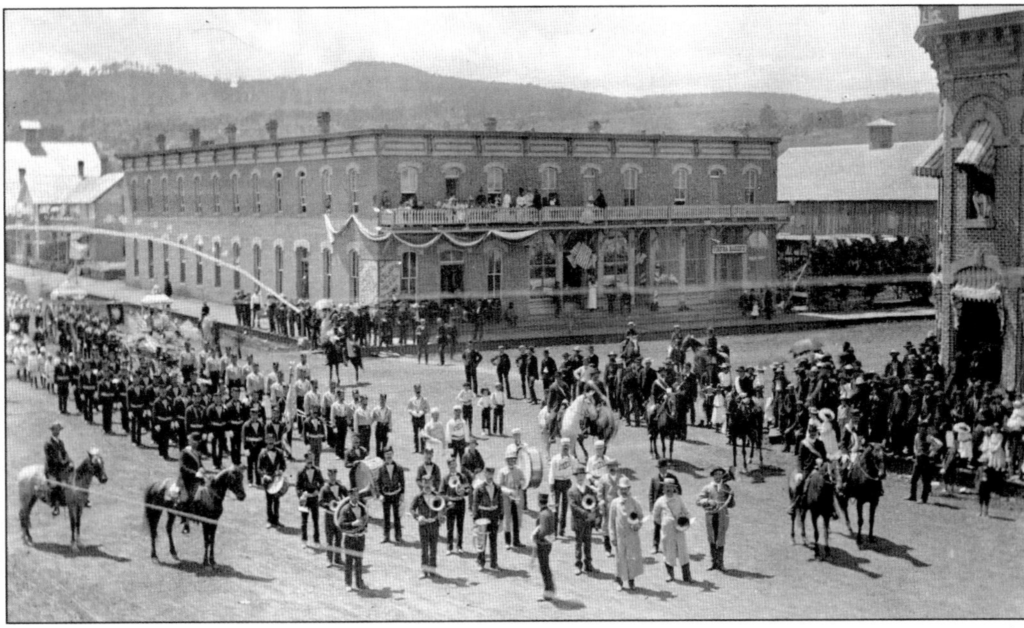

This Fourth of July Spearfish parade was held during the 1887 Firemen's Convention at the intersection of Main and Hudson Streets. The Spearfish Hotel is pictured in the background. The hotel would make headlines in July 26, 1887, when a chandelier fell. The hotel replaced a log cabin hotel in the 1870s, which was destroyed by fire, but it too would also suffer the same fate. It was rebuilt and burned again in 1975, then known as Kelley's Motor Inn.

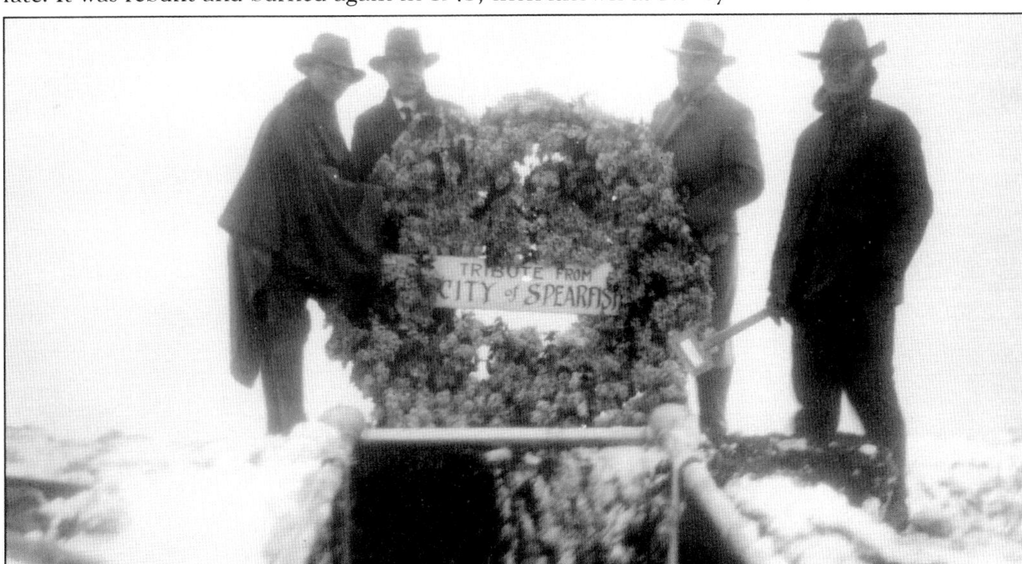

Spearfish pays tribute to Deadwood Dick at his elaborate funeral in 1930. Deadwood Dick became the most sought after name in the Black Hills especially when Ned Buntline wrote novels using Deadwood Dick as the handsome frontier hero. Several Black Hills characters pursued the name of Deadwood Dick. Richard Clark became the last successful Deadwood Dick in the 1920s. The Deadwood Chamber of Commerce persuaded Clark to become Deadwood Dick in the Days of '76 parade. He agreed and assumed the role for the rest of his life.

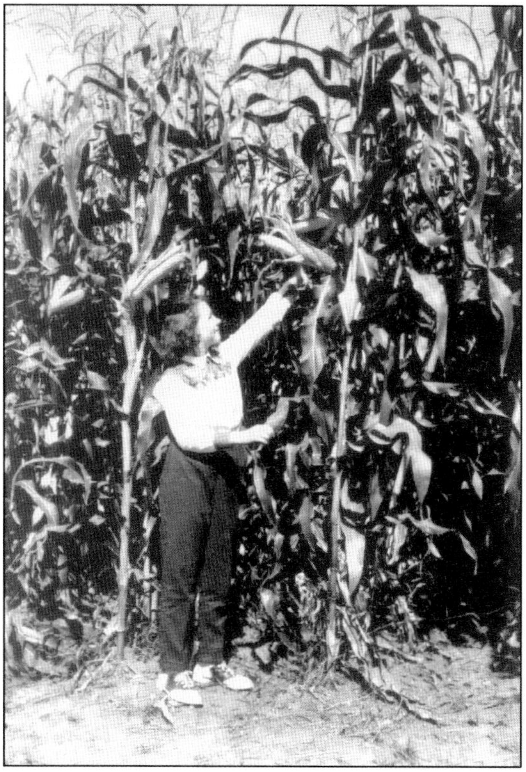

This unidentified young lady helps the reader appreciate the height of the corn that flourishes in Spearfish valley.

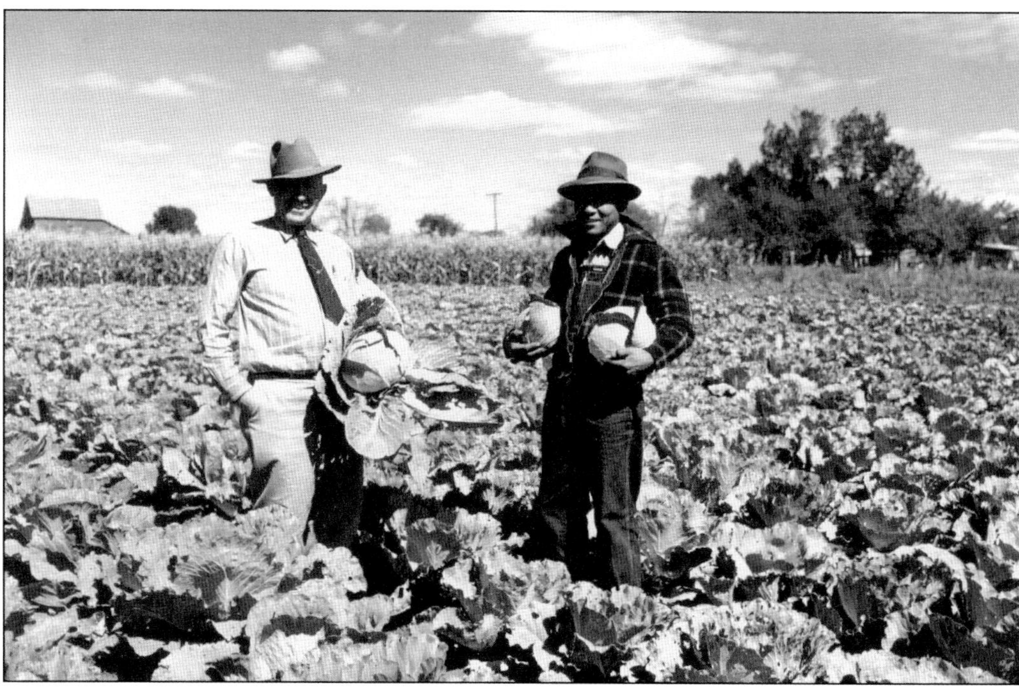

Men in the cabbage field show off the large, succulent heads of cabbage raised in Spearfish valley. Spearfish valley has long been known for its agricultural potential.

The Golden Valley Creamery, which opened in 1914, provided dairy products under the label Golden Valley Dairy and packaged them in cartons decorated with Black Hills scenes. Delivery trucks marketed the products to the Black Hills and eastern Wyoming. On his visit to Spearfish in 1927, Calvin Coolidge sampled the Golden Valley butter, and he wrote a note to the dairy superintendent Harry Linander indicating his wish that the White House serve Golden Valley butter.

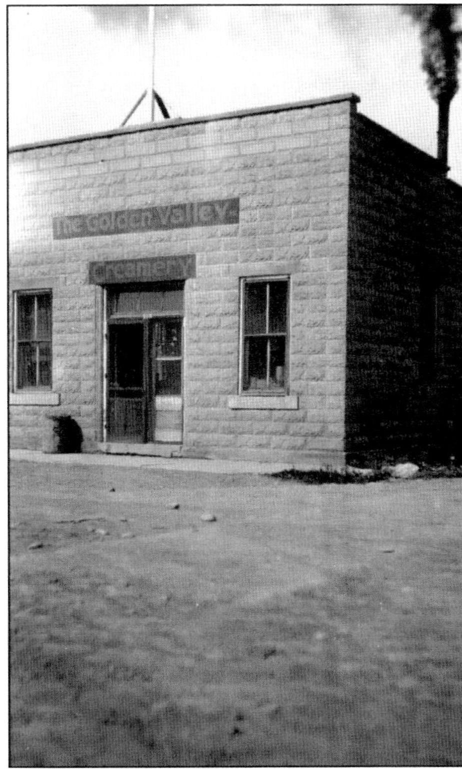

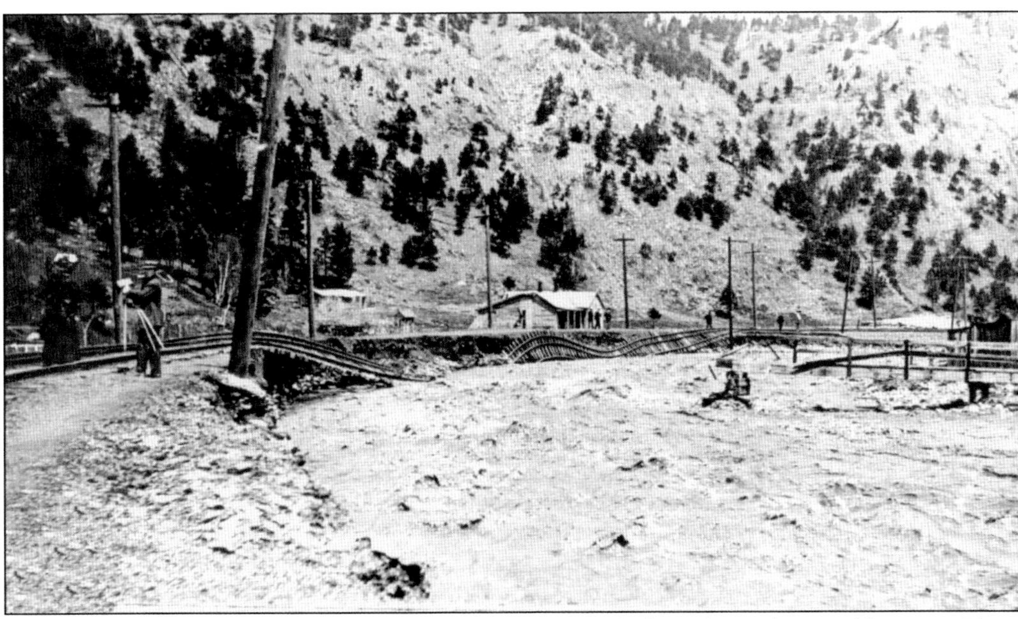

This photograph shows that the Burlington railroad tracks have been damaged between Pluma and Deadwood on White Wood Creek during a June 1909 flood.

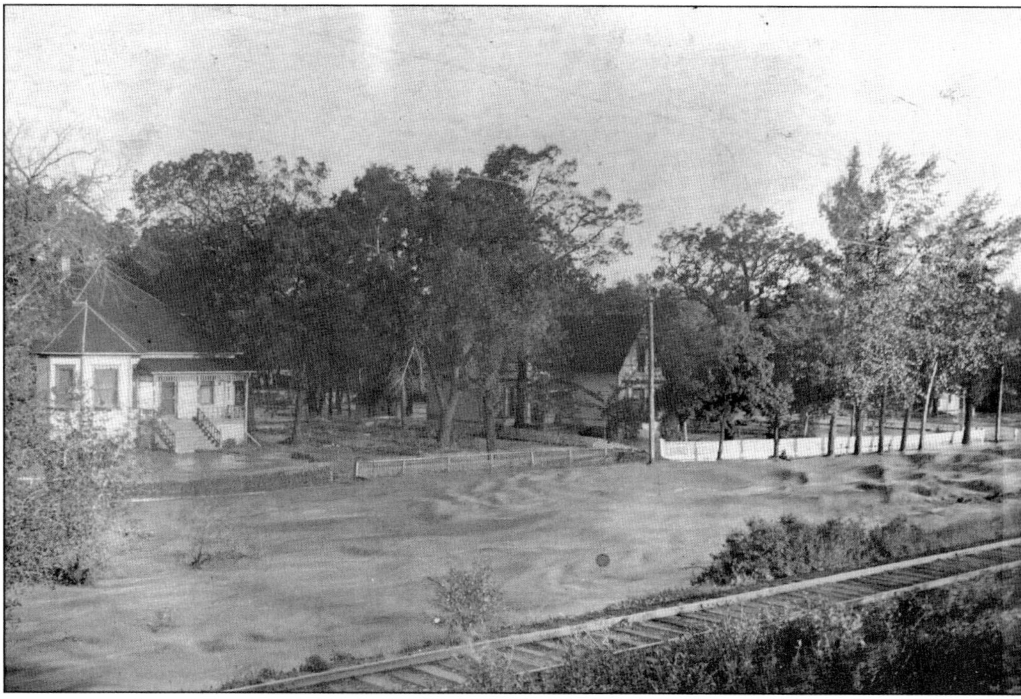

The railroad track is in the foreground of the flooded Canyon Street. Canyon Street flooded when Spearfish Creek rose out of its banks.

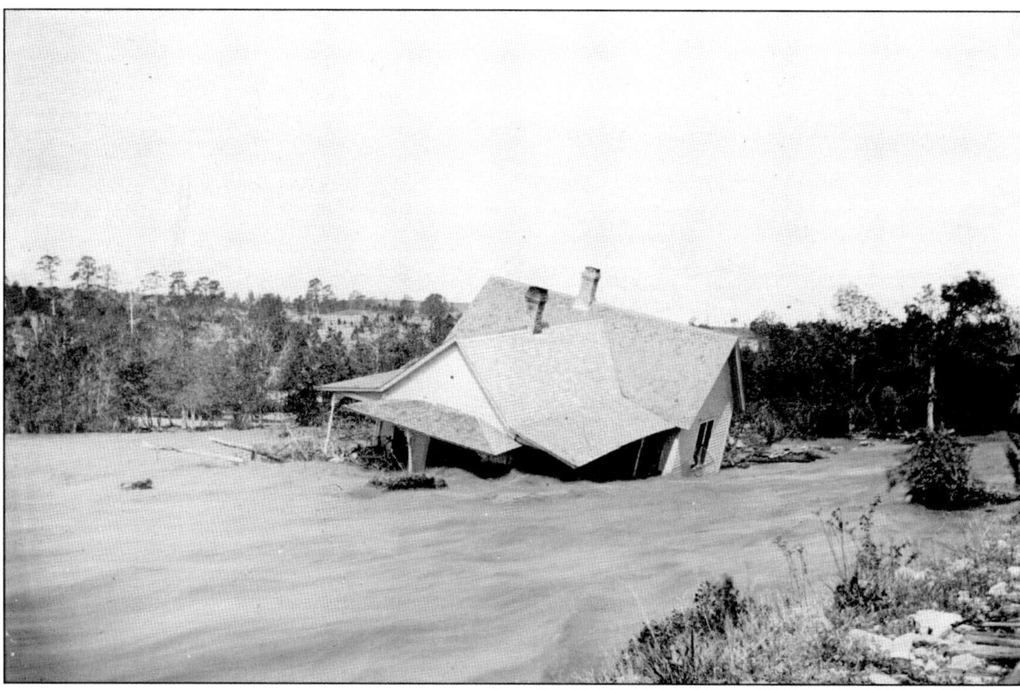

Floods plagued Spearfish from time to time in the early 1900s until the construction of Iron Creek Lake and Homestake mill's diversion of water occurred. The projects lessened the severity of the floods.

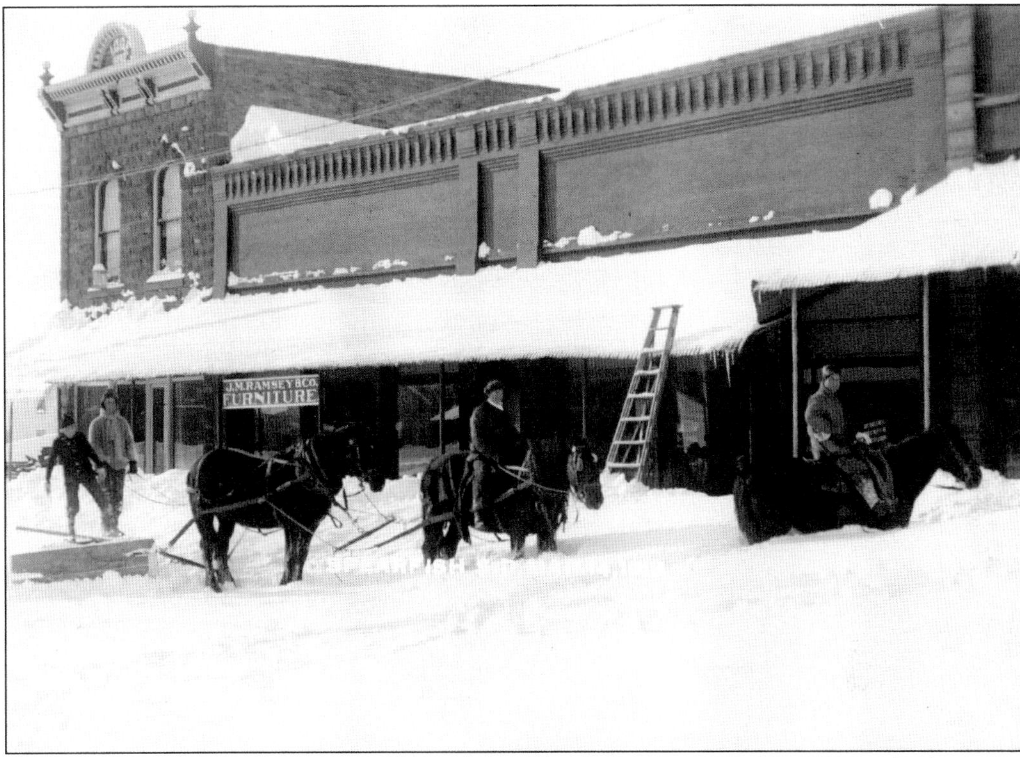

Floods were not the only thing playing havoc with the town; snowstorms were also known to dump large quantities of snow. This snowstorm occurred on December 14, 1913.

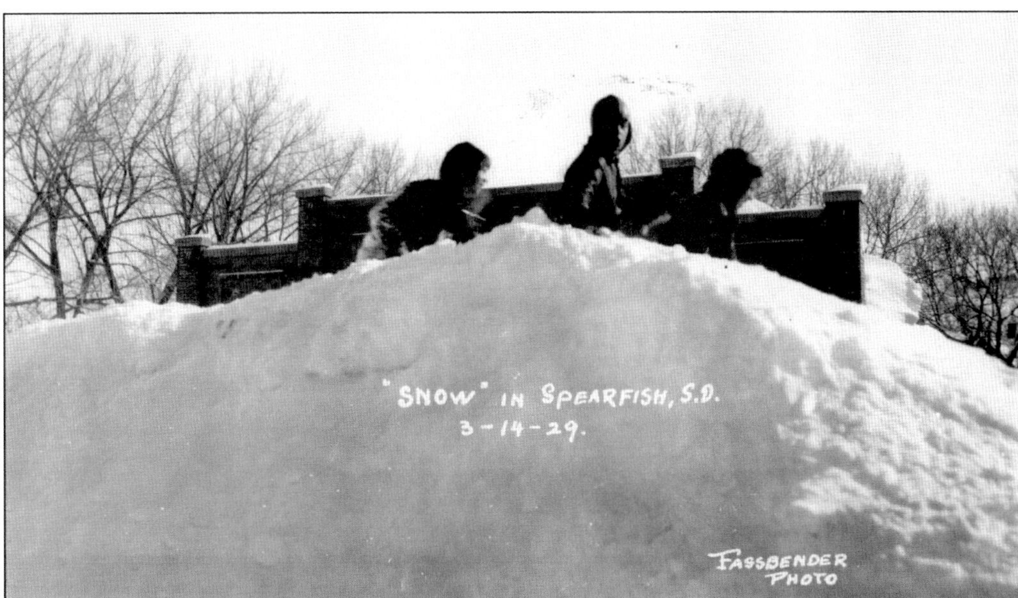

In this photograph, boys enjoy the snowdrifts from a 1929 storm.

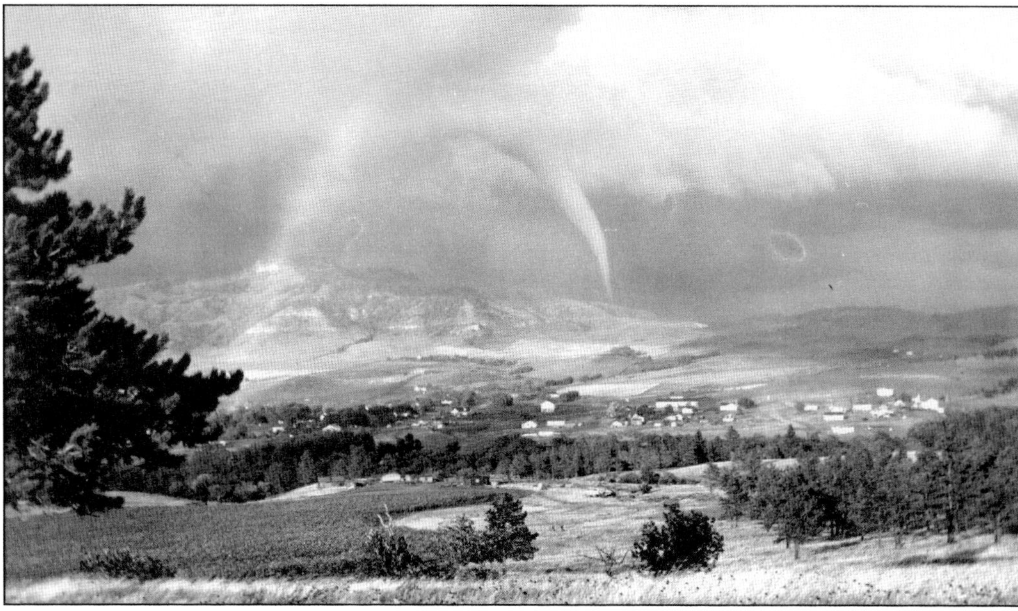

Frank Thomson photographed this funnel cloud over Lookout Mountain on August 4, 1953. The *Queen City Mail* reported on August 6th that staff and tourists at the Spearfish Airport watched the cloud from a basement window and said that it hovered between Lookout Mountain and the airport for 15 to 20 minutes. They reported that the storm moved in from the Northwest and that there were Southeasterly winds blowing into the storm. The funnel cloud dissipated as it neared the corner of the airplane hanger. In addition to pulling out two boundary fences, an old Cessna airplane was destroyed.

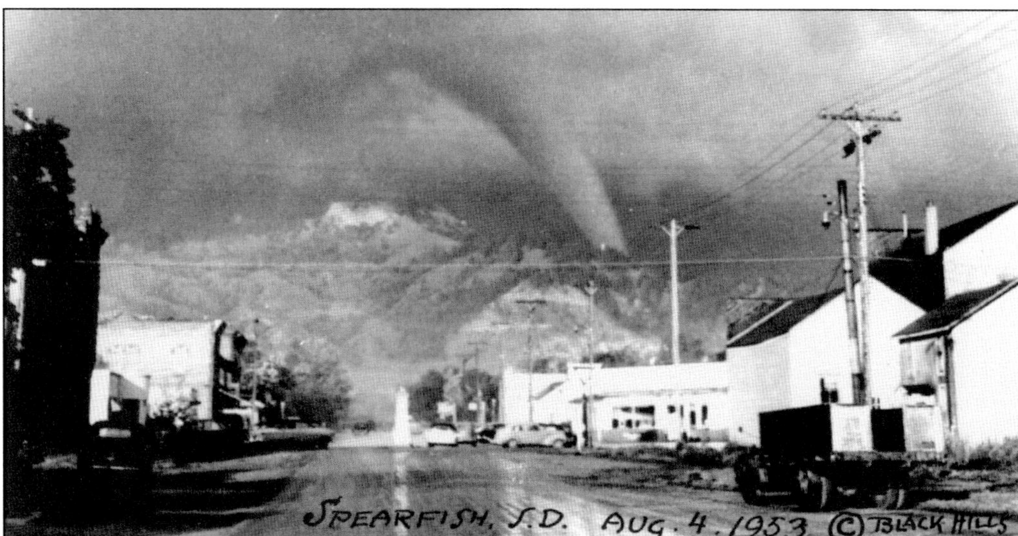

Another view of the 1953 tornado was taken as it threatened the peaceful town. There were no injuries due to the storm, but there was extensive damage done primarily in the business district. The *Queen City Mail* reported on all the trees and shrubs that had been uprooted; "the storm hit its most terrific blow" at the 100F building, a large area of bricks was torn from the east side of the building and deposited on the roof of the Spearfish Implement Company. A large glass door from the implement company shattered, and the storm deposited glass as far as four blocks away.

Four

Spearfish Canyon

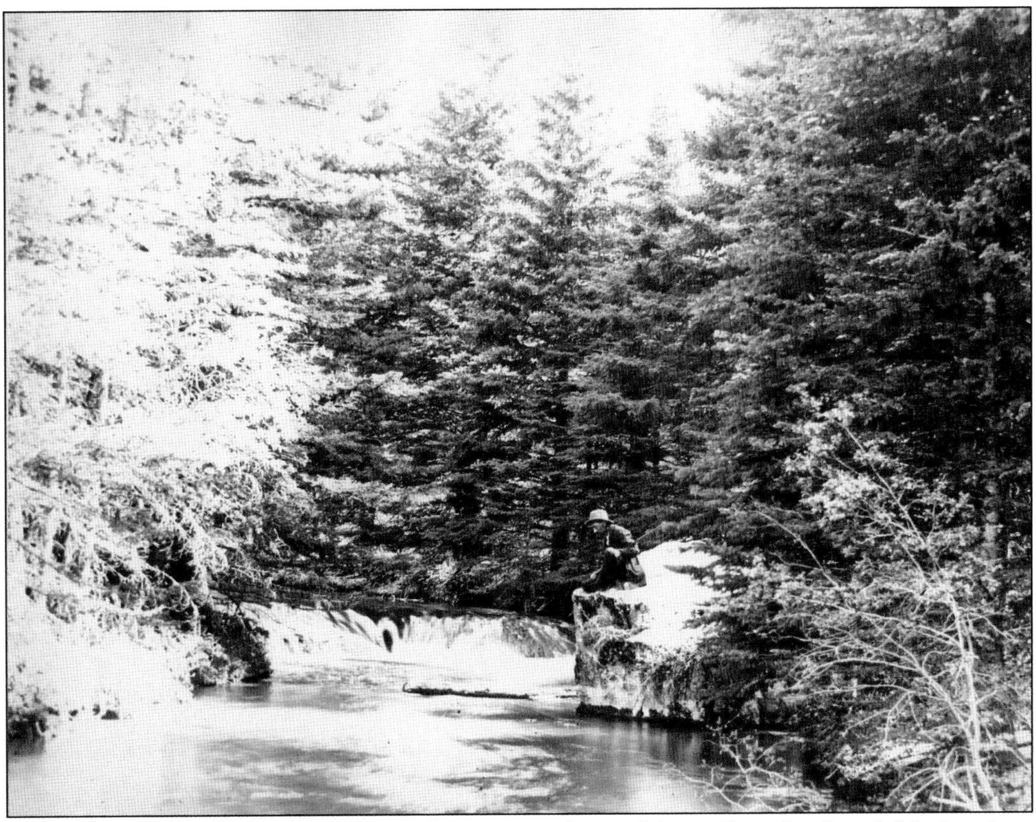

According to legend, Spearfish received its name when a fish swallowed a dwarfed Indian boy. His sister rescued him by throwing a moccasin attached to a rope into the creek. The fish swallowed the moccasin, and the sister pulled it to shore where she used a spear to open the fish and remove her brother. A less imaginative version of how Spearfish got its name is when one man said to another, this is a good place to spear fish.

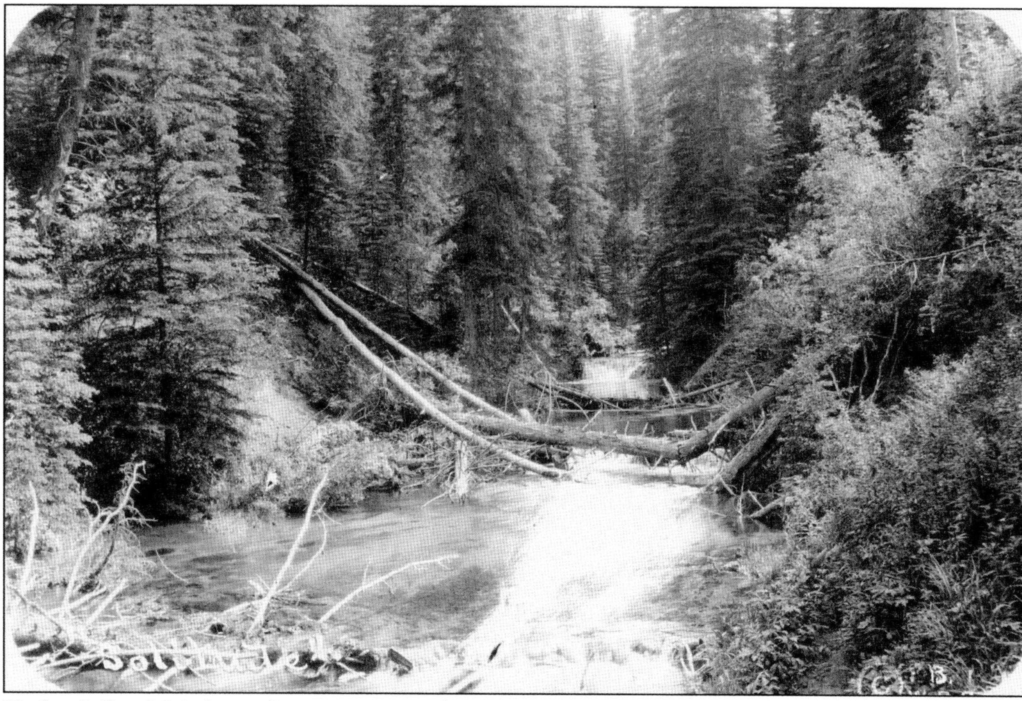

High cliffs of Madison limestone, Ponderosa pine, spruce, aspen, birch, and rushing water dominate the approximately 20-mile-long canyon scene. (Courtesy of the Cook collection.)

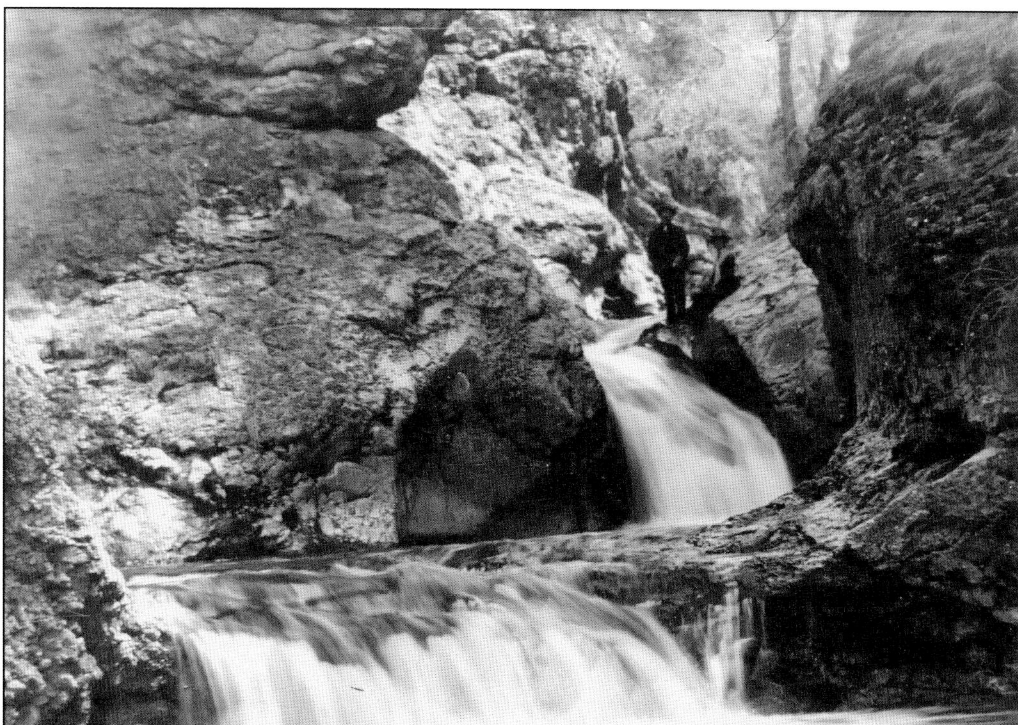

Small waterfalls abound in Spearfish Canyon. (Courtesy of the Cook collection.)

Summer cottages in the canyon offer a secluded getaway for fishing, hiking, or relaxing. (Courtesy of the Cook collection.)

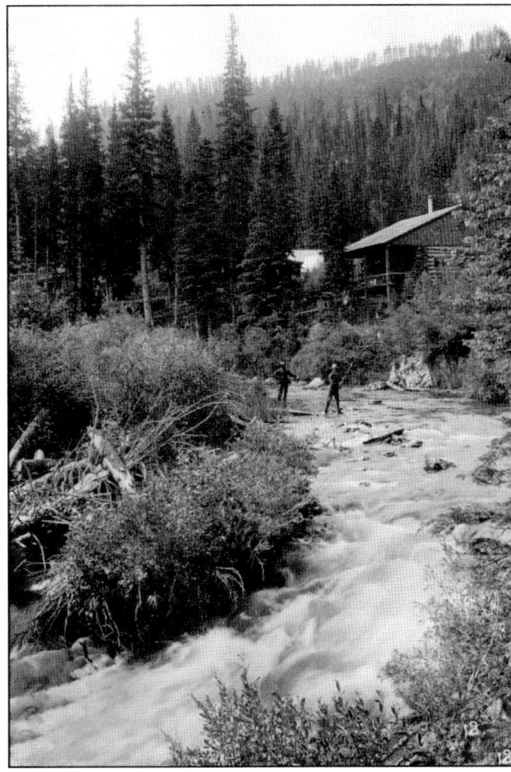

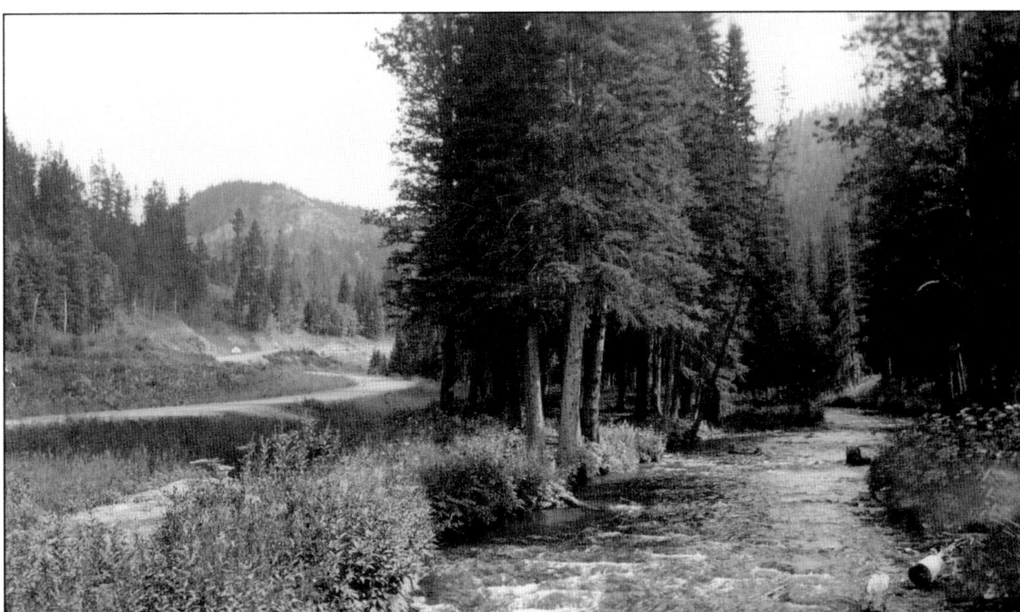

Thomas Odell photographed this tranquil place. Spearfish Creek, the second largest stream in the Black Hills, babbles its way through Spearfish Canyon and into Spearfish, providing a peaceful respite from the hectic demands of life. The creek offers cold, clear water for wading and trout fishing or an opportunity to simply listen to its merry melody.

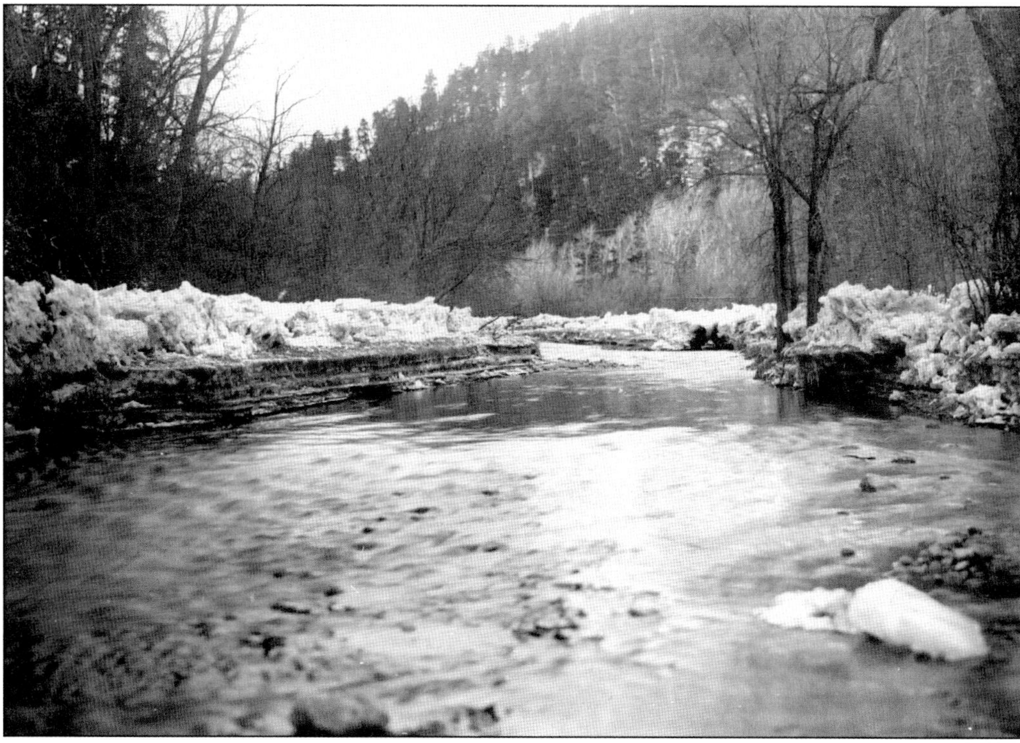

Perkins photographed this winter scene in the canyon in 1908. (Courtesy of the Cook collection.)

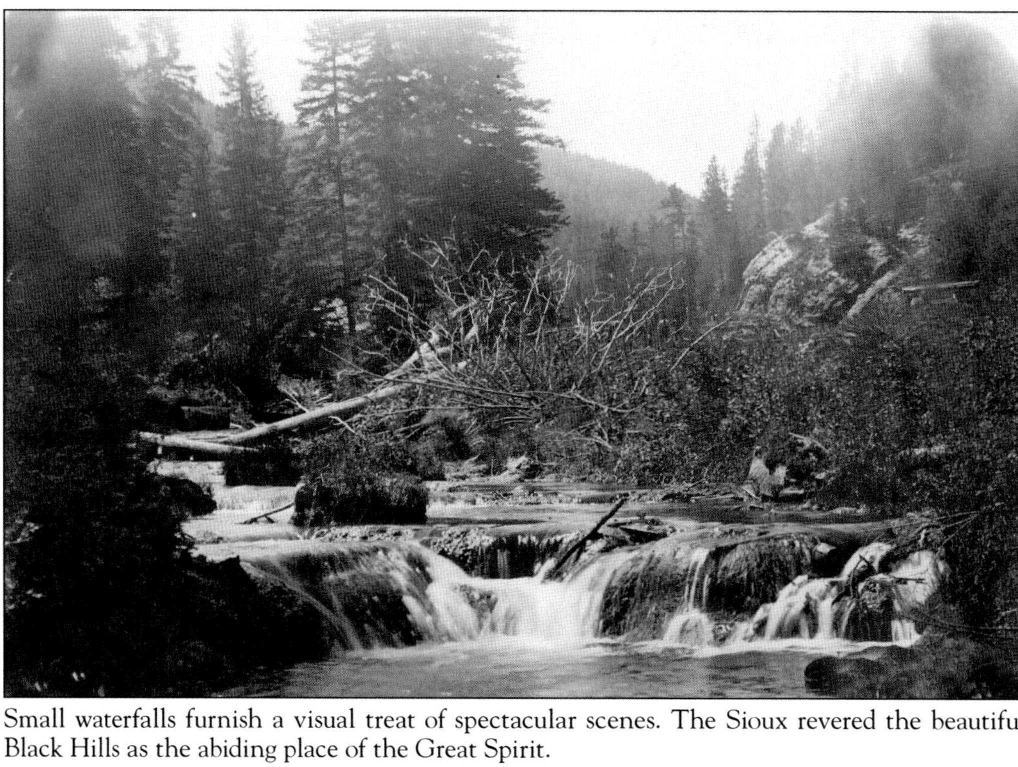

Small waterfalls furnish a visual treat of spectacular scenes. The Sioux revered the beautiful Black Hills as the abiding place of the Great Spirit.

Spearfish Creek has been considered to be one of the best trout fishing streams around because of its perfect habitat for trout. Several species of trout are found in Spearfish Creek. As the creek flows through the town of Spearfish, anglers can catch wild brown trout; wild rainbow and brown trout can be found near the confluence of Squaw Creek in Spearfish Canyon; brook trout are found in Little Spearfish and Hanna Creek; and Iron Creek Lake contains rainbow trout.

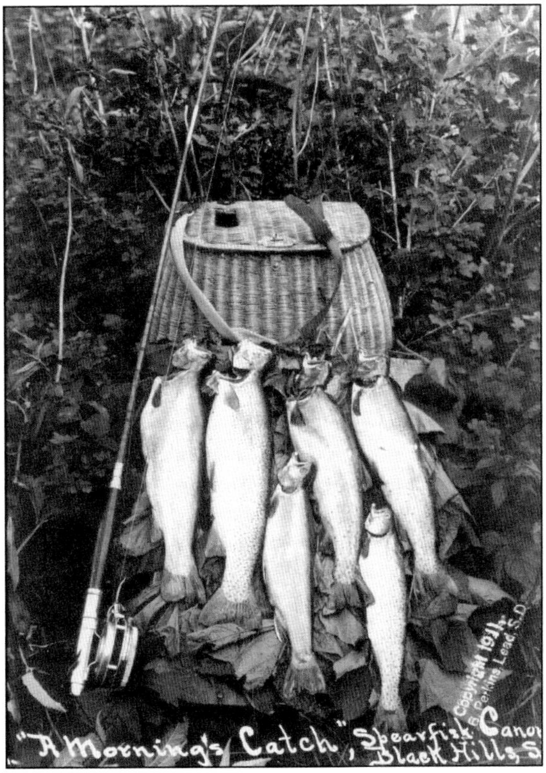

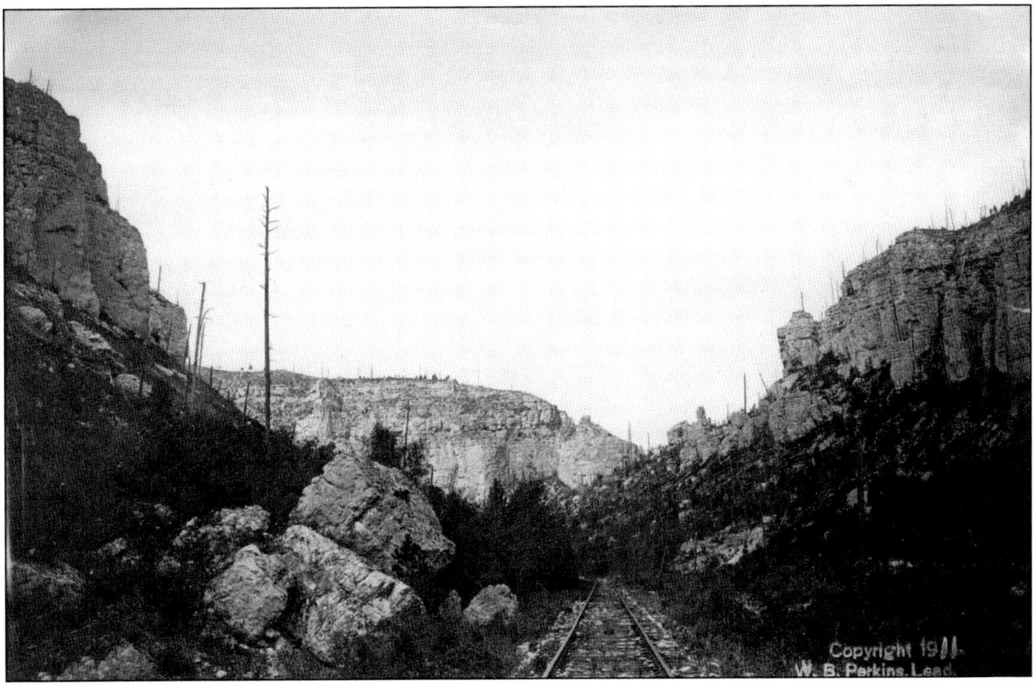

This photograph was taken at the palisades. The only early access to Spearfish Canyon was by rail that was built in 1893. The 31.91-mile mountainous rail line passed through Terry, Trojan, Crown Hill, Spearfish Canyon, Maurice, and Spearfish. (Courtesy of the Cook collection.)

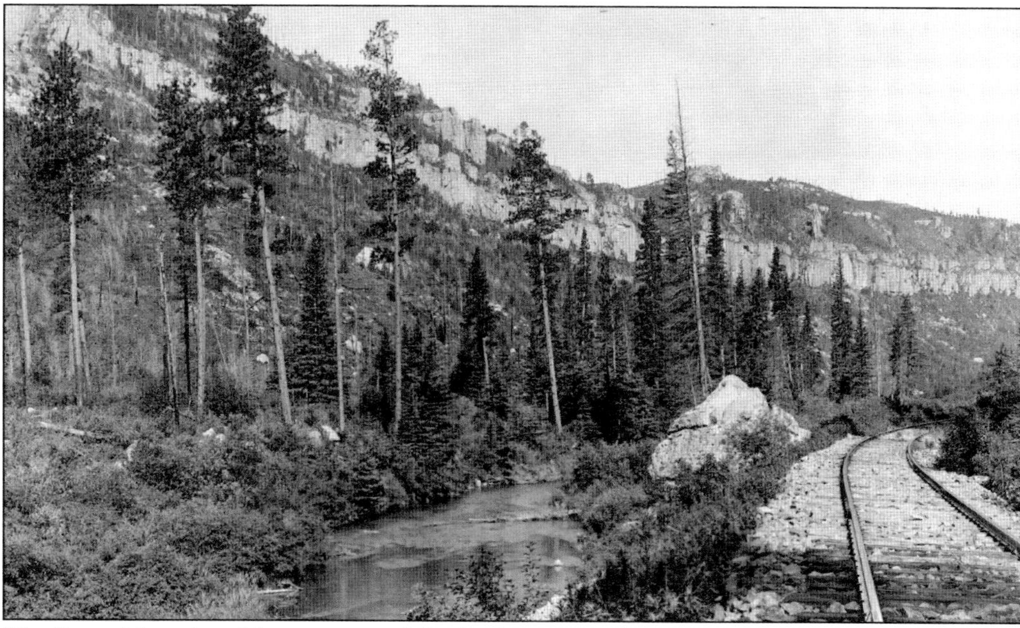

The Spearfish railroad line, a spur of the Burlington and Missouri River Railroad, became of much admired engineering feat. The line cost the Burlington and Missouri River Railroad $2,000,000 from Englewood to Spearfish. It was remarked that it "was the only railroad in the world on which the freight cars had to be chained to the siding to keep them from coming home by themselves."

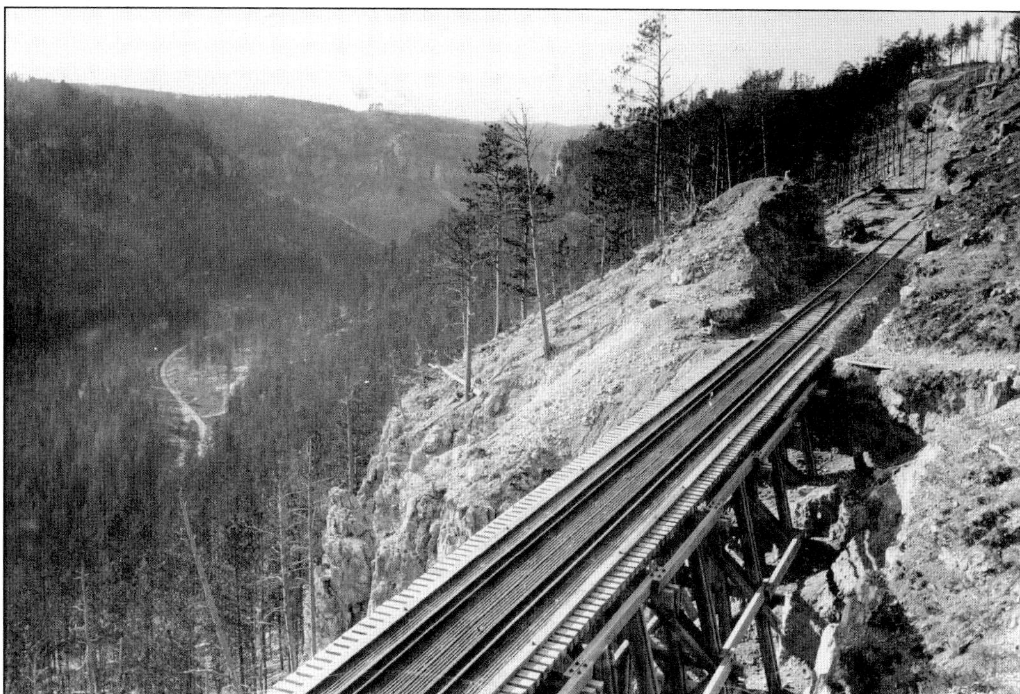

The trestle at Seven Mile Bend overlooks Spearfish Canyon. There were 375 curves in 31 lineal miles on the Spearfish railroad line, a curve for every 436 feet.

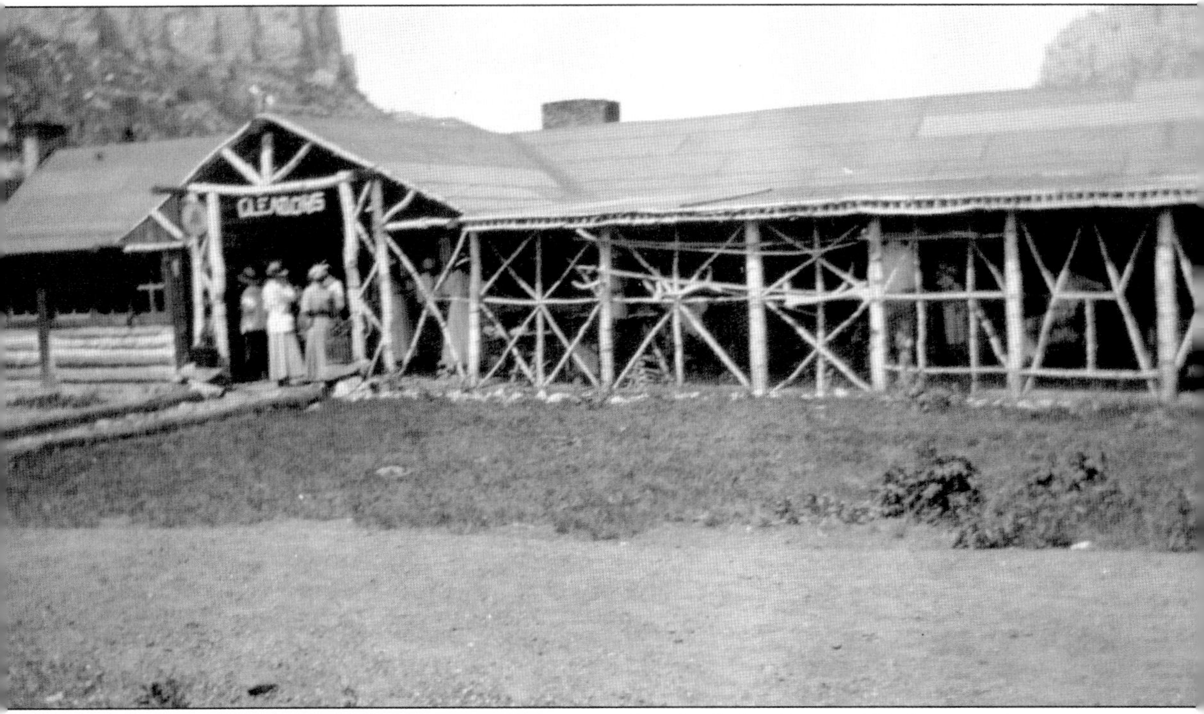

Glendoris, pictured above, began as a one-room cabin built by George Belshaw in the early 1890s. Mr. Lepke and Mr. McLaughlin used it as an office for the sawmill they established across the road in 1892. The Tie and Timber Company owned the sawmill and employed many local men to saw the timbers for the railroad, ranchers, miners, homesteaders, and prospectors. This small settlement became known as Savoy. The Tie and Timber Company left in 1906 and Glen Inglish purchased the cabin. After he married Dorothy Smith they opened it as a lodge, naming it Glendoris using both their names. (Courtesy of the Cook collection.)

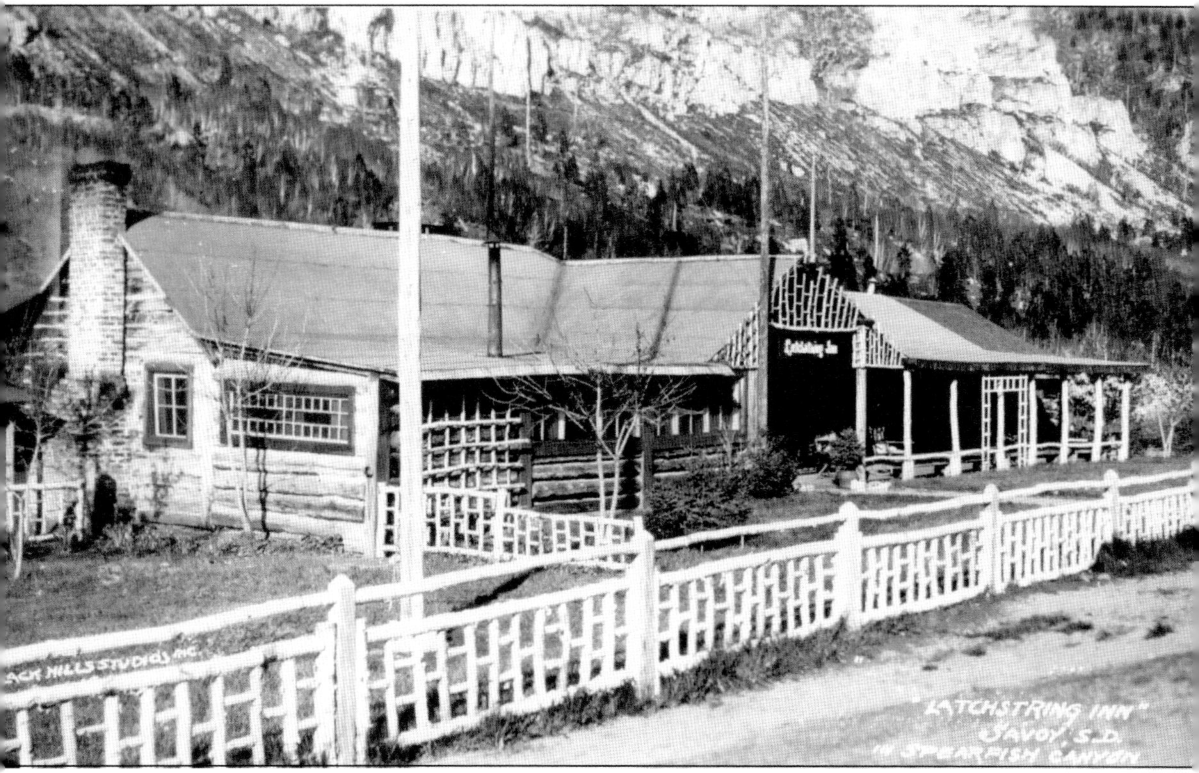

As business grew, Glen and Dorothy Inglish added on to the cabin using vacated buildings. By 1919, when two women, Maude Watts and Martha Railsback, bought the inn, Savoy had grown to include a post office, store, six cottages, and a railroad station. The ladies changed the name to Latchstring Inn since all the heavy doors used latchstrings to open them. Early life at Latchstring Inn was quite primitive and isolated, since only the railroad could reach the inn. Water had to be carried from the creek and kerosene lamps provided the light until the inn was able to generate its own electricity on a limited scale. Watts sold her interest to Railsback in 1929, and Railsback operated the inn alone until she married Lawrence Tinsley the following year. Around 1932, water was piped into the inn, and Black Hills Power and Light provided electricity in 1946. (Courtesy of Roberta Sago.)

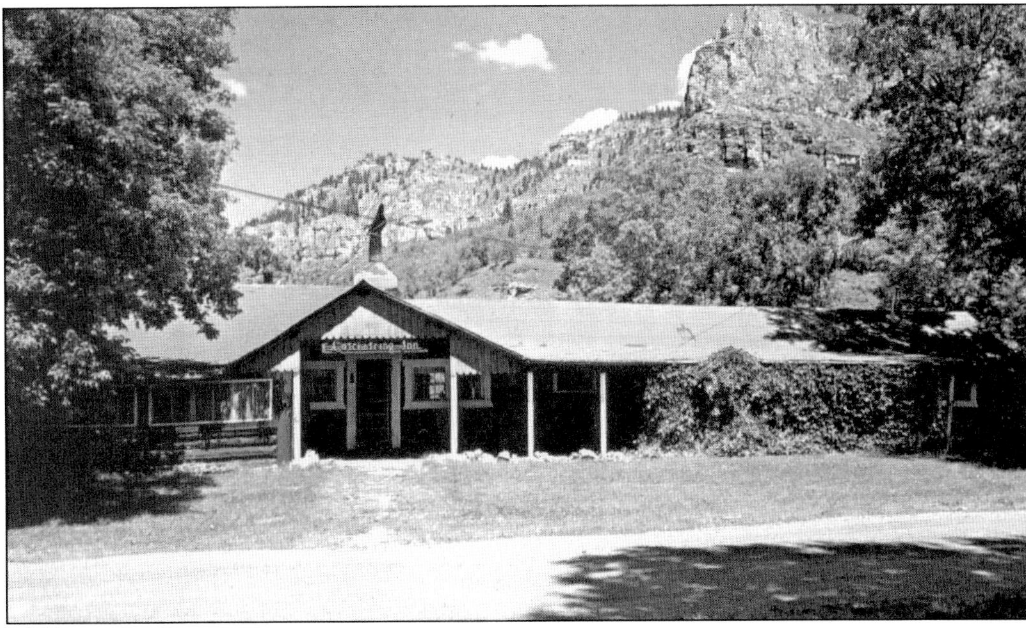

The Tinsleys enclosed the large front porch for a dining room and added a fireplace. Latchstring Inn changed hands several times but continued to be a favorite destination. In 1989, Homestake mill, which had always owned the land where Latchstring stood, announced the inn was beyond repair and would have to come down. Despite petitions to Homestake, the building, cabins, and a chapel were cleared away and a new combination log cultural center and dining establishment was built on the old site. (Courtesy of Roberta Sago.)

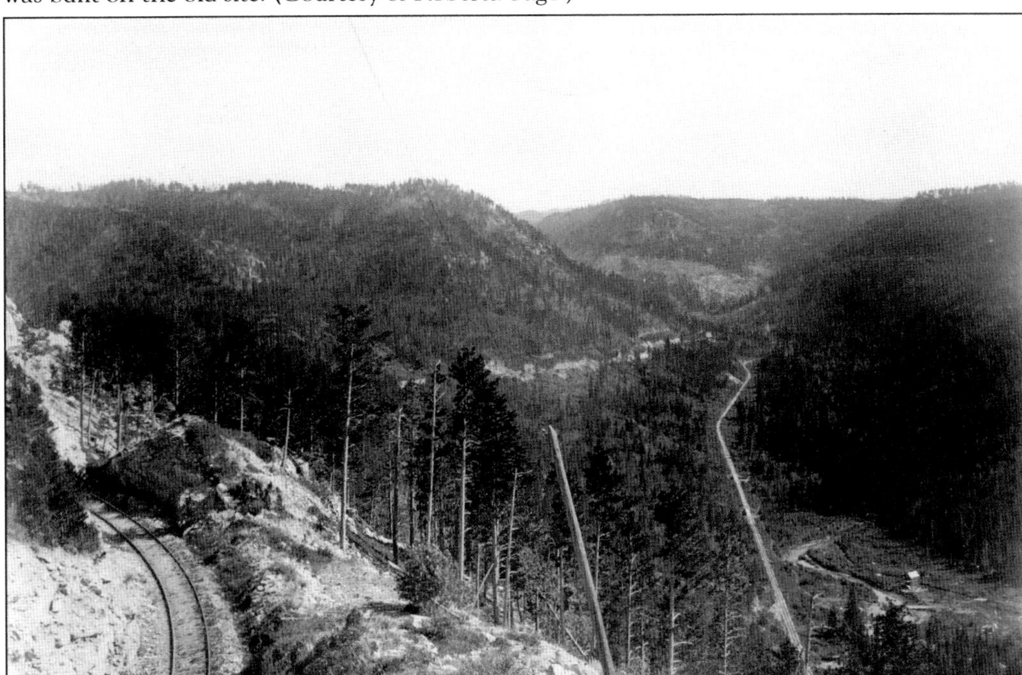

The railroad follows the ridge high above the canyon floor in this 1910 photograph. (Courtesy of the Cook collection.)

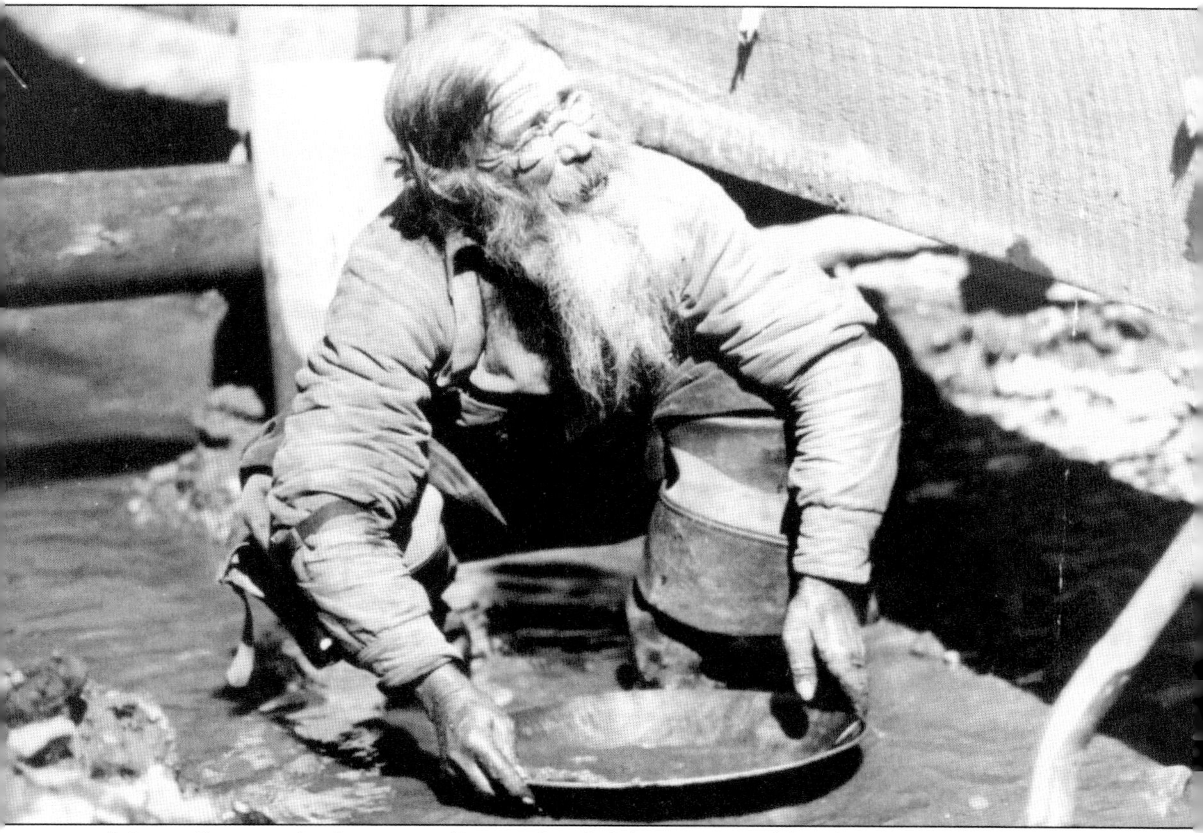

Johnny Perrett, also known as Potato Creek Johnny, earned his fame by discovering one of the largest gold nuggets found in the Black Hills in May 1929, along Potato Creek, a tributary of Spearfish Creek. He sold it for $250 to W. E. Adams. Perrett lived about five miles from Latchstring Inn and became a regular visitor. He purchased groceries with his bag full of gold nuggets. He packed his bacon, beans, and other purchases in a burlap sack, which he carried over his shoulder. Perrett also played the fiddle for dances and was called the Little Iron Creek Fiddler. After Perrett became famous, he showed the tourists how to pan for gold and participated in the Days of '76 parade. He was a well-loved Black Hills character.

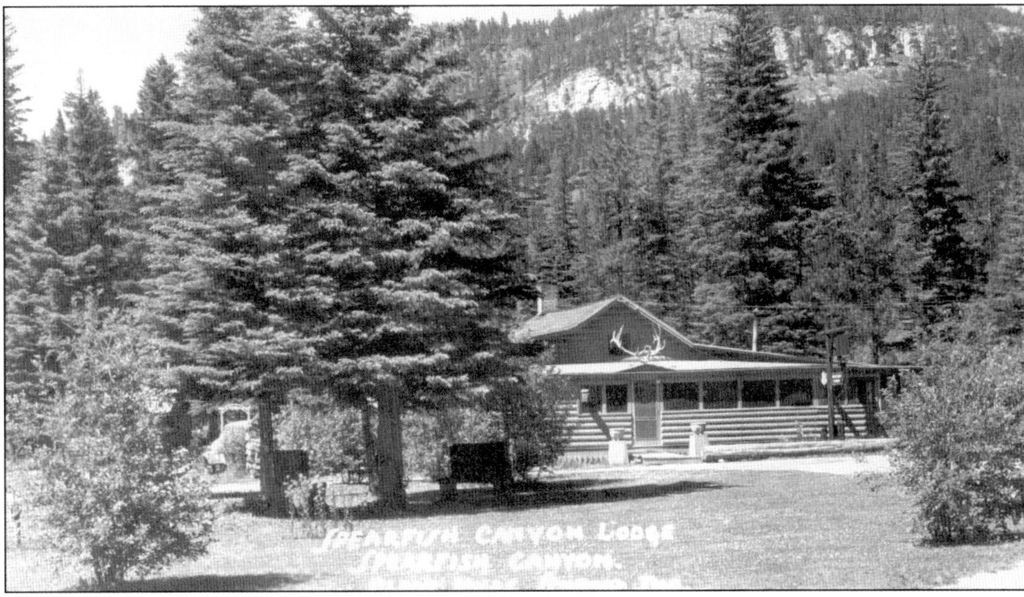

Other lodges were built in the canyon including Spearfish Canyon Lodge. On the back of this postcard this note is written, "Had cokes here." (Courtesy of Roberta Sago.)

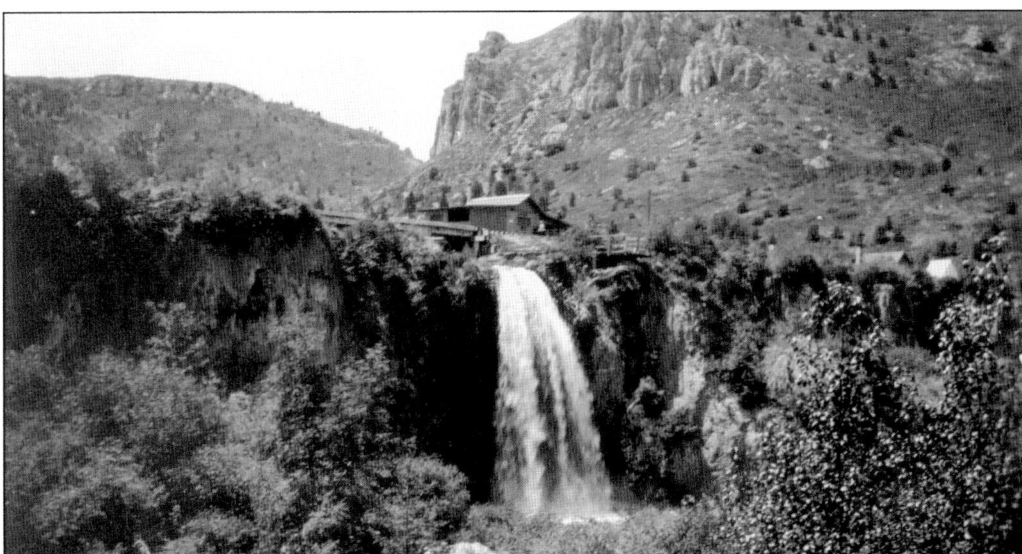

Savoy is perched above Spearfish Falls in this June 30, 1917, photograph. In this same year Homestake mill would divert the water through a tunnel to furnish light and power for Homestake as well as the cites of Lead and Spearfish. Richard Hughes wrote in his book *Pioneer Years in the Black Hills* regarding the falls diversion, "It is much to be regretted that a great part of the district's charm thus has been sacrificed." (Courtesy of the Cook collection.)

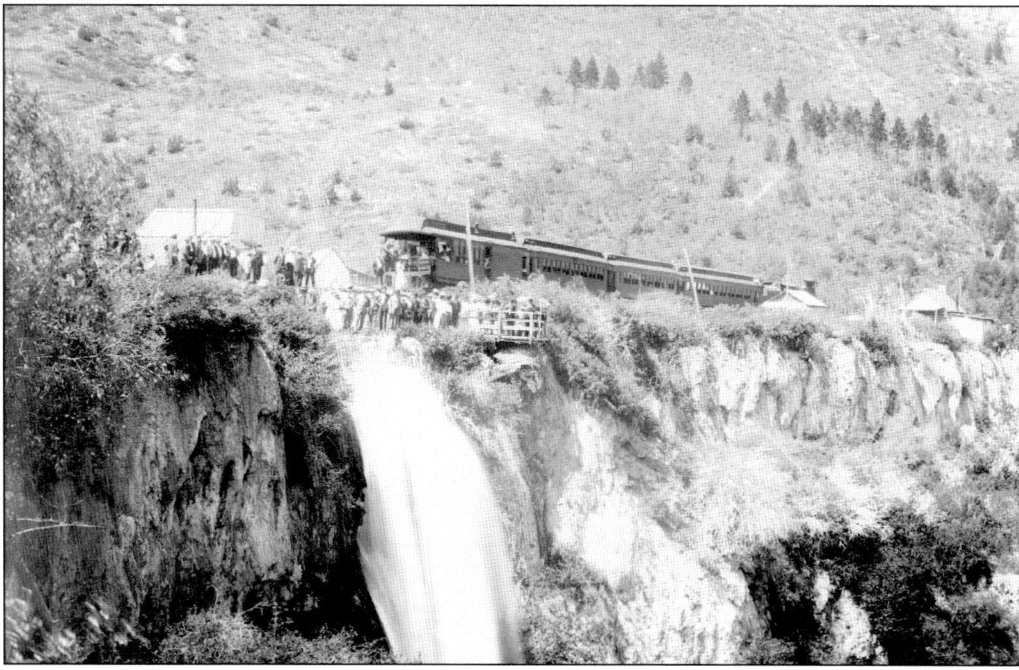

Before the falls was diverted to run hydroelectric plants, the train stopped above Spearfish Falls to let passengers enjoy the thrill and beauty of the thundering water, falling about 60 feet below. The falls was so powerful that it shook the trestle.

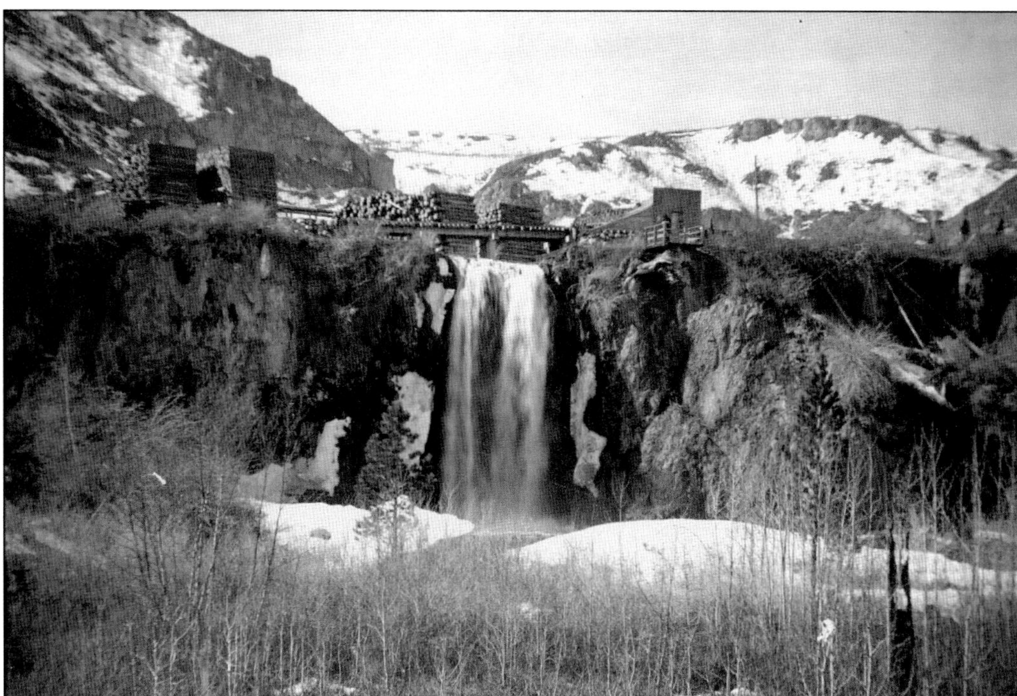

Here is another view of Spearfish Falls, one of the most scenic spots on the Spearfish railroad line, with the trestle and train stopped above.

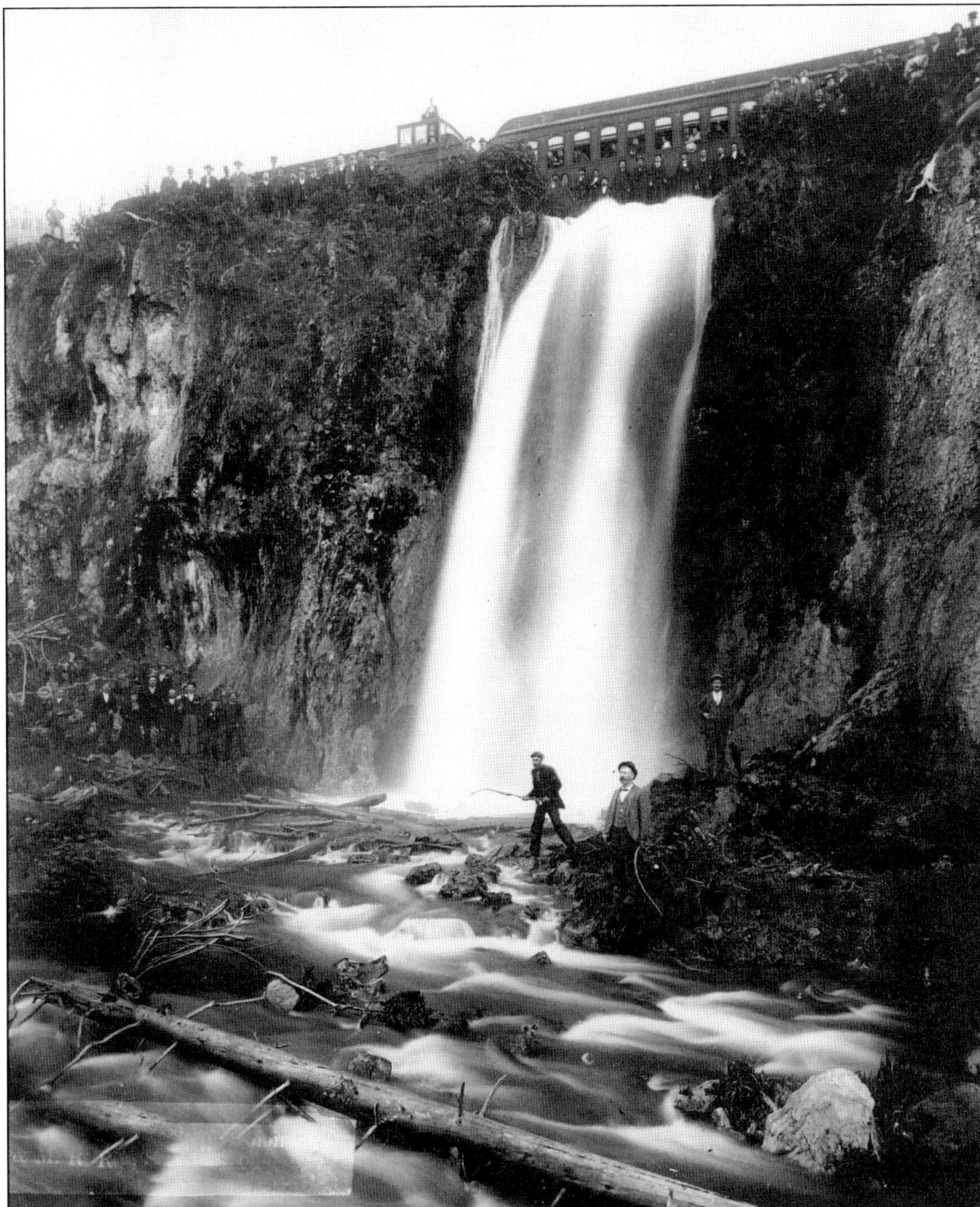

In this photograph, the train stops above Spearfish Falls while two passengers explore the spectacular scene. O. W. Coursey recommended in his book *Beautiful Black Hills* to "leave your car at Spearfish; take the train the next day at noon and go to Spearfish Canyon to Savoy. Get off, stop into the 'Latchstring Inn' register and secure a room for the night . . . take your tackle along; fishing is good—the best in the Hills."

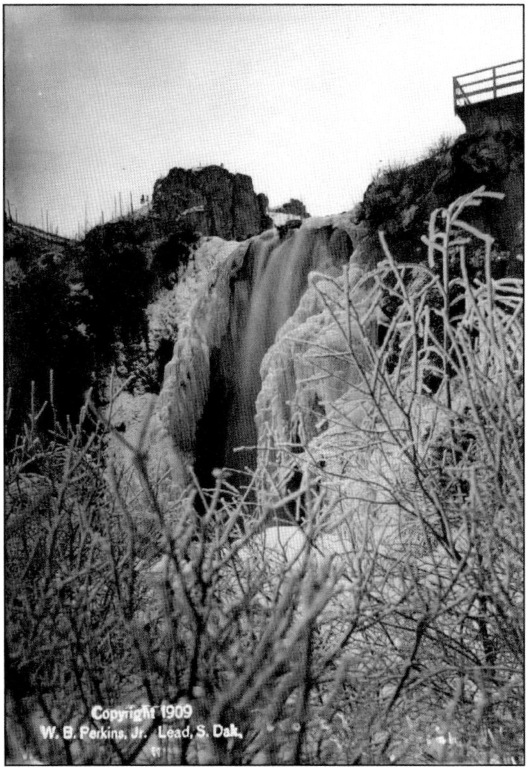

Once again, Spearfish Falls is the subject for a photographer. The falls is seen here in winter splendor. Winter added another dimension of beauty to Spearfish Canyon. Rock and snow slides made for interesting stories along the Spearfish railroad line in the early years.

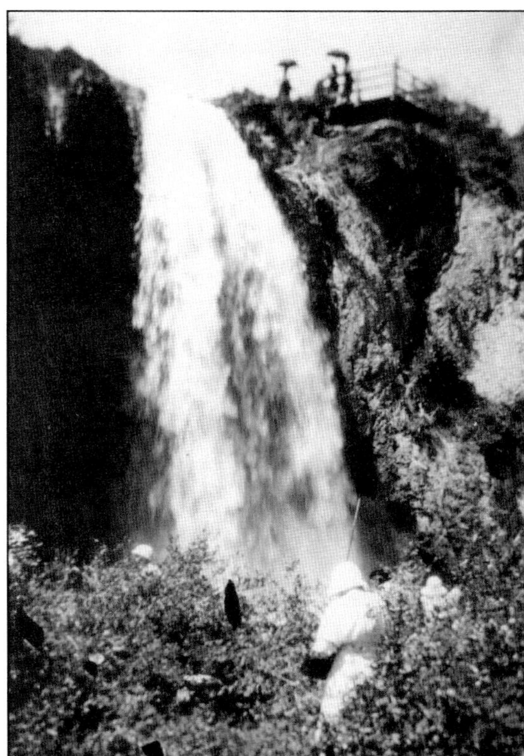

A group of people listen to the thunderous roar of the Spearfish Falls and seem to be preparing themselves for the droplets of mist it sprayed upon spectators.

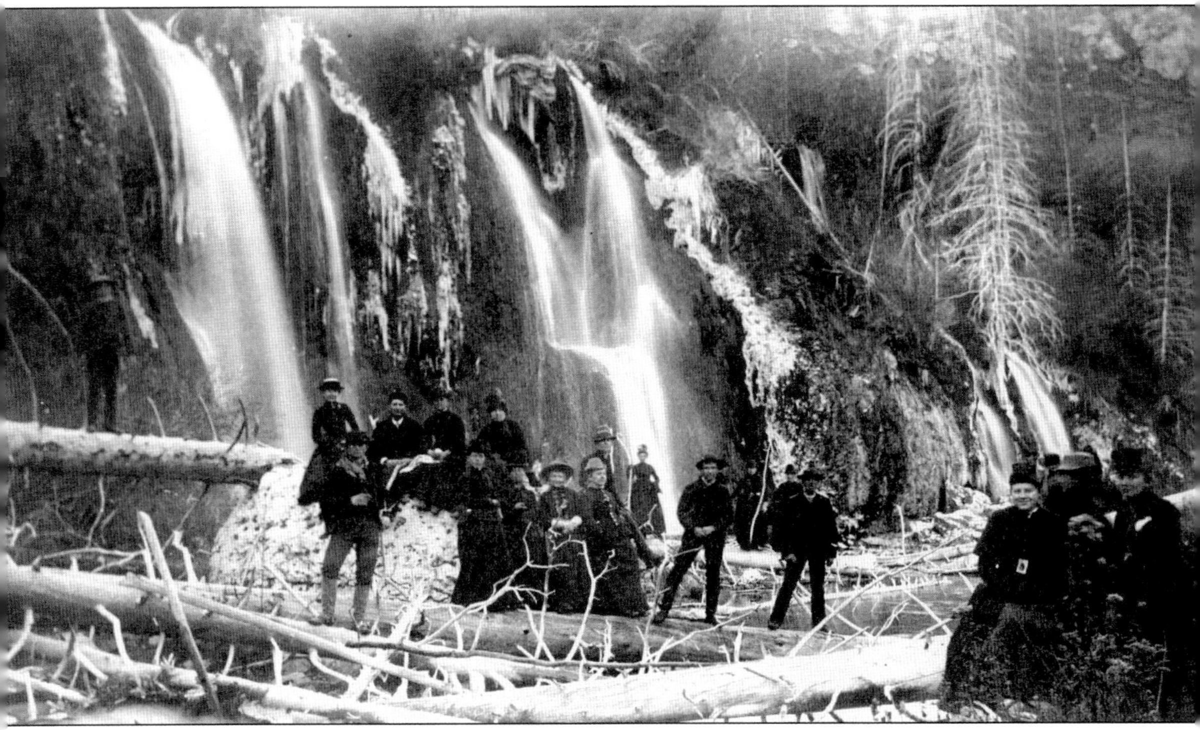

Visitors to Spearfish Falls pose for this 1889 photograph. Fishermen, picnickers, and berry pickers could take the train to Spearfish Canyon and stay for the day. The return train would blast a warning whistle and everyone would scurry to board the train at a railway stop for their return home. (Courtesy of the Cook collection.)

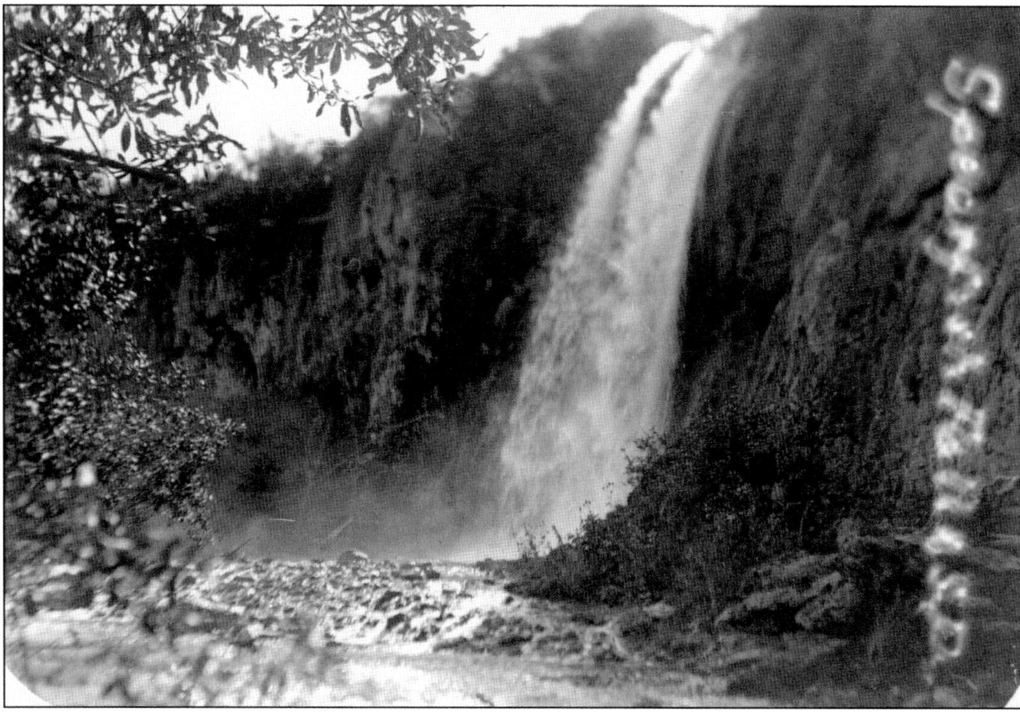

A favorite subject for photographers, this view of Spearfish Falls was taken in 1906. Spearfish Falls was nicknamed "Baby Niagara."

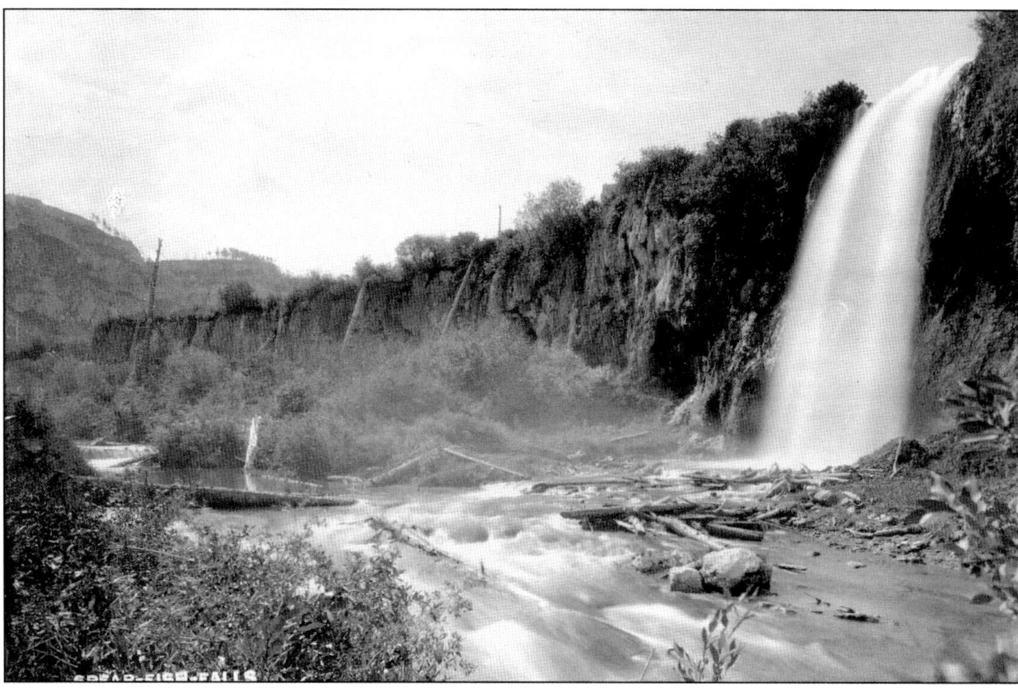

The beauty of Spearfish Falls became only a memory after the water's diversion in 1917. It was not until 2003 that Homestake allowed the water to flow freely once again. (Courtesy of the Cook collection.)

Beautiful Rough Lock Falls was named because of a steep hill near the falls that required wagon wheels to be rough locked or chained to brake the wheels coming down the hill so wagons would not run into the horses. This didn't always work, as a nearby canyon was named Breakneck Canyon, because wagons coming down the steep terrain pitched over horses, breaking their necks.

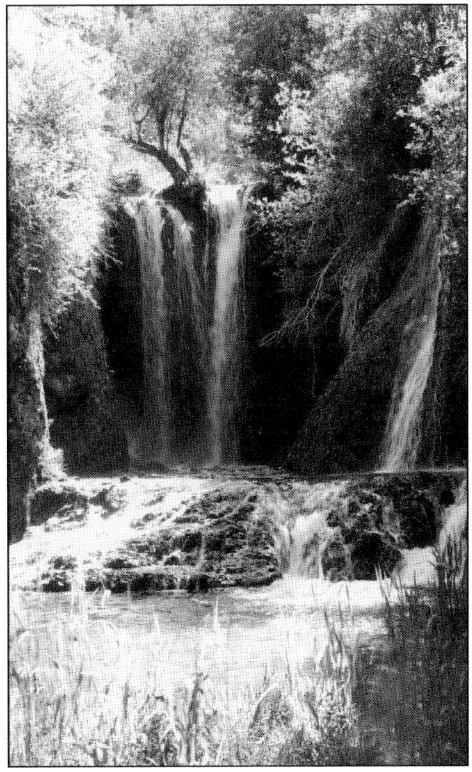

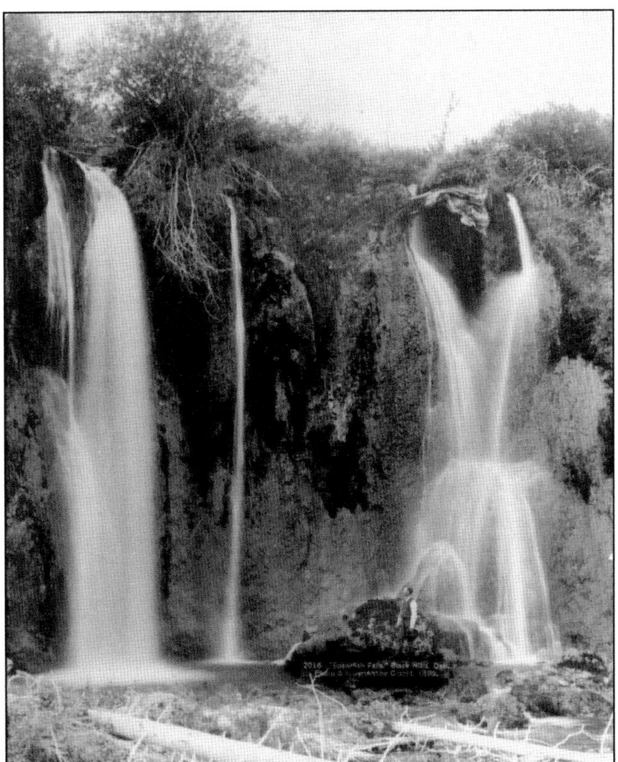

Above Rough Lock Falls, Little Spearfish Creek merrily babbles along until it thunders over the edge, creating a spectacular sight.

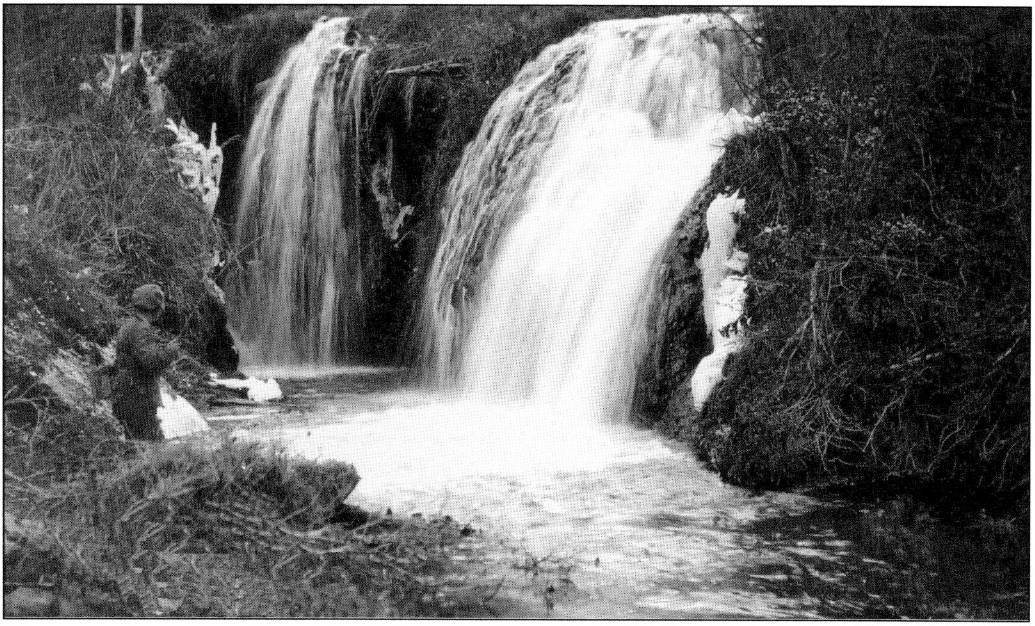

This is another view of Rough Lock Falls by photographer Thomas Odell.

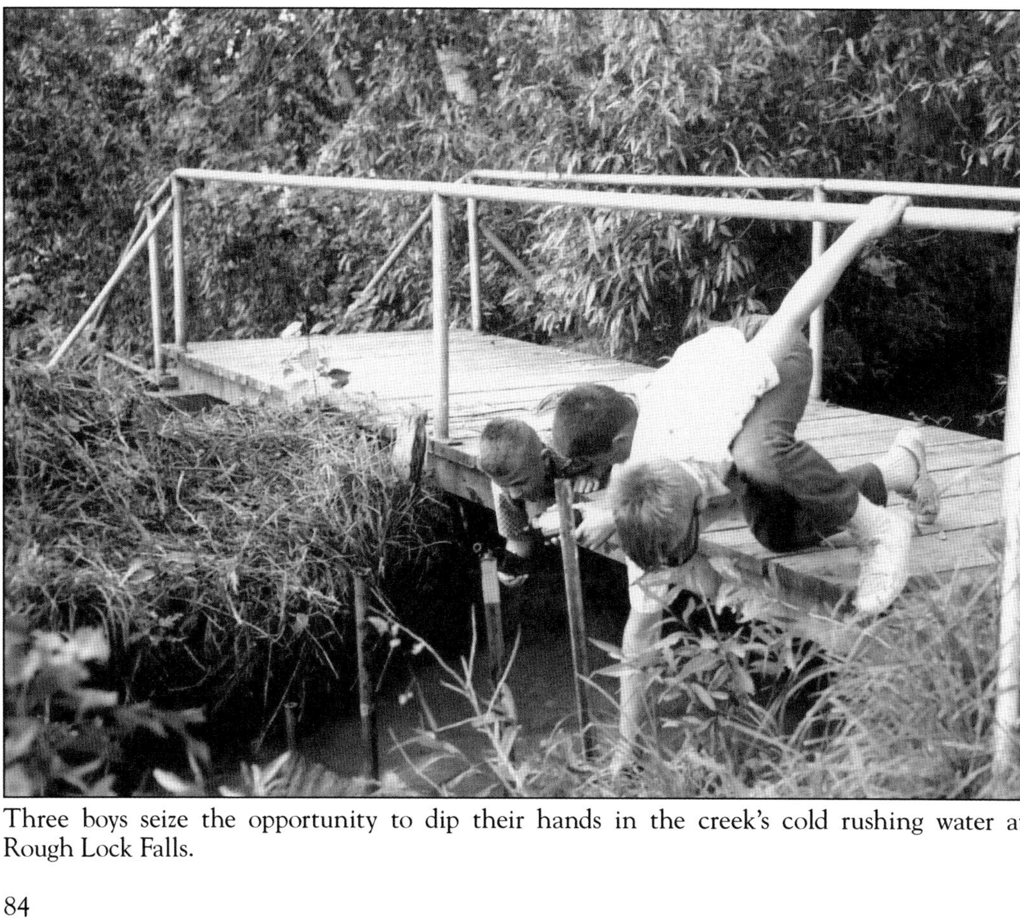

Three boys seize the opportunity to dip their hands in the creek's cold rushing water at Rough Lock Falls.

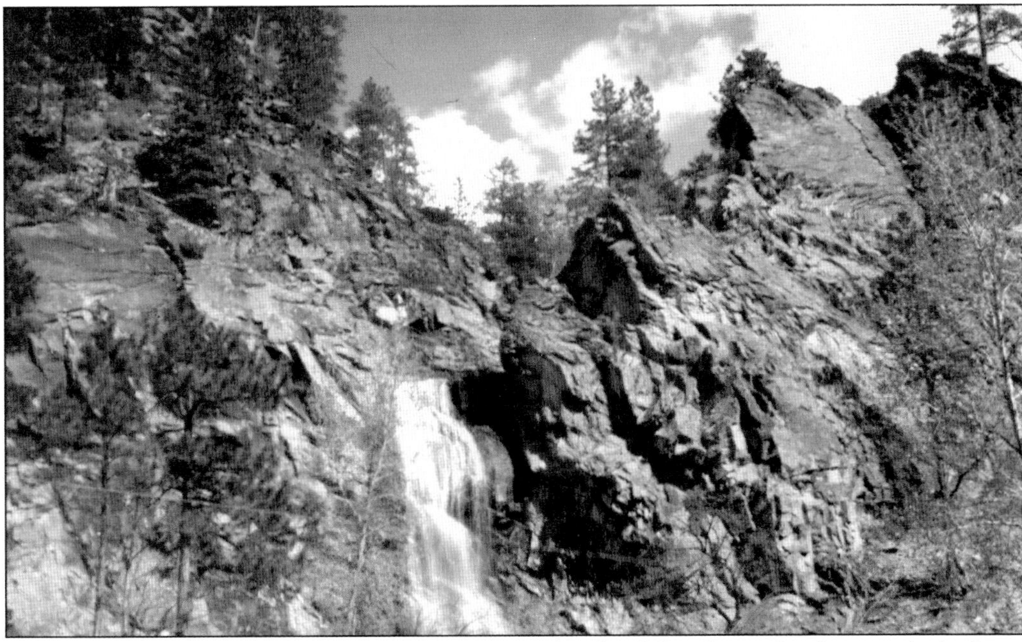

Another falls in Spearfish Canyon is Bridal Veil Falls. This falls is located right near the highway. The falls cascade down the mountainside simulating a flowing bridal veil.

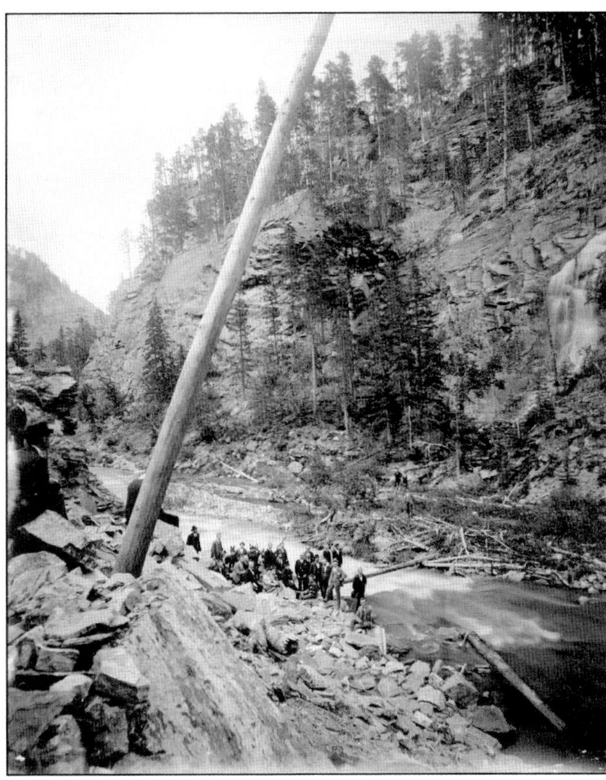

A group of people edge closer to view Bridal Veil Falls. The train ran above Spearfish Falls while it ran below Bridal Veil Falls. The train often let passengers off to spend the day.

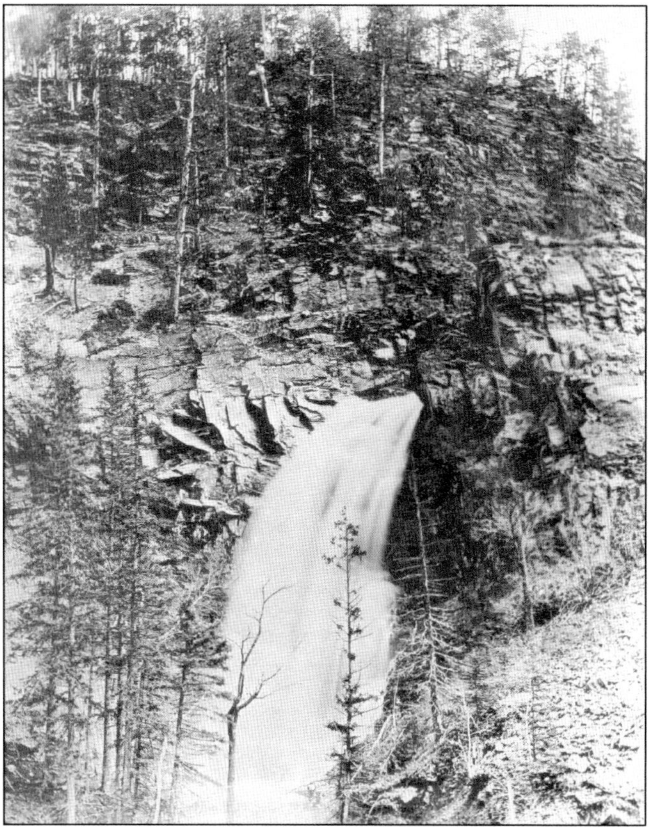

Here Bridal Veil Falls is seen at its best. In the spring the falls tends to run fuller than in the summer. In the 1990s, rock climbers began to expand their sport to Spearfish Canyon. When Bridal Veil Falls freezes over in the winter, it presents a challenge to the best of ice climbers. The ever changing ice offers a dangerous but exhilarating experience.

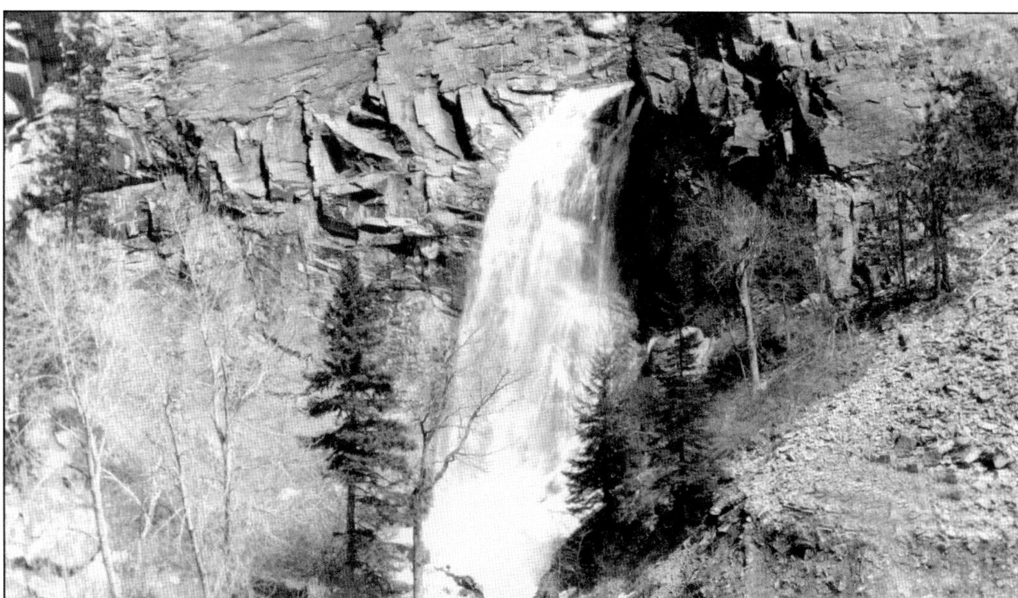

Thomas Odell captured Bridal Veil Falls flowing in full splendor. Through the years, however, Bridal Veil has diminished because of drought and overuse.

Iron Mountain Road, as seen here, is typical of many of the back roads near Spearfish Canyon. In 1877, miners established a mining camp in the Iron Creek area.

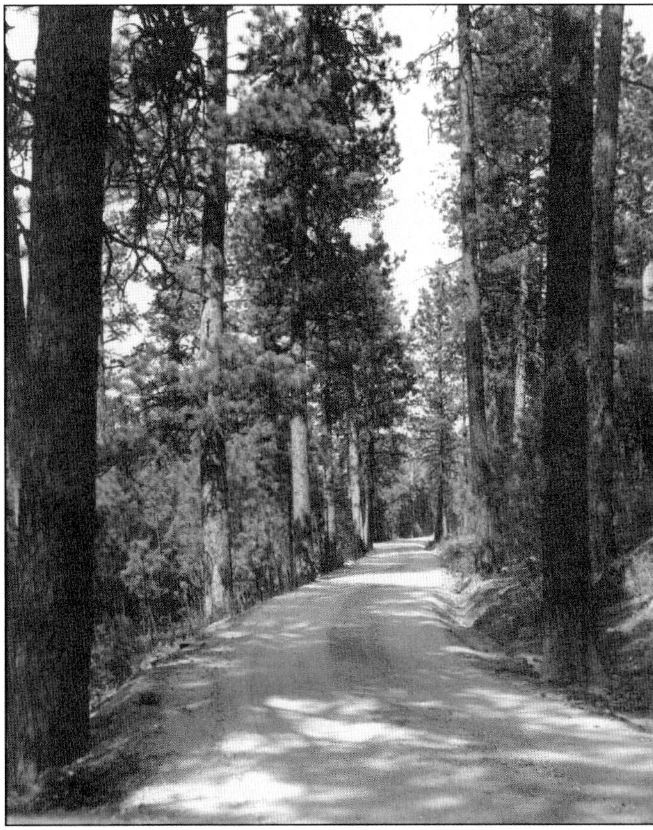

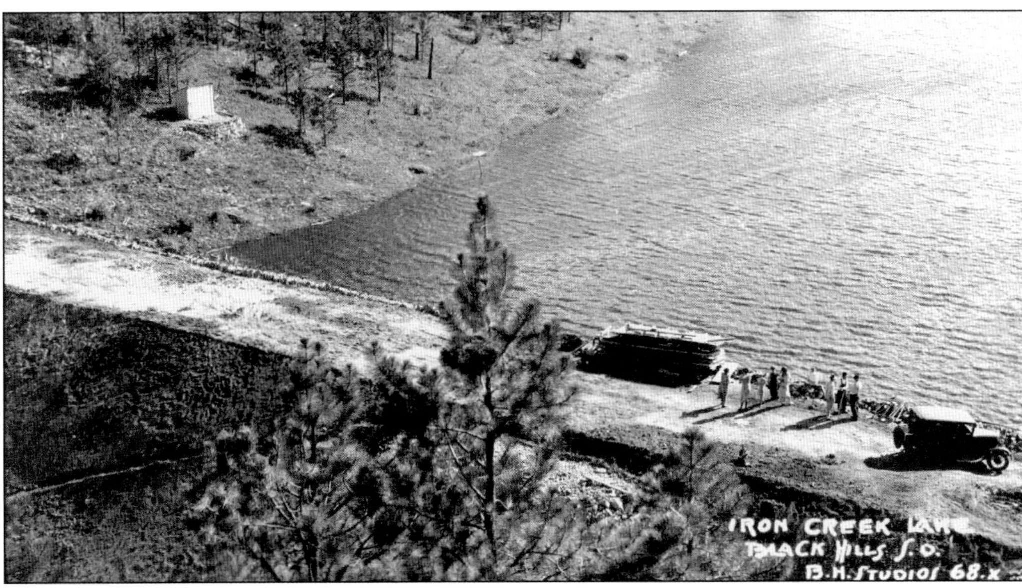

Here is a photograph by Thomas Odell of Iron Creek Lake, a popular recreation spot. The Works Progress Administration constructed the lake in 1937. A heavy rain in the vicinity of Iron Creek Canyon in 1933 caused a flash flood that ripped through the canyon carrying boulders the size of houses with it. The torrent of water washed out two miles of track and closed the road to traffic.

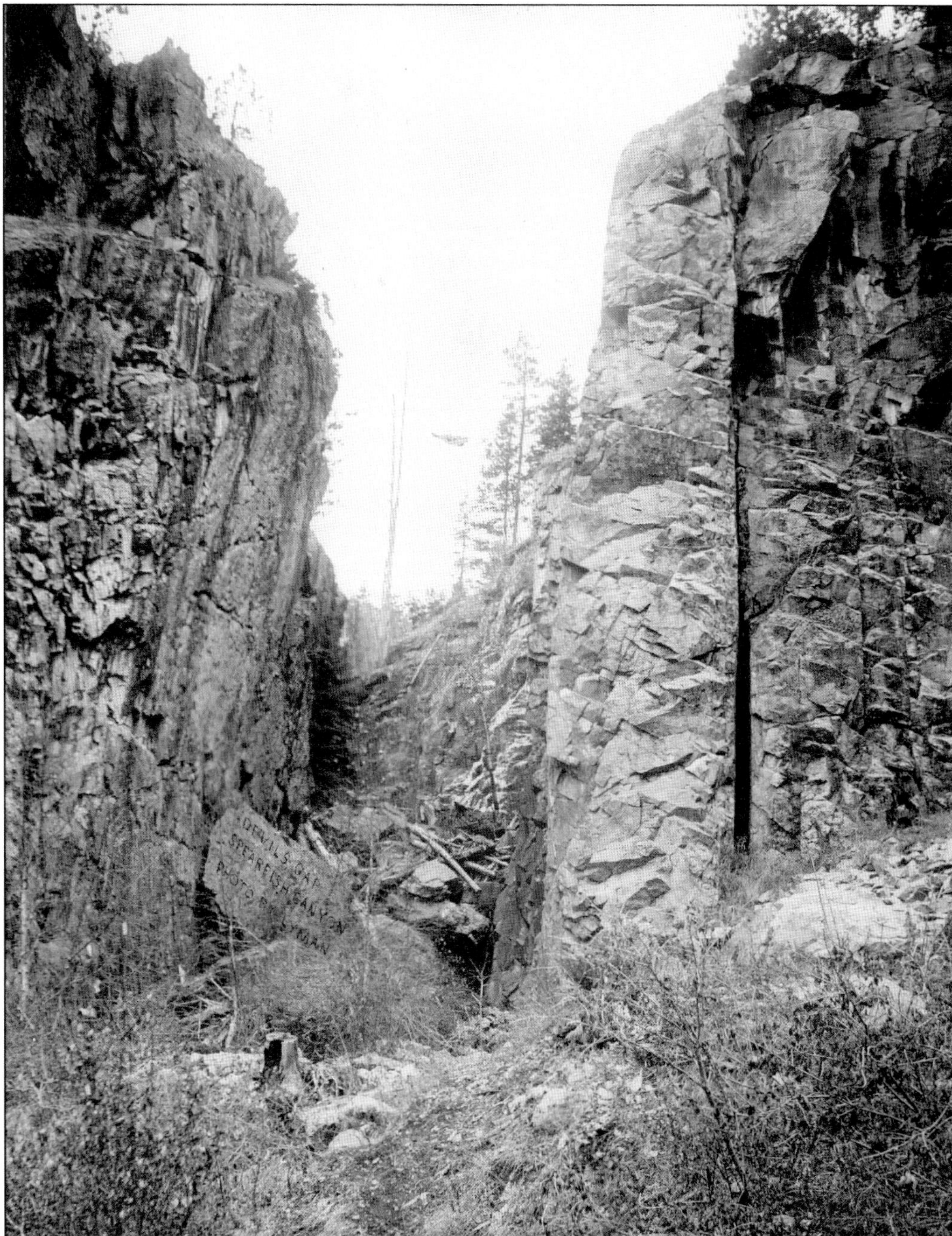

This early photograph is of Spearfish Canyon's Hell Gate. Frank Lloyd Wright, the famous architect, rode through Spearfish Canyon a few years after the road was built. Unprepared for the marvelous scene before him, he described the canyon in a flourish of words and compared it to paintings of the Chinese masters: "We would be headed straight for gigantic white walls trabeated in ledges from which pines sprouted and grew in precisely the manner of the pictorial dreams of the great Chinese painter, the greatest painters who ever lived." (Courtesy of the Cook collection.)

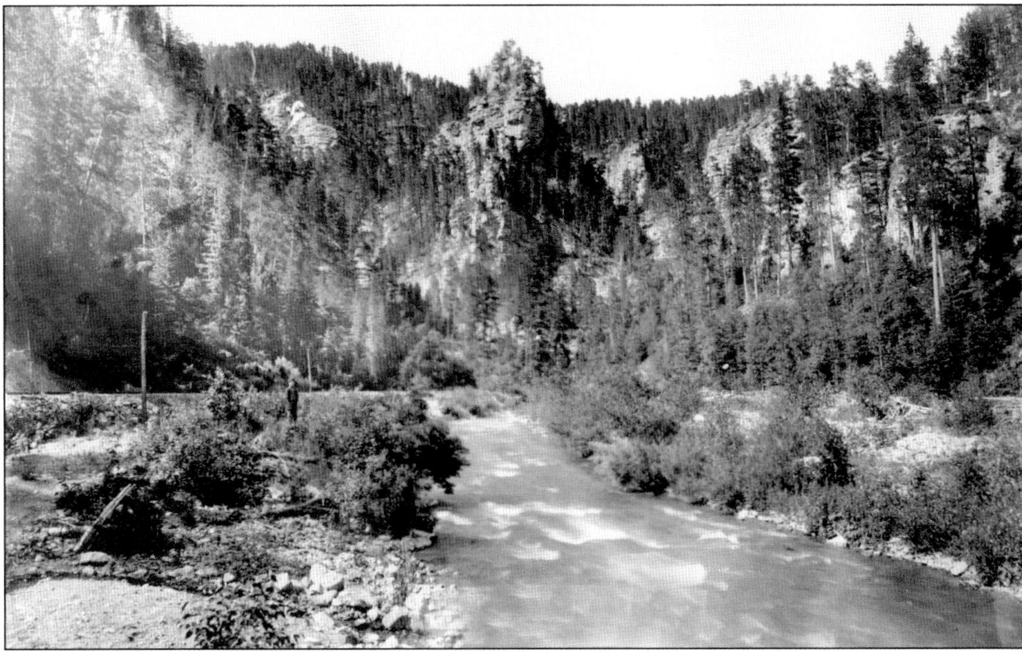

Locke and Peterson photographed this scene. Wright continues with his fascination, "We were in the land of the Sung and Ming masters. Whoever knows their idealizations of nature in the Chinese landscape painting of those great periods, and they were mostly landscapes, can see the character of the Spearfish ensemble."

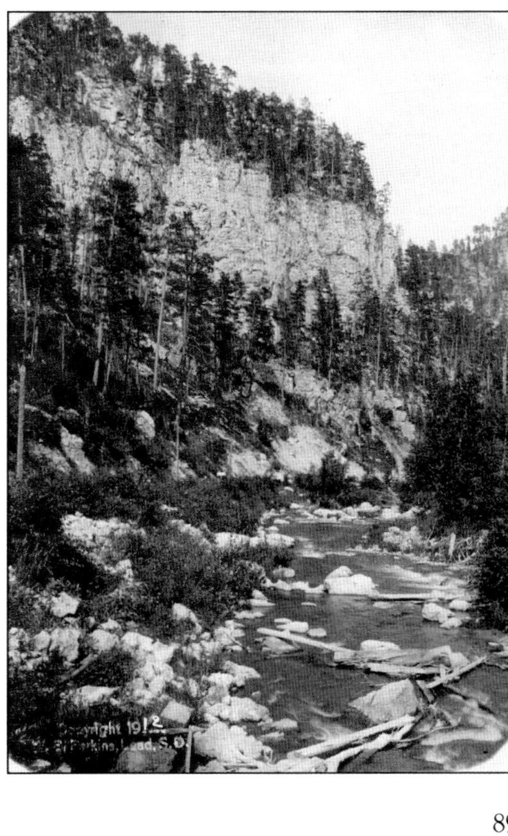

Overtaken with the canyon's beauty, Wright adds further, "Great horizontal rock walls abruptly rising above torrential streams, their stratified surfaces decorated (it is the word) with red pine stems carving stratified branches in horizontal textures over the cream white walls." (Courtesy of the Cook collection.)

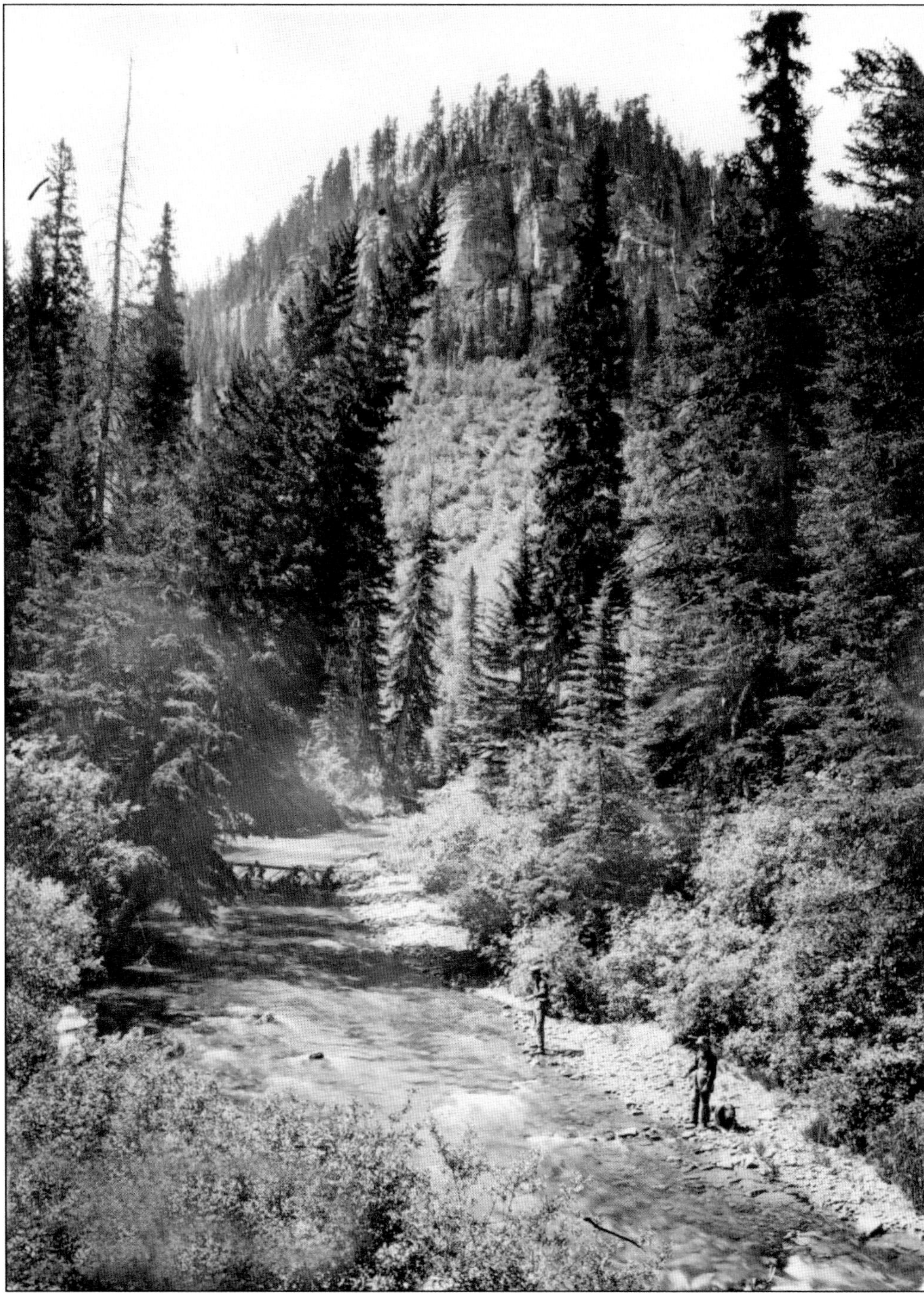

Here is a Perkins photograph of another 1910 canyon scene. Fortunately Spearfish Canyon's scenery is as spectacular now as it was then. Wright continued to describe it as "multiplied red pine trunks and the black green masses of the pine rhythmically repeating pattern, climbing, climbing until the sky disappeared or was a narrow rift of blue as the clear water poured over pebbles or pooled under the heavy masses of green at the foot of the grand rock walls."

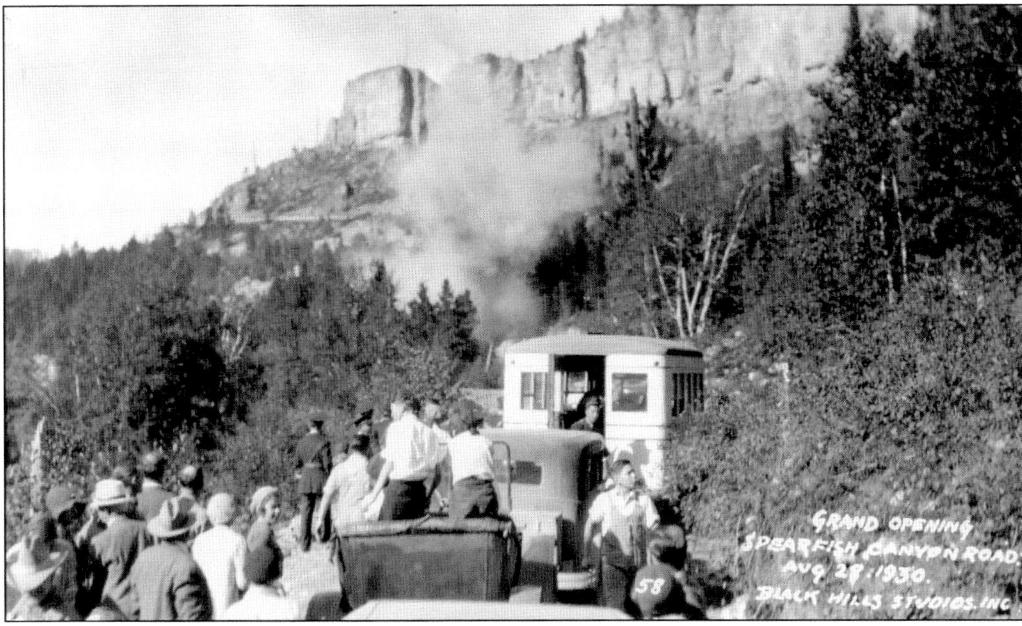

The Spearfish Canyon Road was opened in August 1930. Automobiles had become the preferred mode of travel while the railroad service was coming to an end. In 1934, the Spearfish railroad line was abandoned and the only access to the canyon was by car. A disastrous 1933 flood washed out parts of the highway and railroad in the canyon. The highway was rebuilt but the railroad was not.

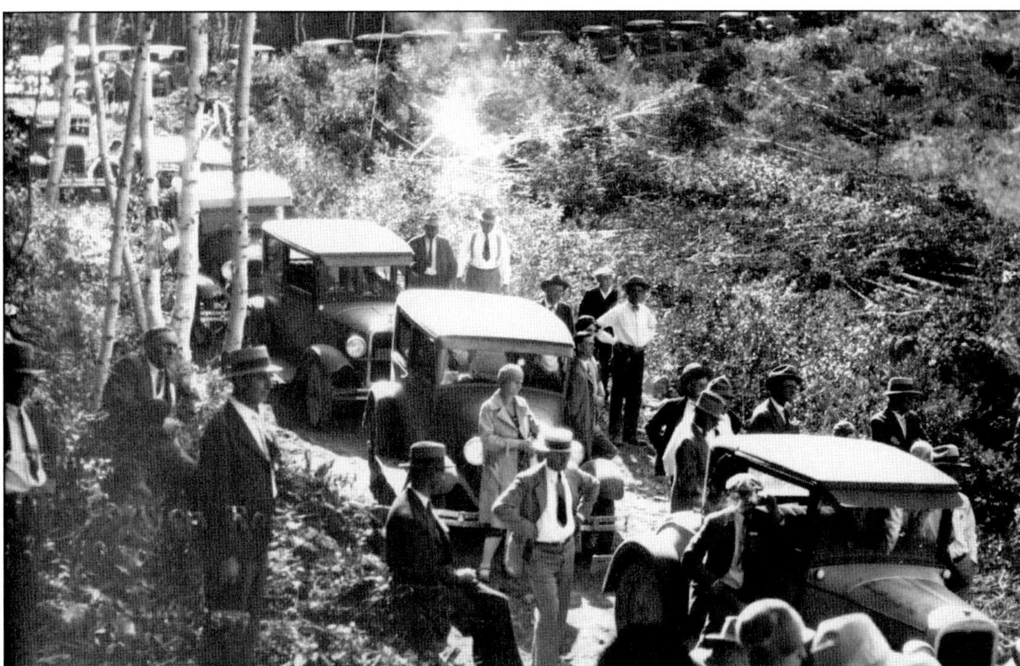

Gov. W. J. Bulow set off dynamite at the Spearfish Canyon gravel highway dedication, removing boulders that stood in the way. On that day in August 1930, a total of 367 cars drove the newly opened highway.

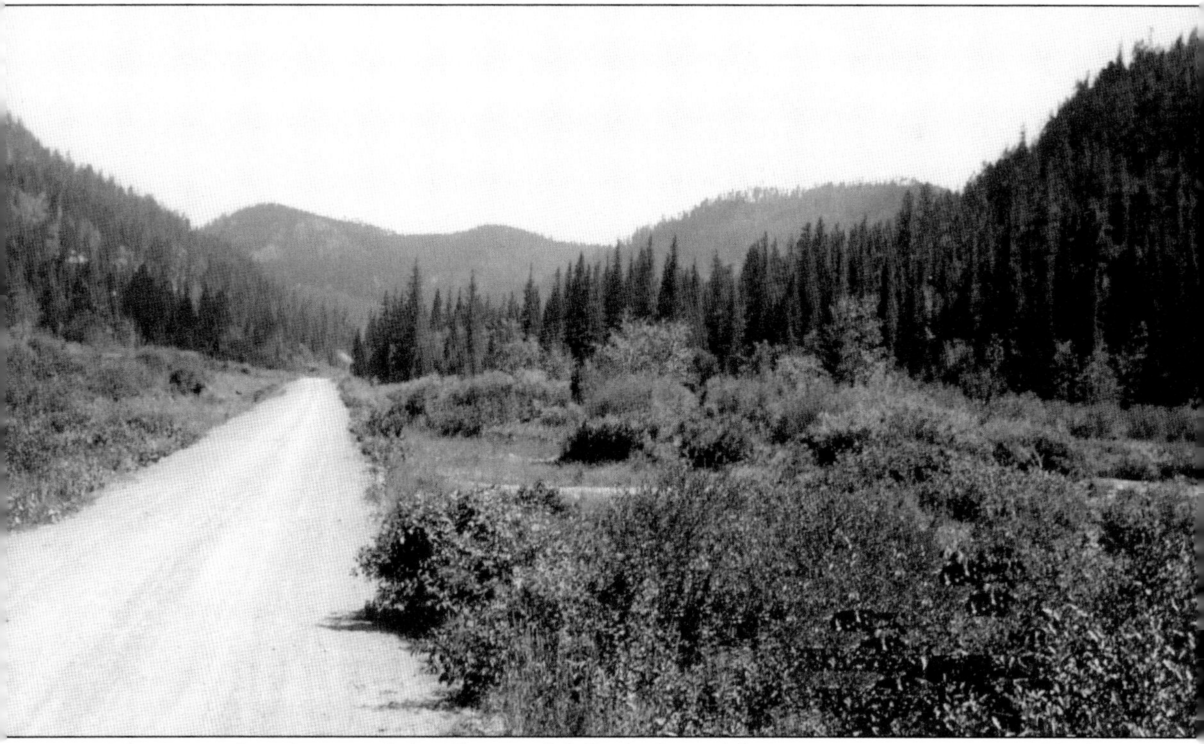

This is another photograph by Thomas Odell of a Spearfish Canyon scene. In 1950, a blacktop highway pushed its way through Spearfish Canyon. Because of its convenience, tourism to the Northern Black Hills increased. Bicycling, snowmobiling, hiking, and cross-country skiing are other popular ways to see the canyon.

Five

Black Hills Passion Play

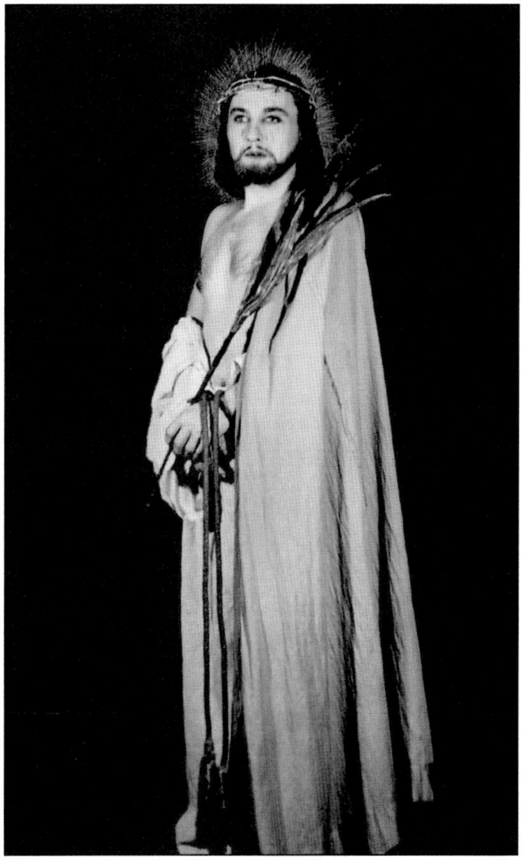

The Black Hills Passion Play has been a renowned Spearfish institution since 1938. Josef Meier, shown here in the role of Christ, was born in Luenen, Germany, home of the Luenen Passion Play. The Luenen Passion Play had been performed as an Easter week event since 1242. For seven generations the Meier family had portrayed the Christus. When the Nazis were rising to power in 1932, Josef Meier, with a dozen cast members, brought the Passion Play to the United States. The production, deeply rooted in the German tradition, first played to German speaking audiences. Meier soon realized that many more people could be reached with an English version and translated the play. Chicago actress Clare Hume joined the company in 1935 and she and Meier were soon married. Their daughter Johanna began performing the role of the Christ child as an infant, as her father had before her. The core company would travel from town to town and extras would be drawn from the hosting community. (Courtesy of the Meier collection.)

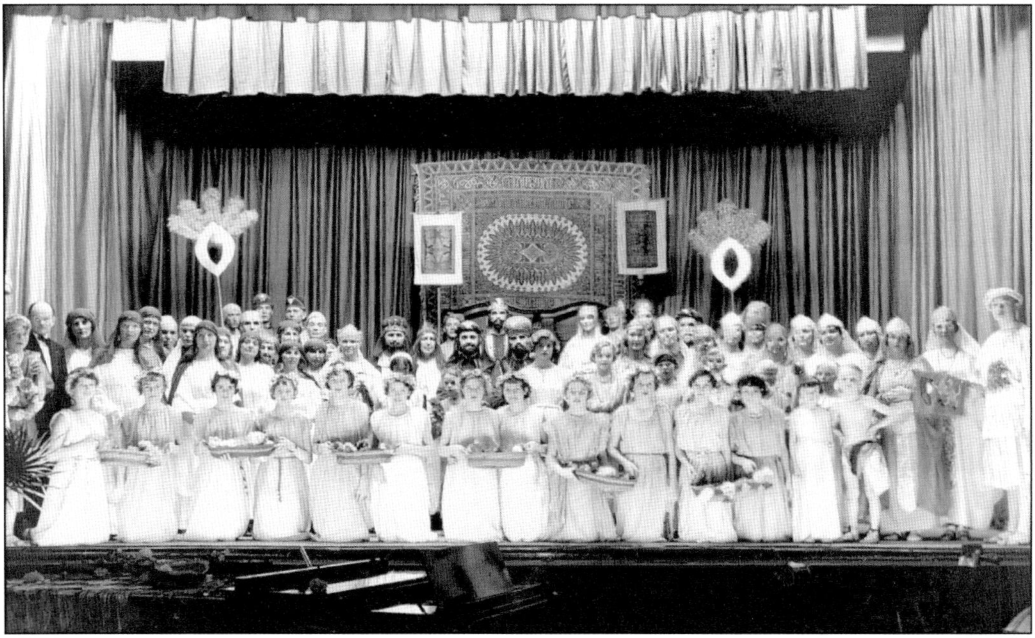

In 1938, the Passion Play came to the Black Hills and Spearfish for nine performances in the college auditorium. Spearfish residents enthusiastically received the production. Josef Meier had been looking for a site to locate an outdoor theater and in Spearfish the Passion Play found a permanent summer home. They would continue to tour during the winter months for a number of years. Before the company left on their 1938–1939 winter tour, Josef Meier announced that the production would be renamed the Black Hills Passion Play. (Courtesy of the Lown collection.)

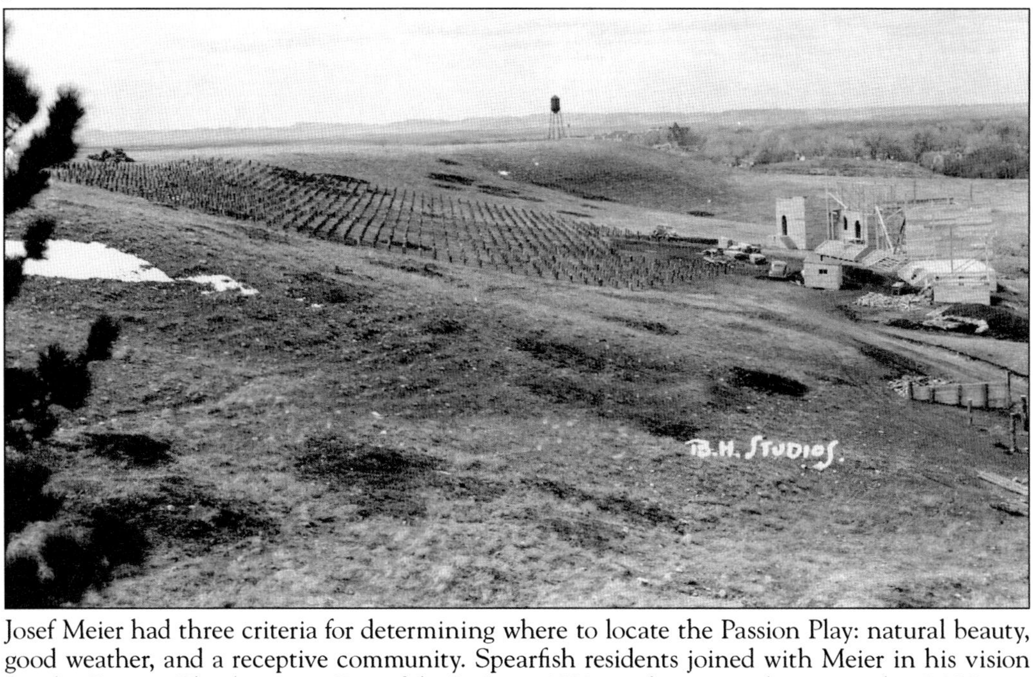

Josef Meier had three criteria for determining where to locate the Passion Play: natural beauty, good weather, and a receptive community. Spearfish residents joined with Meier in his vision for the Passion Play home in Spearfish. In June 1939, performances began in the 8,000-seat amphitheater. (Courtesy of the Thomas Odell collection.)

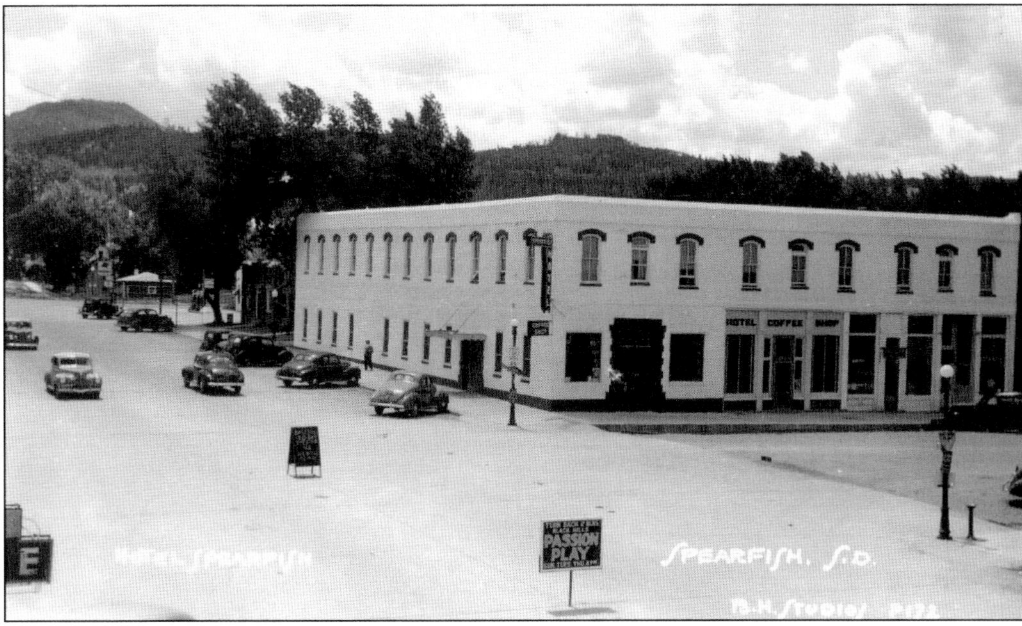

Signs posted around Spearfish still direct patrons to the site of the Passion Play. This image shows a sign on Main Street with the Hotel Spearfish in the background. For many years tourists came to the Passion Play in droves. One long-time Spearfish resident recalls that locals knew not to try to dine out on any of the three nights that the Passion Play performed. Passion Play patrons filled the restaurants and hotels and were a terrific boon to the Spearfish economy. (Courtesy of the Thomas Odell collection.)

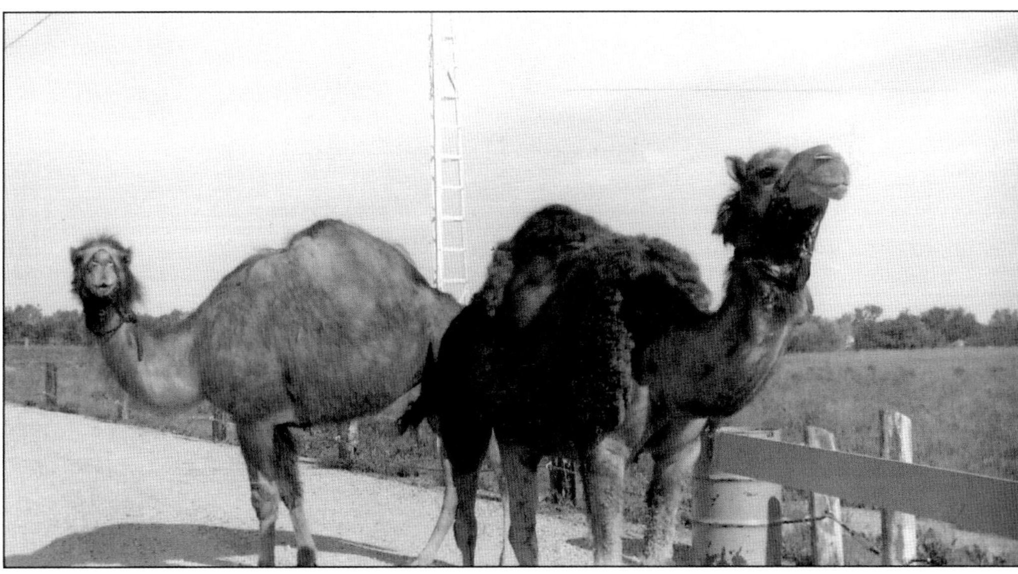

The Passion Play cast also included several four-legged members. Two camels carry the Magi, and Jesus makes his triumphal entrance into Jerusalem on a real donkey. As noted in the *Queen City Mail*, Spearfish's newspaper, the sheep, horses, and donkey helped to create a sense of realism. (Courtesy of the Frank Thomson collection.)

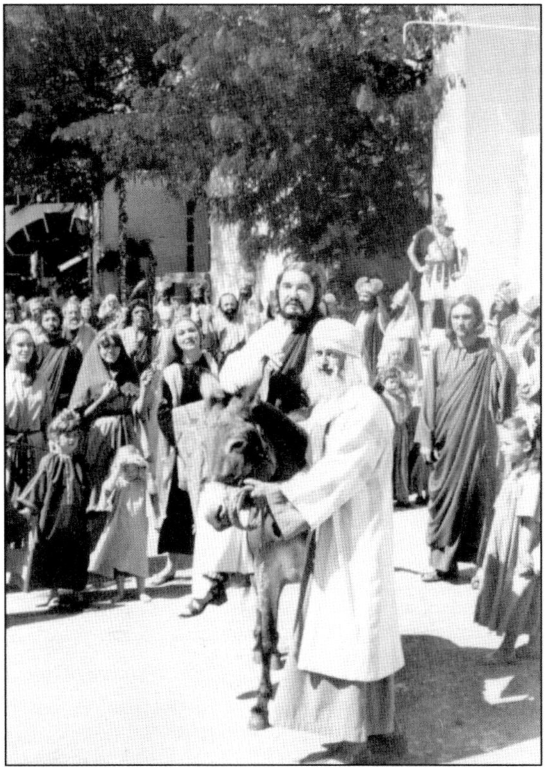

In the summer of 1939, approximately 15,000 people attended the Passion Play. When attendance dropped the next year, Josef Meier realized that most of the residents in the Black Hills had seen the play the previous year. As the company toured throughout the winter, they promoted the Passion Play and the Black Hills. These efforts contributed greatly to tourism in the Black Hills. (Courtesy of the Bob Lee collection.)

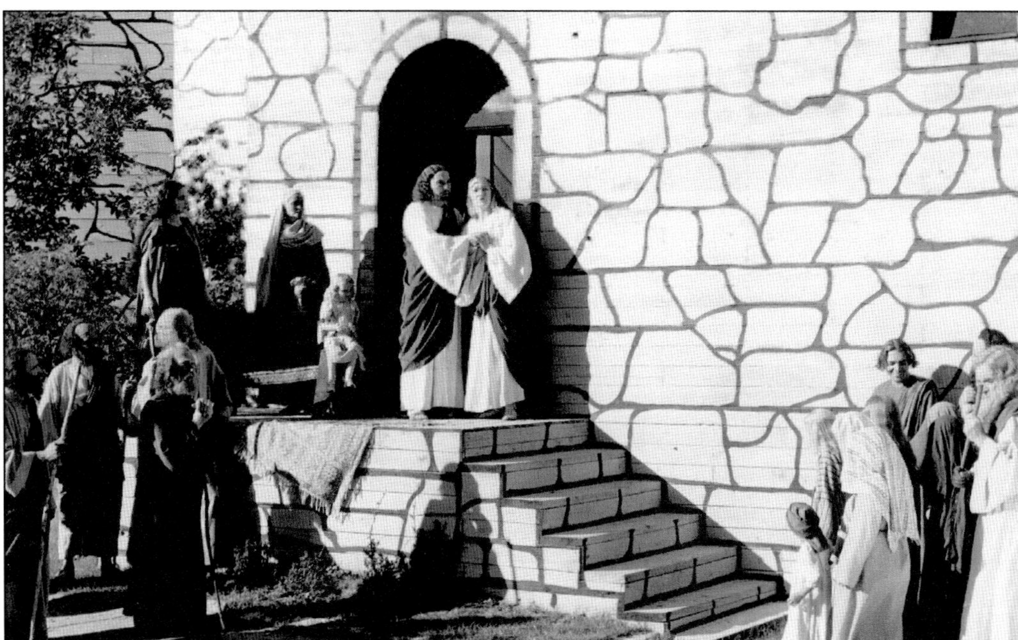

Due to gas rationing during World War II, attendance declined and the Passion Play went back to touring year-round. The company's premier performance in Washington, D.C., was a benefit for the Community War Fund. The audience included many notables such as the Belgian ambassador. (Courtesy of the Meier collection.)

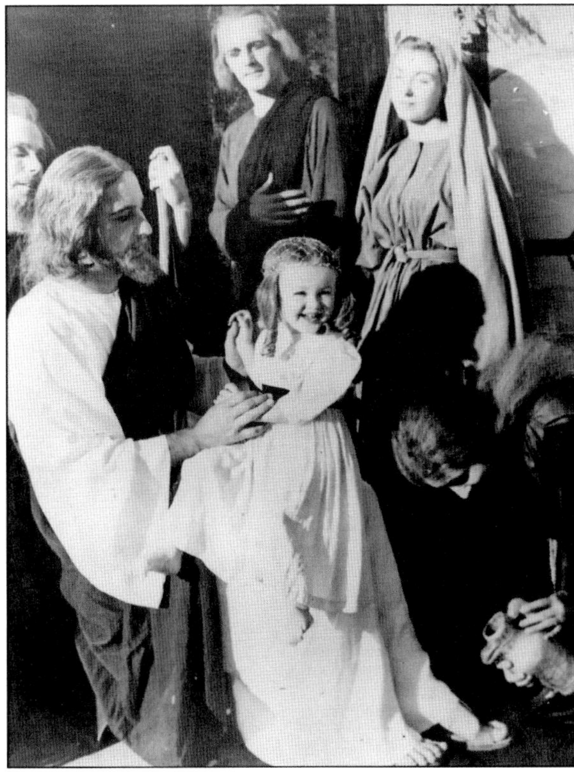

In this photograph from 1940, showing Christ blessing the children in Bethany, young Johanna Meier sits on her father's knee. As an adult she followed in her mother's footsteps playing the role of Mary Magdalene, which was Clare Hume Meier's first role in the Passion Play. In 1994, she took over her mother's role as Mary, the mother of Jesus. (Courtesy of the Black Hills Passion Play.)

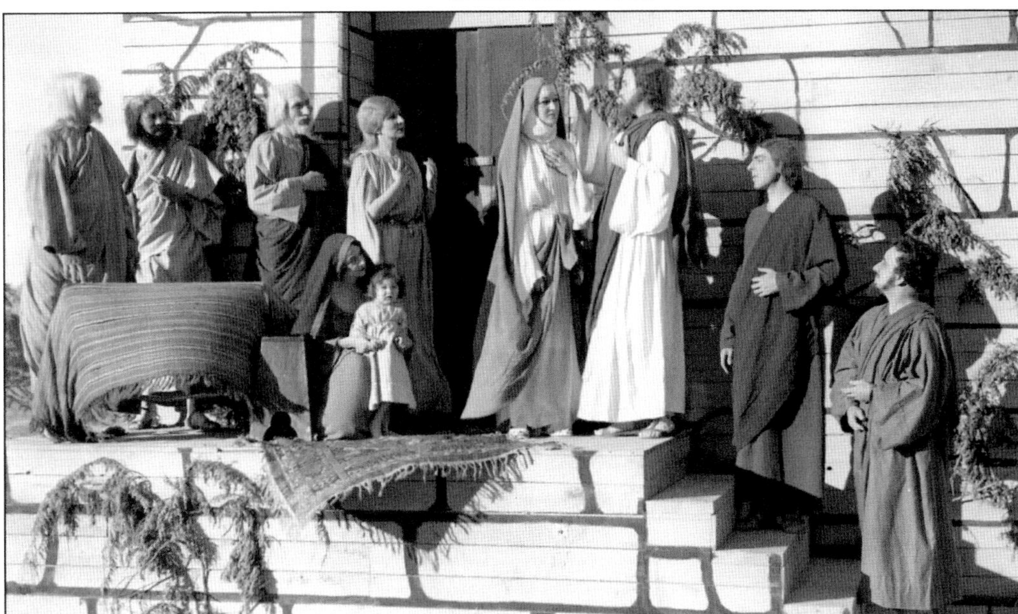

Clare Hume Meier spoke of her role as Mary, the mother of Jesus, in a 1959 newspaper. She spoke of the tremendous responsibility of playing Mary as she endeavored to portray Mary's human qualities as well as her spiritual nature to make her "everyone's ideal Mother of Jesus." She added, "I try to leave the audience with a memory of a radiant Mary at the time of Ascension . . . not leaving merely the memory of the moments of agony both under went." (Courtesy of the Lown collection.)

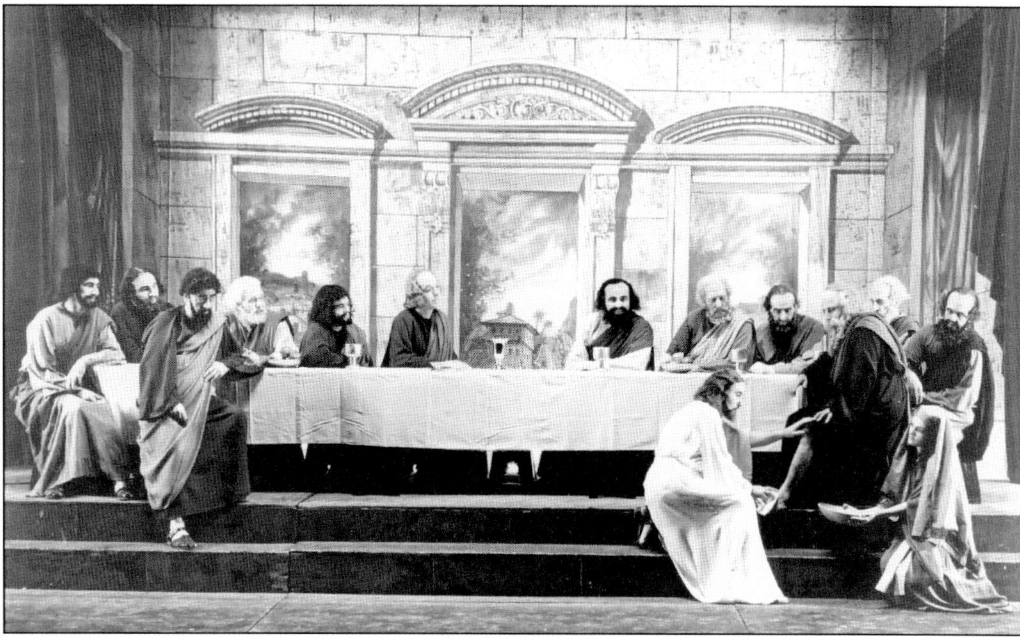

The company continued to tour the United States and Canada until 1954, when they established a winter home in Lake Whales, Florida. That same year, the Black Hills Passion Play received the Freedom Foundation George Washington Medal for "helping to bring about a better understanding of the American way of life." (Courtesy of the Black Hills Passion Play.)

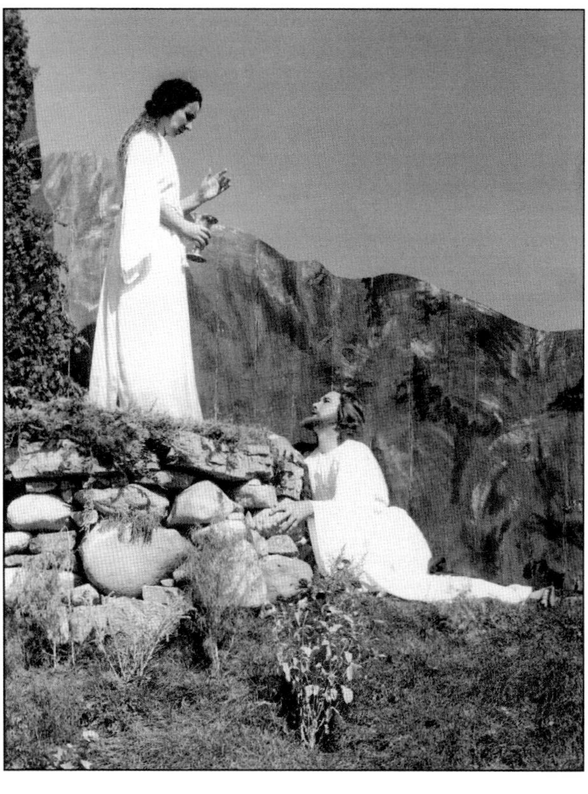

Josef Meier earned international acclaim as an actor for his role as Christ. In 1984, Meier's 80th year, South Dakota governor Bill Janklow declared October 10th to be Josef Meier Day. As the Black Hills Passion Play marked its golden anniversary, Gov. George Mickelson stated, "The play has grown into one of the state's major cultural productions." He further stated, "It is well deserving of its worldwide recognition." (Courtesy of the Meier collection.)

This scene is in the court of Caiaphas. The Passion Play relies very heavily on community members as extras, many of whom return year after year. In a 1990 article from the *Lawrence County Centennial*, a former motel owner and 29-year veteran comments about the start of his years at the Passion Play: "Being in the motel business, we thought it behooved us to see that the play was successful." For many, participation was a social event. Children formed lasting friendships playing in the dressing rooms between scenes. (Courtesy of the Black Hills Passion Play.)

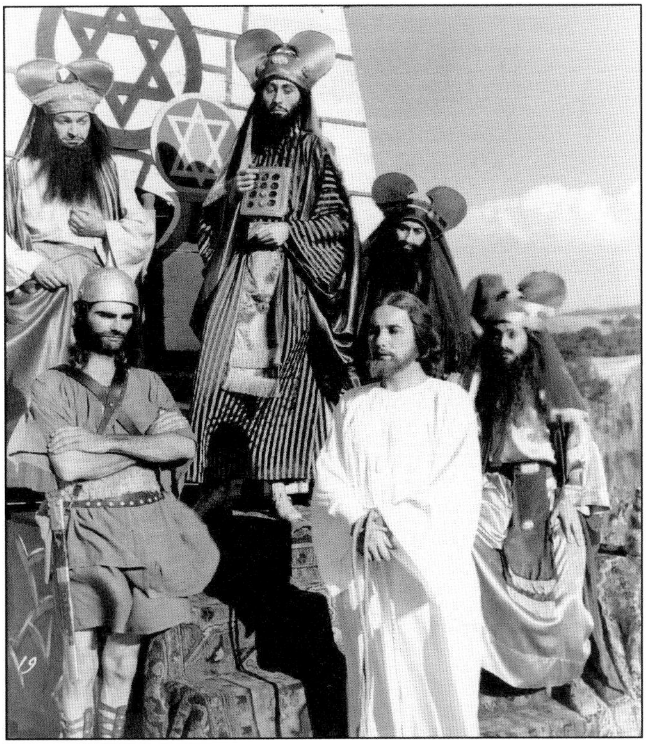

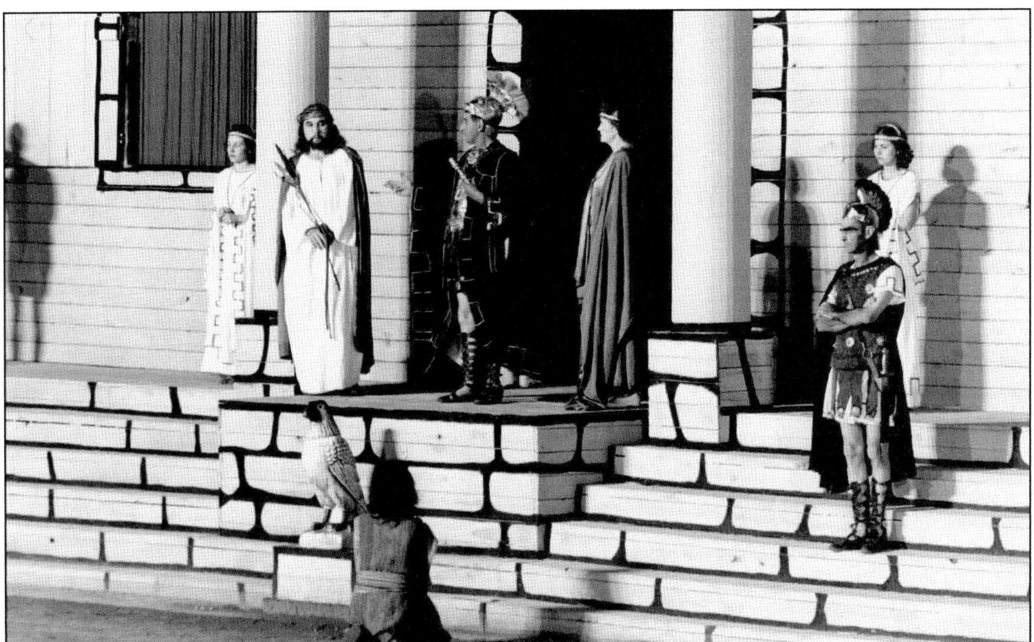

In return for the community support as supernumeraries, actors with non-speaking walk-on roles, the Passion Play makes donations to the local churches. On July 24, 1985, the *Queen City Mail* reported that a special performance was given on July 20th; the gate receipts totaling $6,313 were given to the Spearfish Chamber of Commerce for distribution among area churches. (Courtesy of the Black Hills Passion Play.)

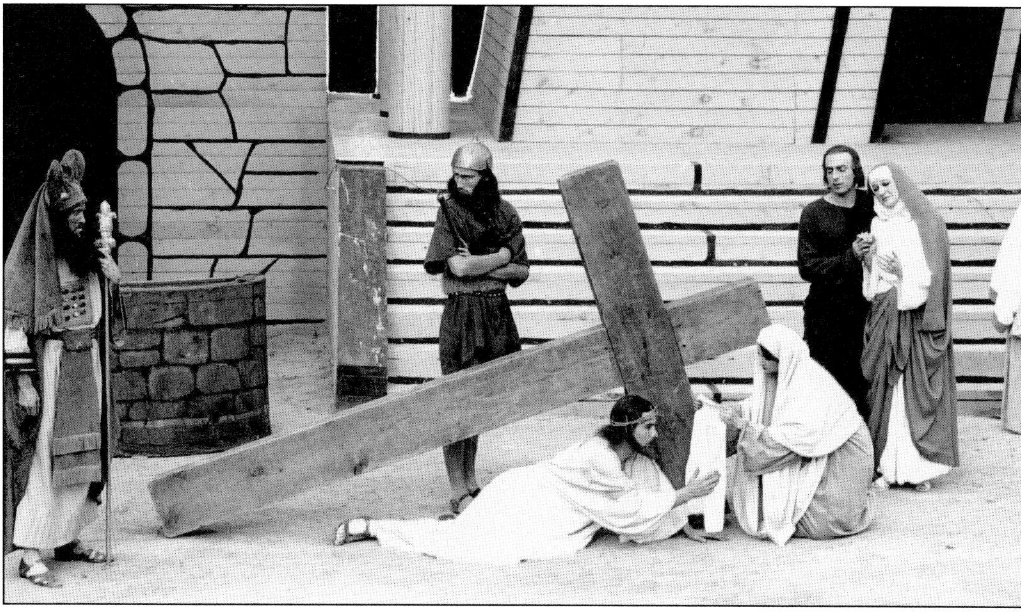

Josef Meier considered producing the Passion Play and playing the role of Christ as a spiritual endeavor. When a newspaper reporter asked him if after 15,000 performances the role had become monotonous, he replied, "There is immeasurable depth to repeating the Scriptures, and we try to penetrate that depth to project across the footlights, it brings a constant growing realization of Him." (Courtesy of the Meier collection.)

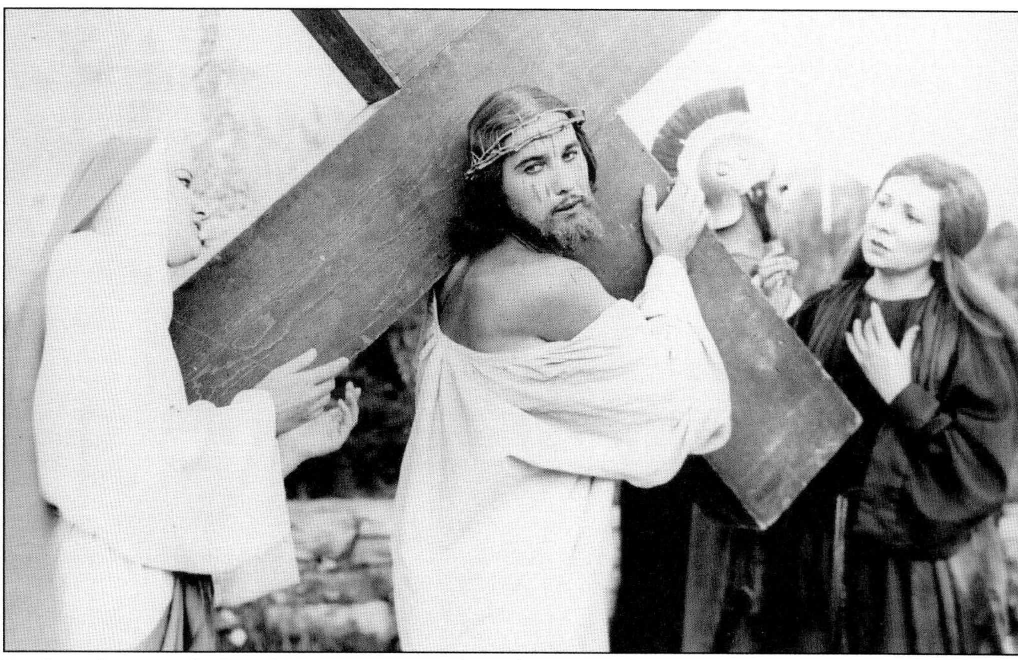

In this photograph, Josef Meier portrays the Christus as he meets his mother on the road to Golgotha. In 1965, Josef Meier received the papal honor called *Pontifice Et Ecclesia* (for the pope and church). It is the highest honor given to a layman by the Catholic Church and was granted by Pope Paul VI. (Courtesy of the Black Hills Passion Play.)

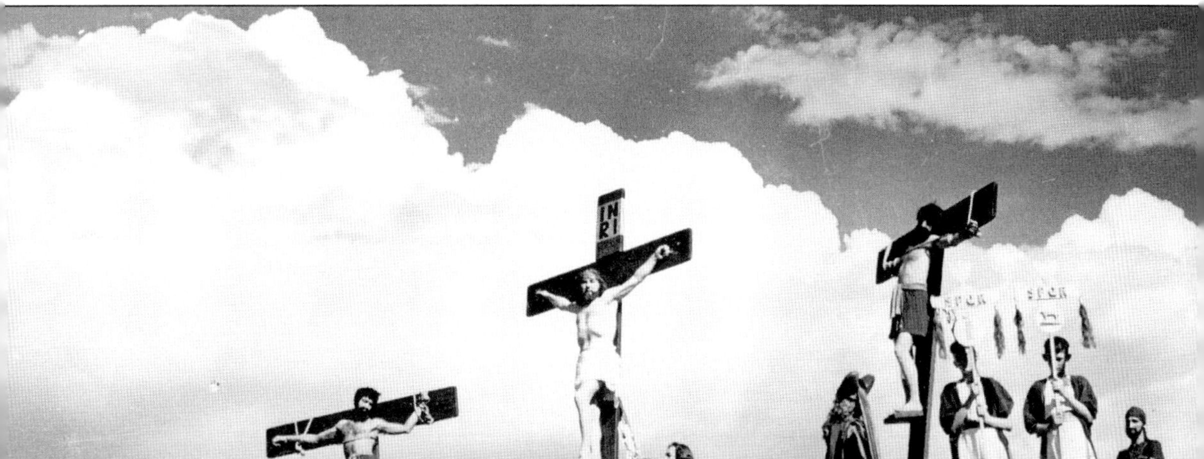

The papal honor is granted to "those who have contributed to the good of religion and to advance a deeper and wider appreciation of virtue and culture." This honor was granted to Meier because of his "dignified and impressive presentation of the Passion Play" and his portrayal of the Christus. Pope John Paul II conferred a similar honor upon Meier in 1994. In 1994, Josef and Clare Meier retired. Direction and management of the Black Hills Passion Play was turned over to their daughter Johanna and her husband Guido Della Vecchia. (Courtesy of the Black Hills Passion Play.)

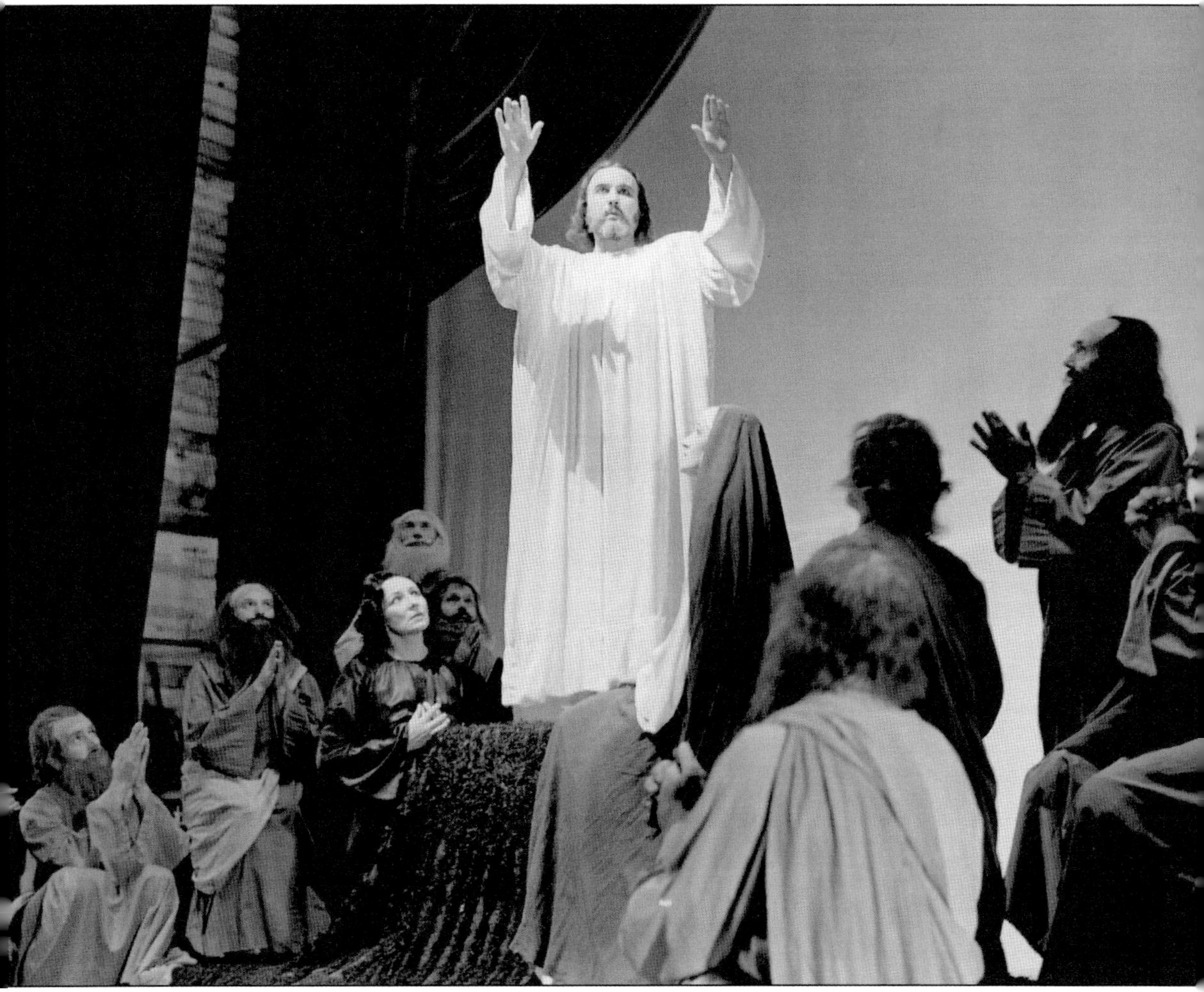

The Meier family continues to have a strong relationship with Black Hills State University where they first performed in Spearfish in Woodburn Auditorium. Each summer, Johanna Meier, a professional opera singer, directs an opera workshop and festival at the university. The building that houses a concert hall as well as music class and practice rooms bears the Meier family name. In 2006, Johanna Meier was inducted into the South Dakota Hall of Fame for directing the Black Hills Passion Play and for establishing the Johanna Meier Opera Theater Institute at Black Hills State University. Her father was bestowed the honor in 1989. (Courtesy of the Black Hills Passion Play.)

Six

Black Hills State University

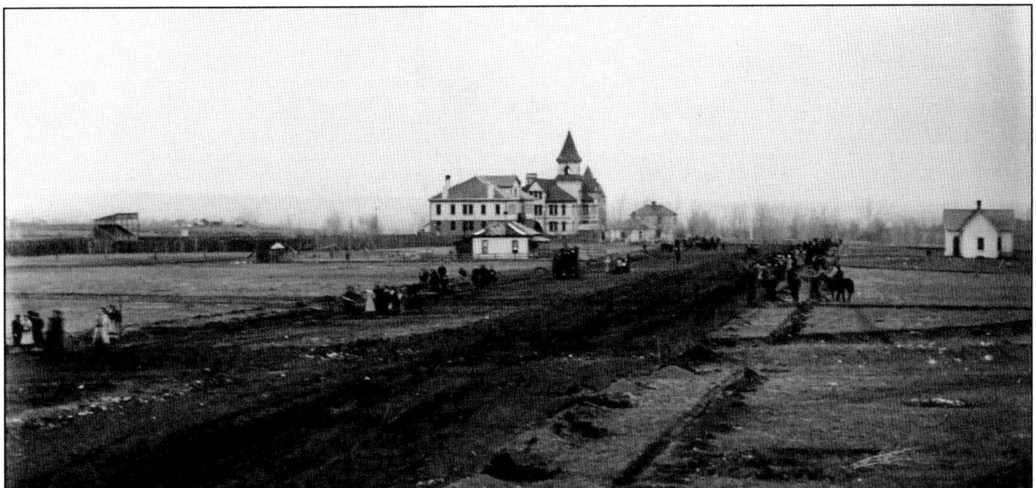

In February 1881, the territorial legislature passed an act to establish a Territorial Normal School to be located at Spearfish in Lawrence County, Dakota Territory. In addition to instructing both male and female students in good common school teaching practices, the curriculum was to include mechanical arts, husbandry and agricultural chemistry, fundamental laws of the nation, and citizens rights and responsibilities. However, it was three years before the Territorial Normal School would open its doors. In 1883, the legislature reenacted the 1881 legislation with amendments. Spearfish residents worked together to make the 20 sections of land adjacent to Spearfish available, as required by the law. The school has gone through several name changes throughout its history. When South Dakota gained statehood in 1889, it became State Normal School. The name became Black Hills Teachers College in 1941. In 1964, the name was changed to Black Hills State College. Then became Black Hills State University in 1990. This photograph shows the State Normal School as it appeared in 1906. (Courtesy of the University Archives.)

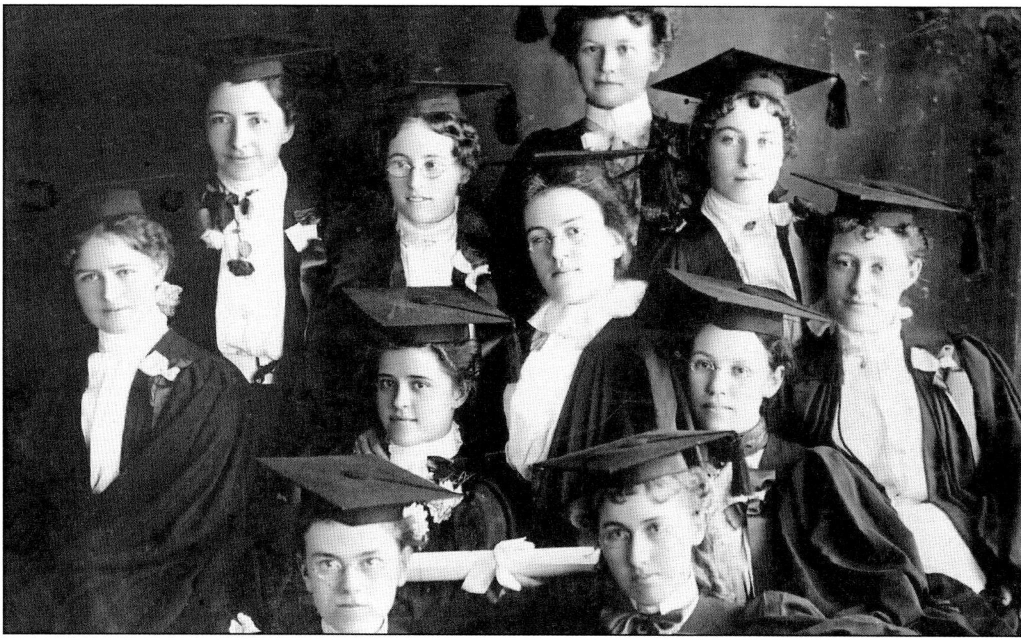

The Territorial Normal School started classes April 14, 1884. The class of 1889 was the first graduating class from the State Normal School. Members of this class listed in the 1889–1900 bulletin include: Carrie A. Anderson, Pearle Gilbert, Arloa B. Greenleaf, Katherina Hough, Frances Murrin, Irene D. Pringle, Evangeline Winyall, Gertrude Tutty, Emma T. Wood, Marcia Rich, and Jennie B. Wright. (Courtesy of the University Archives.)

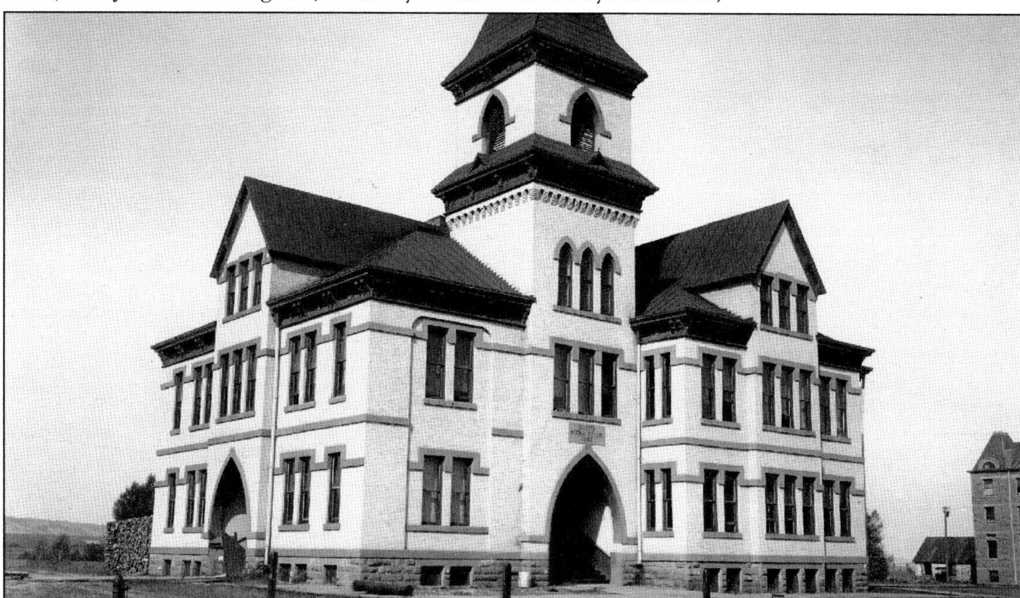

After a rocky first year Fayette L. Cook took over management of the Territorial Normal School in 1885. Despite much adversity in the first years of his tenure, the school experienced tremendous growth under Professor Cook's administration. Enrollment increased as Cook's reputation as a man of principle spread. After a year of planning, the new main building opened in 1889. (Courtesy of the University Archives.)

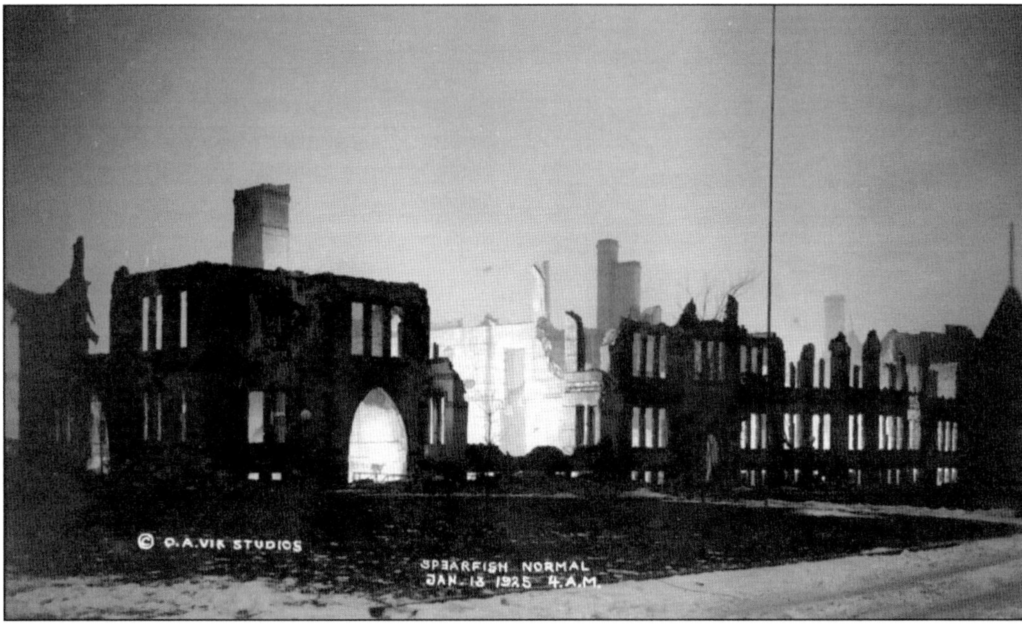

A joyful beginning to the winter term was shattered when State Normal School students and Spearfish residents were awakened by a fire in the school's main building in the early morning hours of January 13, 1925. An electrical short was determined to be the cause of the fire. (Courtesy of the University Archives.)

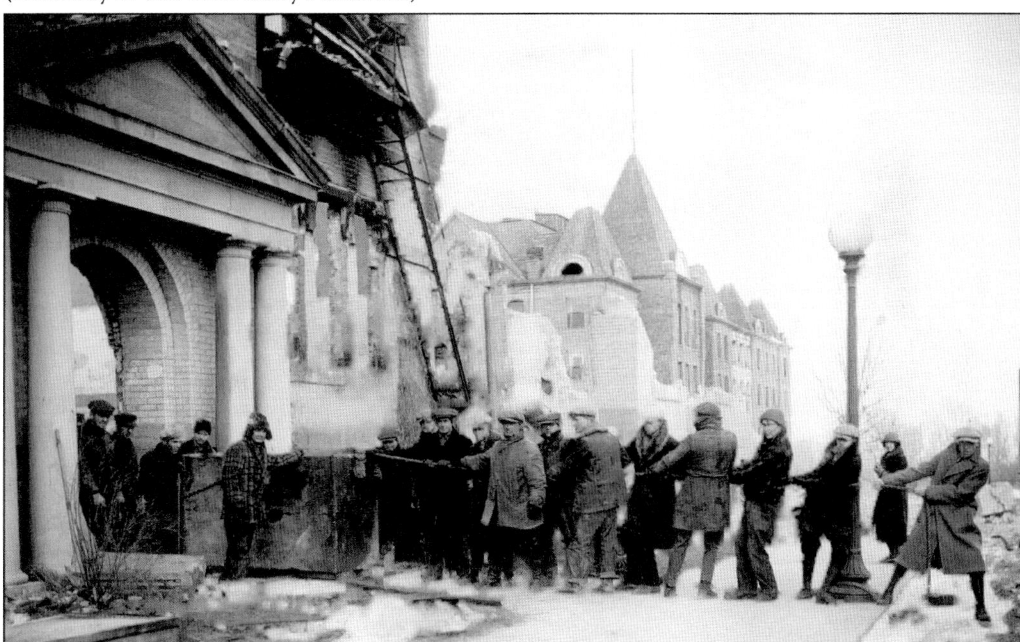

During the blaze, students tried to save library books, but the fire was too far advanced. The volumes that were checked out did survive and the community donated many others to refill the library shelves. Some students did successfully save some of the costly equipment from the physics lab. Salvage continued throughout the next day. This photograph shows the 40 years of records stored in an all-steel safe that survived the blaze. (Courtesy of the University Archives.)

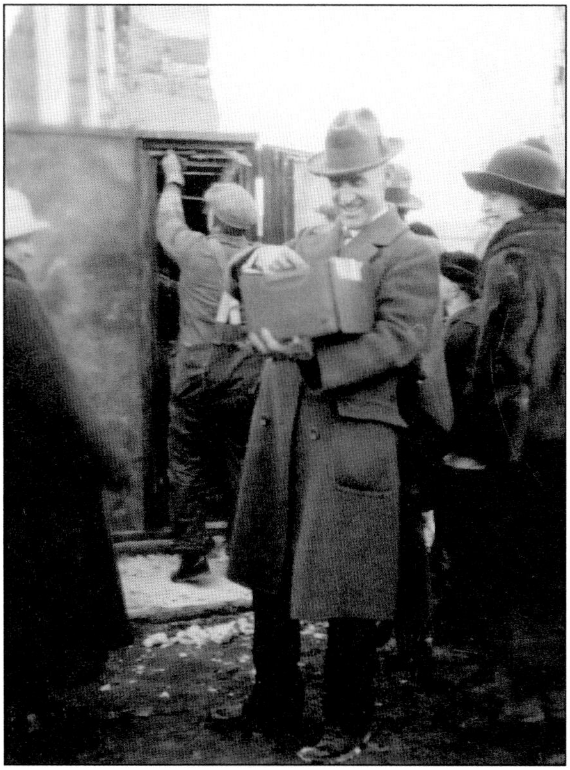

Pres. Ethelbert Cooke Woodburn examines the contents of the all-steel safe during the salvage operation. On January 16, 1925, the campus newspaper published his message regarding the fire. He begins, "A calamity of the sort we have just experienced seems at first to stun." He goes on to talk about rising to the challenge. He concludes his message saying that the actions of the students, staff, and community at this time of crisis gave him "a renewed confidence in the underlying goodness of 'folks' and a new pride in the group of people, young and old, with whom it is my privilege to work." (Courtesy of the University Archives.)

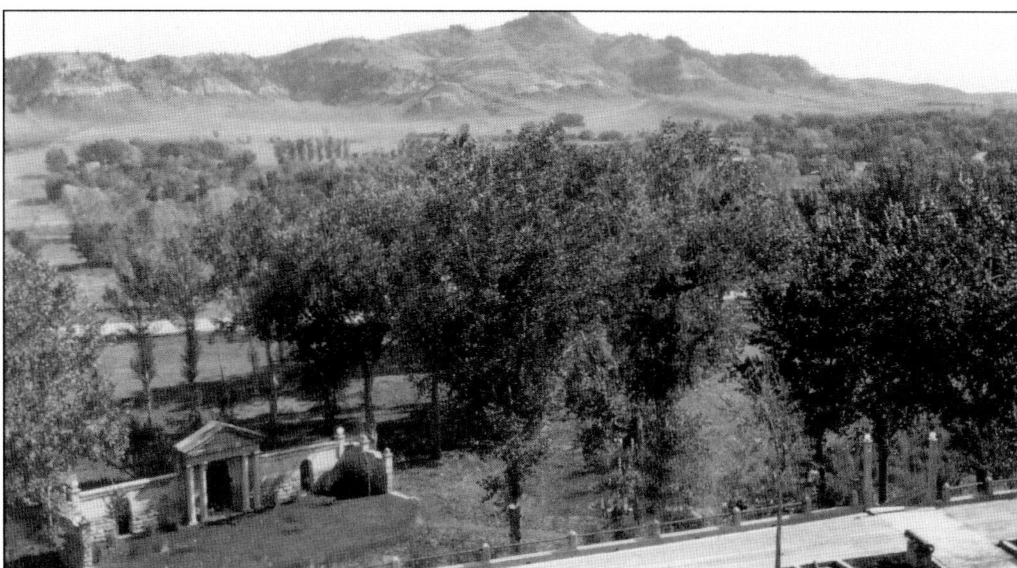

A portion of the facade of the old main building was saved. It was moved to the orchard directly below where the building originally stood. A grassy hillside made a natural amphitheater to create an outdoor theater. The orchard is long gone and the area is now known as Ida Henton Park after one of the school's teachers who served for 43 years. Lookout Mountain is seen in the background.

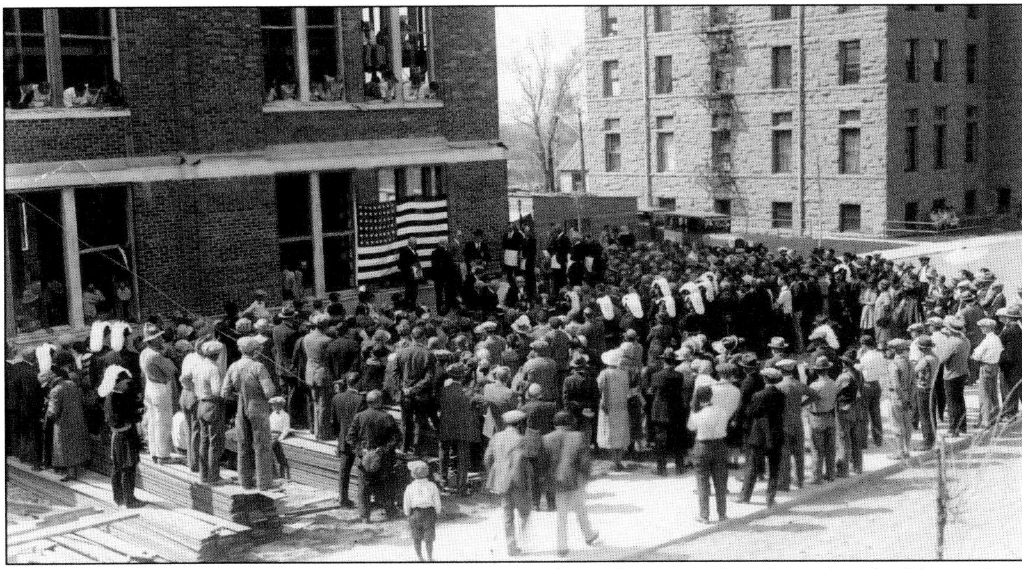

The state legislature appropriated $315,000 to replace the main building that had burned on the normal school campus. They also appropriated $35,000 to partially equip the new hall. Construction of a new main building began during the summer of 1925. The ceremonial laying of the cornerstone was celebrated April 30, 1926. Use of the partially completed building began in the fall of 1926. (Courtesy of the University Archives.)

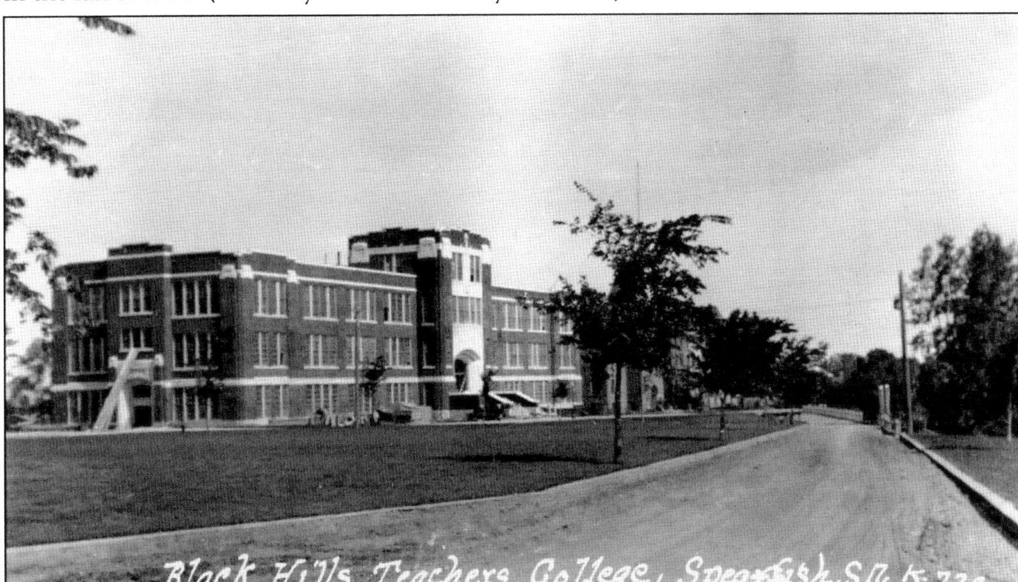

The regents named the new main building Woodburn Hall in 1944. Ethelbert Cooke Woodburn served as president from July 1, 1919, until he retired in 1942. He came to South Dakota as a book salesman. He then became the superintendent of schools in Elk Point, South Dakota, from 1905 until 1907, then in Canton, South Dakota. Due to his good reputation, he became the head of the Training School at Northern Normal and Industrial School in Aberdeen, South Dakota. He rose through the ranks, becoming head of the education department, and then in 1915, he became vice president and acting vice president for one year before moving to Spearfish. He died in June 1958. (Courtesy of the Thomas Odell collection.)

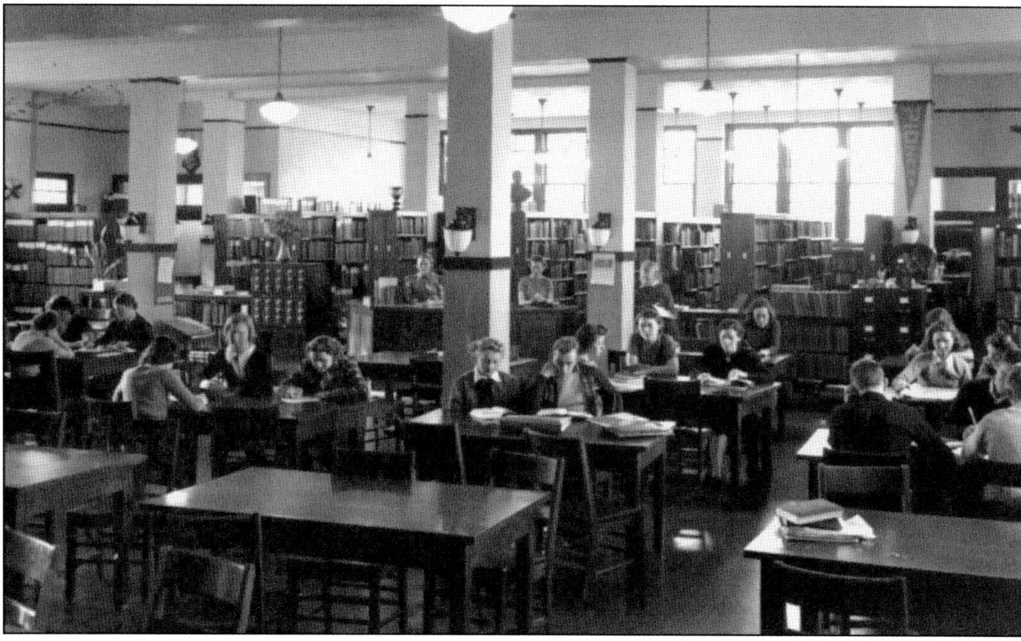

The school library was housed in several locations on campus. It was in the main building when it burned in 1925 and was nearly a complete loss. When the new main building, Woodburn Hall, was built, it too housed the campus library. In 1972, a separate library building opened. It was named the E. Y. Berry Library and Learning Center. It is the building that houses the library today. This photograph shows the library in Woodburn Hall in about 1938. (Courtesy of the Mar Gretta Cocking Scrapbook, the University Archives.)

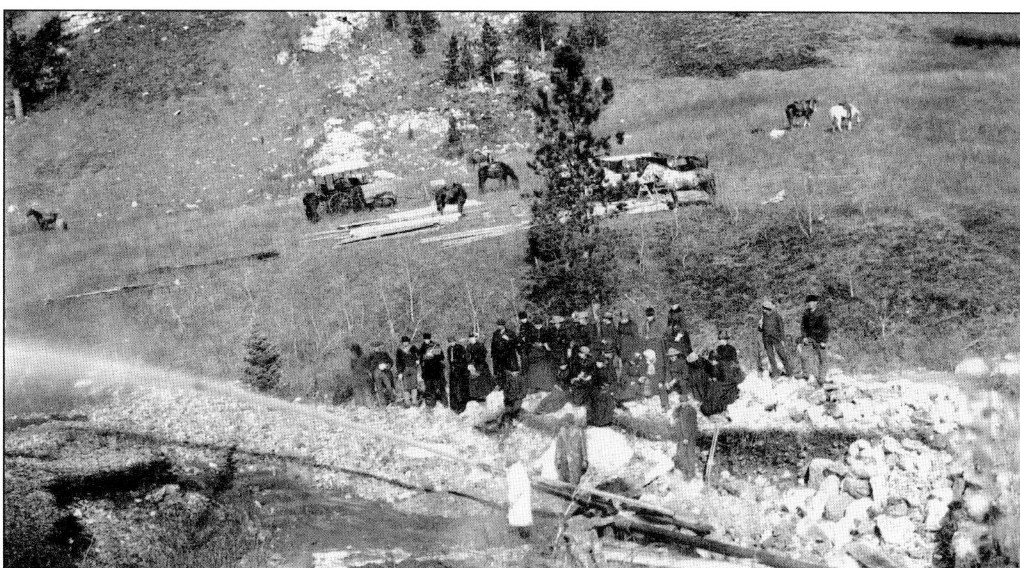

From the beginning, students and faculty took advantage of the natural resources and beauty of the Northern Black Hills. This photograph shows a geology class field trip from 1888. Under the instruction of Katherine J. Bingham, the class studies hydraulic mining. (Courtesy of the University Archives.)

State Normal School faculty also enjoyed outings in Spearfish Canyon. This photograph was taken in 1927. The teachers here are identified in the 1927 yearbook by their faculty portraits as Mabel Ewing, voice and public school music teacher; Leona B. Jones, upper grade supervisor; and Ruberta M. Olds, Spanish language teacher. (Courtesy of the University Archives.)

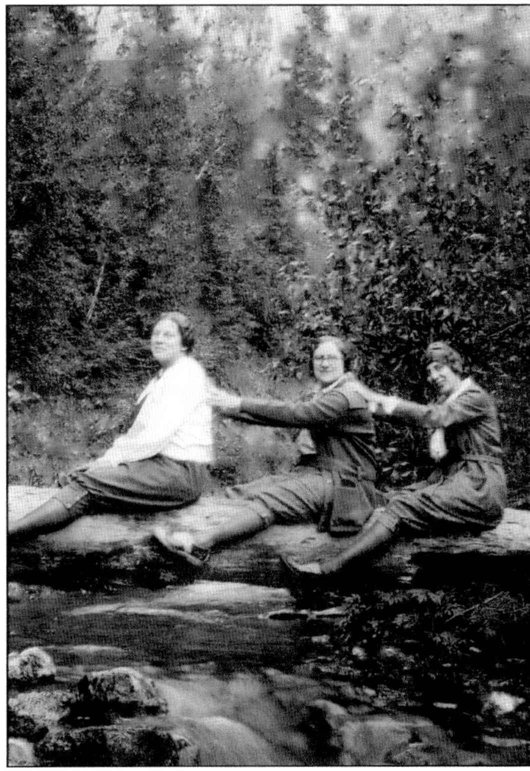

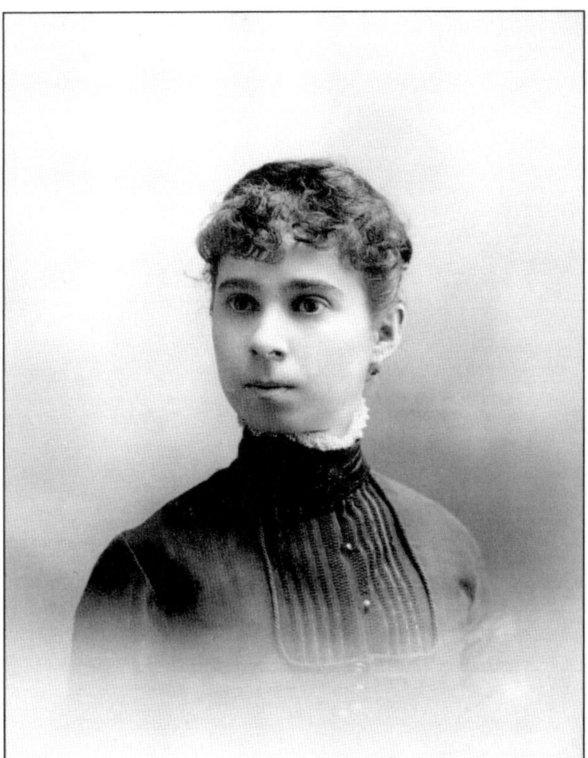

Wenona Culbertson joined the model school department staff in 1888. The purpose of the model school department was to prepare those not yet ready to enter the normal school. In 1892, Culbertson and Professor Cook were married. She then moved to teaching at the normal school and began the first art department. In addition to teaching art, she taught penmanship and served for many years as the school bookkeeper. (Courtesy of the University Archives.)

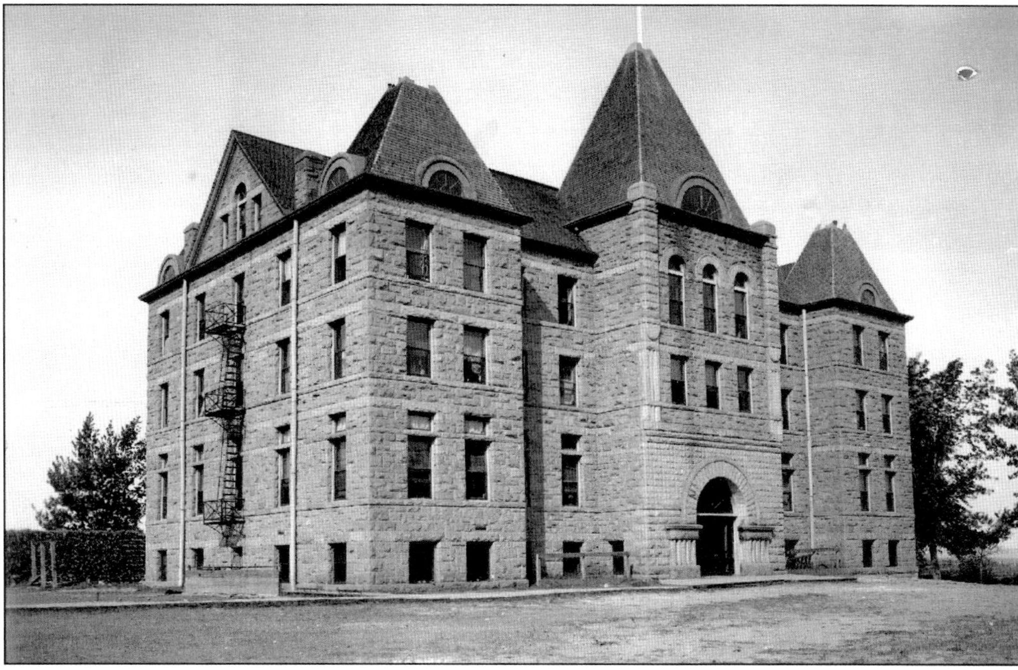

The first women's dormitory, completed in 1899, was named for Wenona Cook. Although there have been many renovations and changes in use, Wenona Cook Hall still stands on the Black Hills State University campus. (Courtesy of the University Archives.)

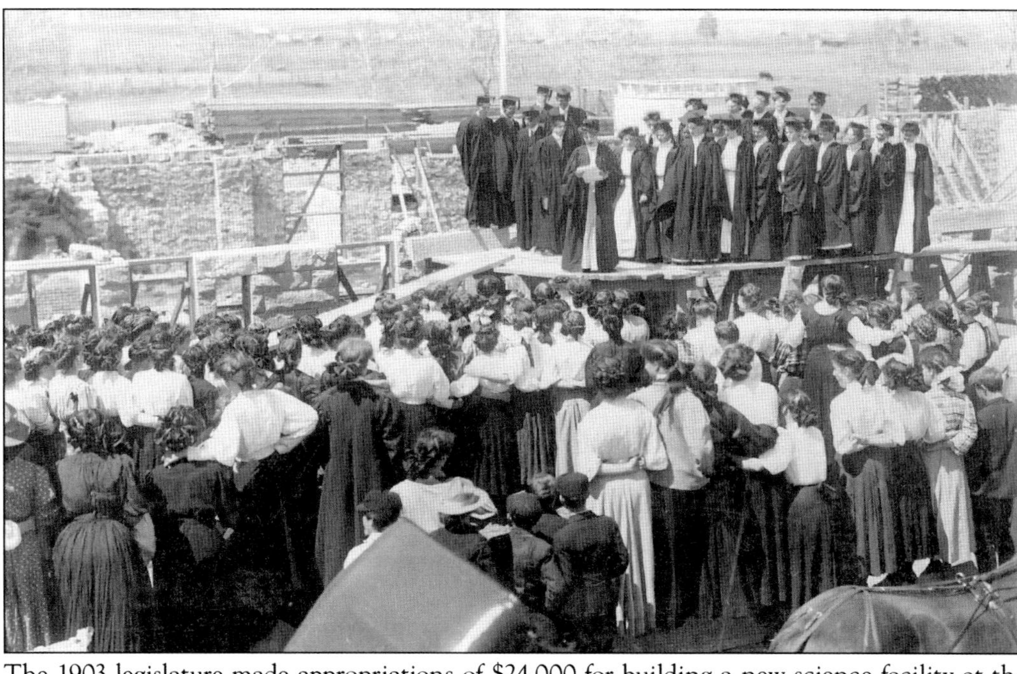

The 1903 legislature made appropriations of $24,000 for building a new science facility at the State Normal School. The regents of education approved the plans submitted by C. A. Randall of Deadwood. This picture of the science hall dedication in the fall of 1903 shows Spearfish valley behind the campus. (Courtesy of the University Archives.)

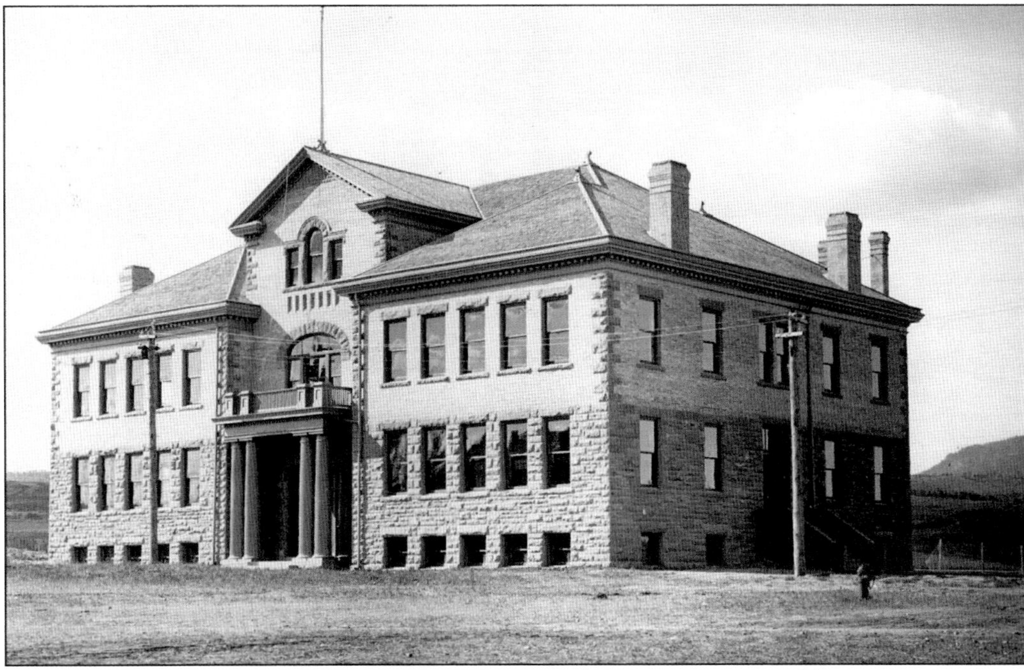

Completed in 1904, the building contained science laboratories, a new library, a gymnasium, domestic economy apartments, and manual training facilities. Due to a lack of equipment, the building was only partially available until the fall of 1905. (Courtesy of the University Archives.)

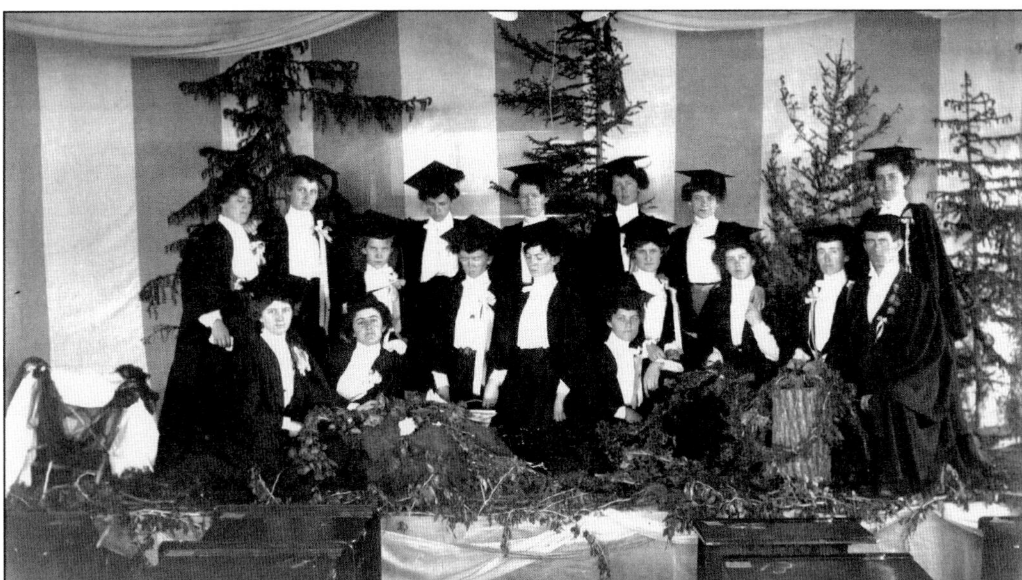

Shown in this photograph is the class of 1902 graduation ceremony. Students pictured are (first row) Bertha Gibson, Lena Odou, and Anna Uhlig; (second row) Mabel Peterson, Estella Robins, Helen Carpenter, Margaret "Daisy" Thomas, Emma Walton, Miss Preston, and Frank Thomson; (third row) Elva Russell, Bessie Wilcox, Pearl Beckwith, Agnes Anderson, Bertha Burris, Percy Tracy, and Edith Earl. Frank Thomson later authored *The Thoen Stone: A Saga of the Black Hills*, one of the resources used in chapter 1. (Courtesy of the University Archives.)

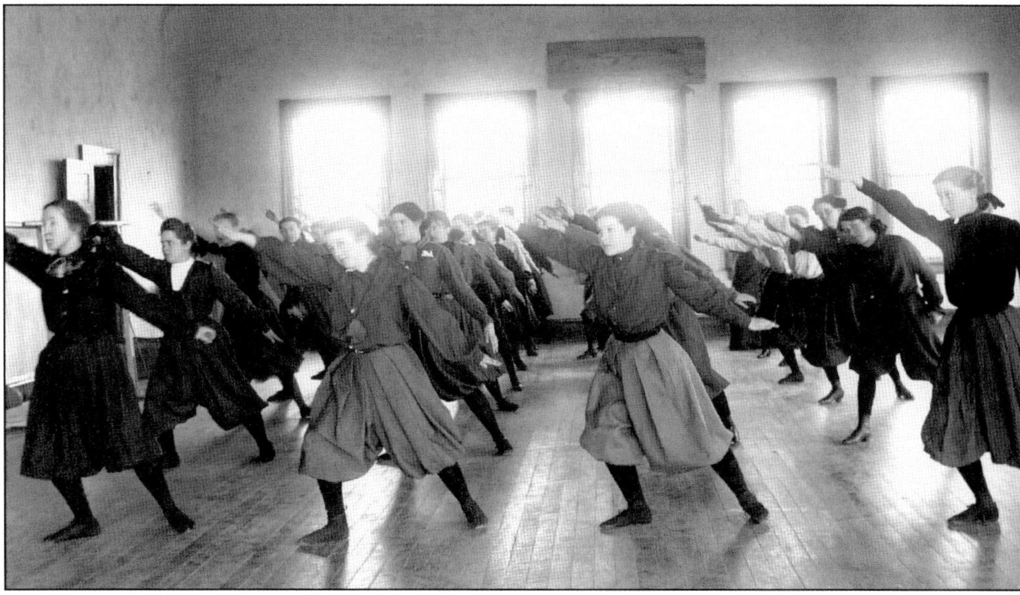

The 1906–1907 catalogue states, "Believing that the health of the body is as important as health of mind and that the latter is impossible without the former, extraordinary efforts have been made to provide facilities for physical training." The catalogue continues to describe the athletic facilities including a new gymnasium "equipped with lockers and the use of the bathrooms is free to all." This 1907 photograph shows the gym class. (Courtesy of the University Archives.)

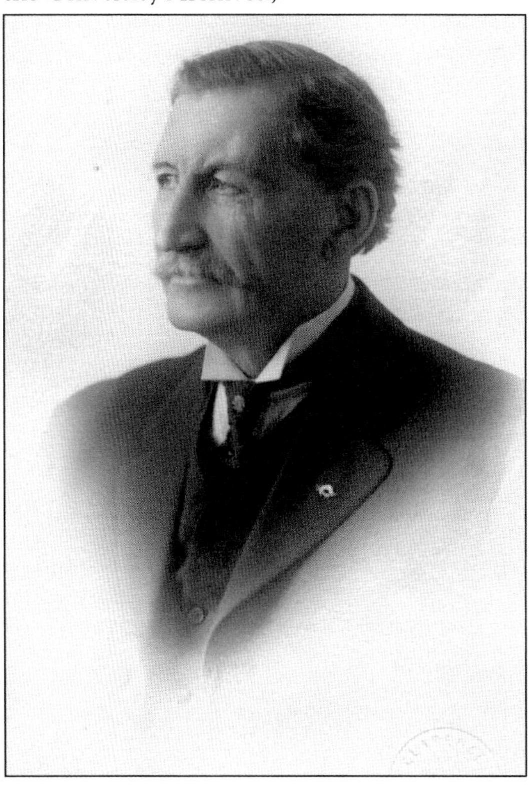

Fayette L. Cook (1850–1922) served as the first president of the normal school from 1885 until 1919. Born in Grand Rapid, Michigan, he served as superintendent of schools for Olmsted County, Minnesota, prior to coming to the Territorial Normal School. An article in the campus newspaper from September 26, 1924, discusses the tribute to him on the second anniversary of his death. In the library, his portrait was draped in school colors. The words inscribed under the portrait are reported to have read, "He fought a good fight, he has finished the course, he has kept the faith." (Courtesy of the University Archives.)

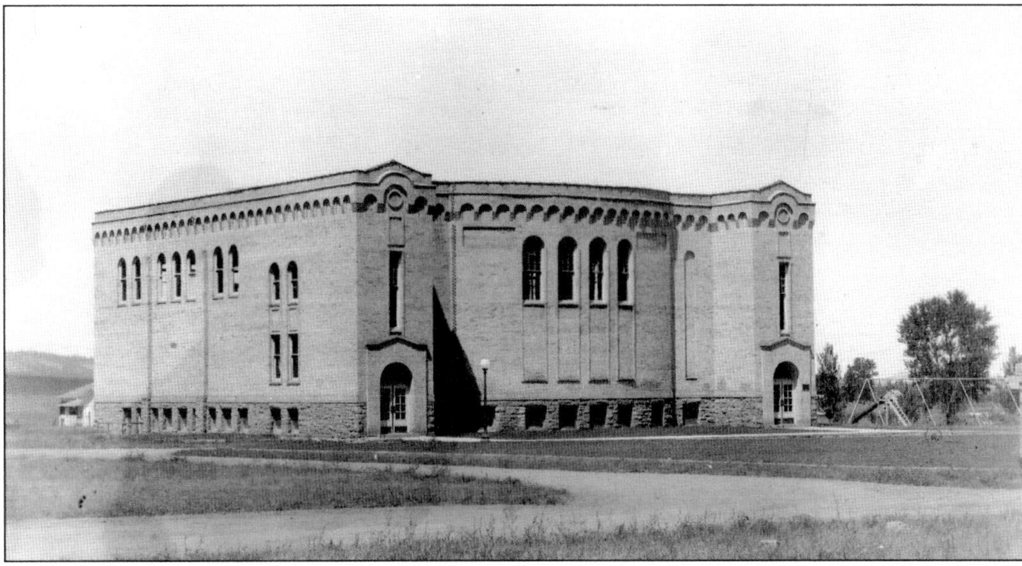

Pres. Fayette L. Cook's 18-year dream of a new gymnasium for the school came to fruition in 1918. The building was later named Cook Gym. The gym could seat 1,200 and housed an elevated track that could double as a spectator's gallery. A swimming pool, reputed to be one of the first indoor pools in the area, was in the basement. This was the first swimming pool on a higher education campus in the state. The swimming pool was still in use after Cook Gym was razed in 1966, and another building, also called Cook Gym, was built in its place. (Courtesy of the University Archives.)

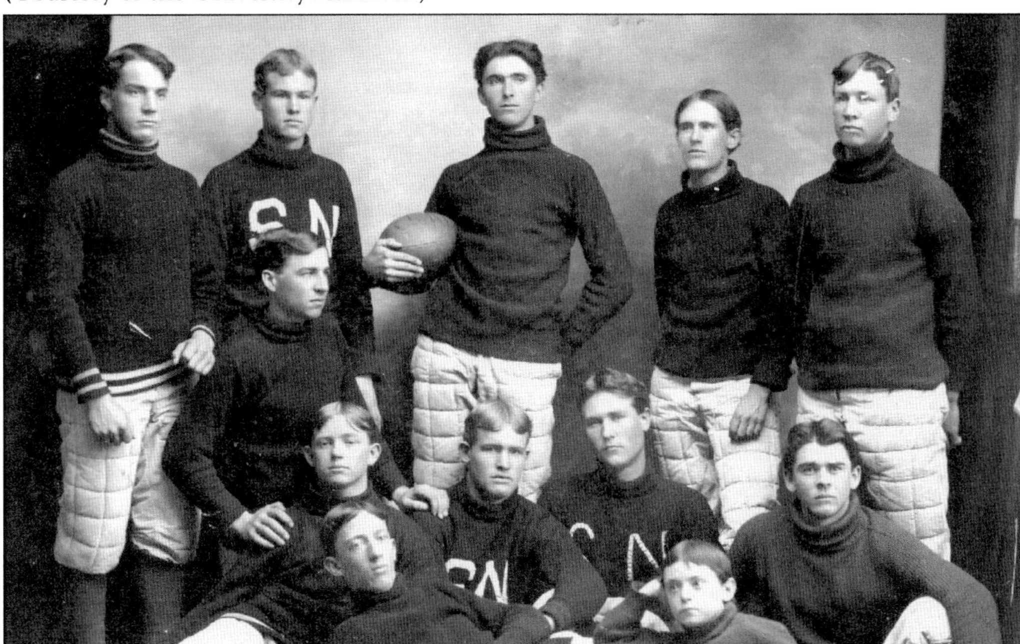

Athletics began at Spearfish's State Normal School in the late 1890s. Although they never had a game off campus, in 1898, a rugby football team was formed. The following year the first football team was organized. However, they did not compete out of town until 1904. The first football team is shown here. (Courtesy of the University Archives.)

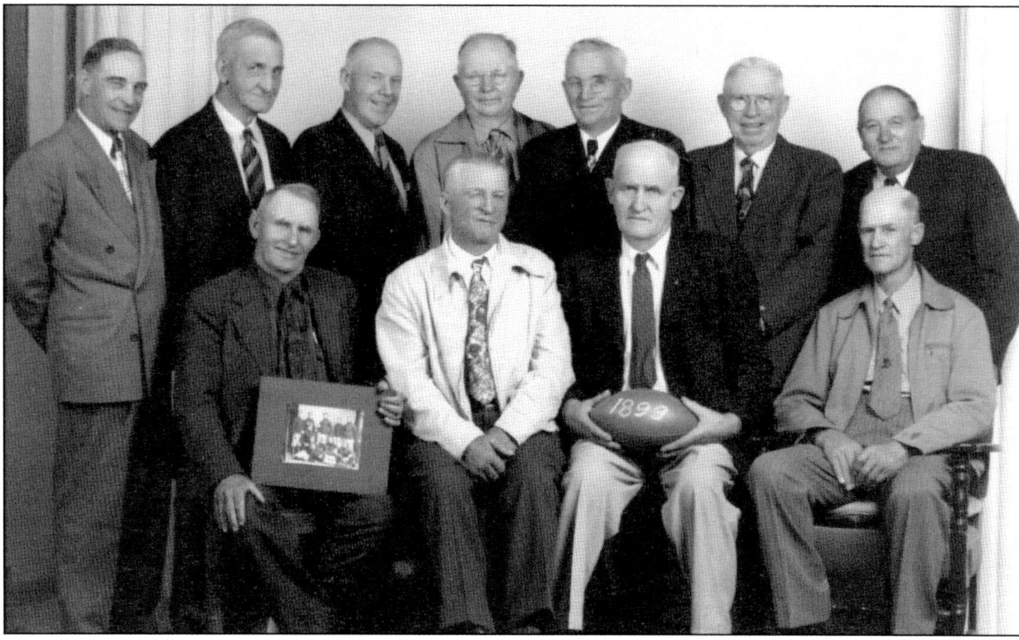

In 1949, at a 50-year reunion, members of the 1889 football team gathered. Pictured are, from left to right, (first row) Frank Thomson, Carl Blatt, Chris Thybo, and Andrew Thybo; (second row) Ernest Lown, Roy Cook, Jesse L. Driskill Jr., Len Chiesman, O. Allen Anderson, Charlie Thomson, and Chas (Brownie) Lown. (Courtesy of the University Archives.)

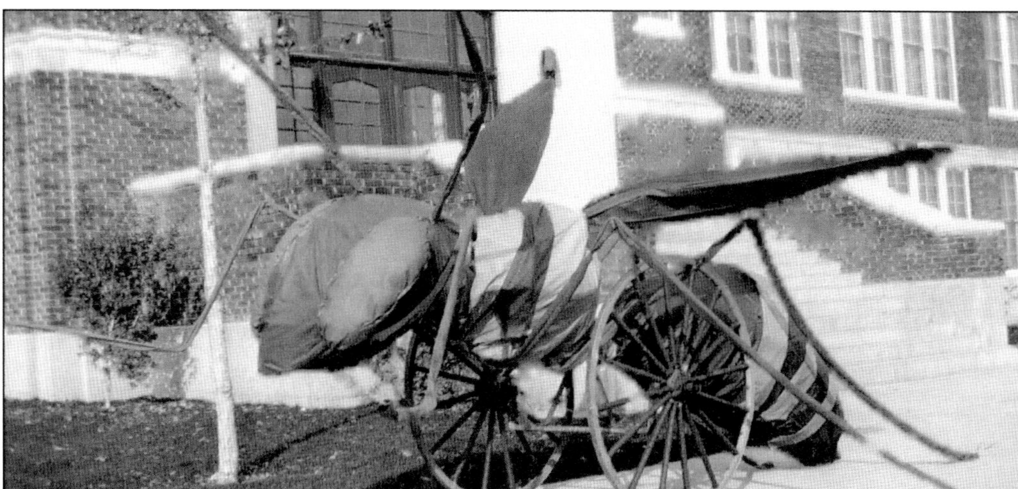

It was 1922 when the school mascot became the yellow jacket. There are several stories of how the school adopted that name. One says that they were called the yellow jackets because of the football team's striped socks. Similarly the *Anemone* reported that the football players themselves, chose the moniker. Another story is that they wore yellow jackets over their uniforms; at one game, a fan stood and spontaneously started cheering, "Go yellow jackets." This photograph shows the mascot as a Swarm Day parade float from 1930. Swarm Day was the name adopted for homecoming in 1928. Prior homecomings had been called Pioneer Day, Gypsy Day, and Hobo Day. It should be noted that yellow jackets do not swarm as bees do. The name Swarm Day is still used today. (Courtesy of the University Archives.)

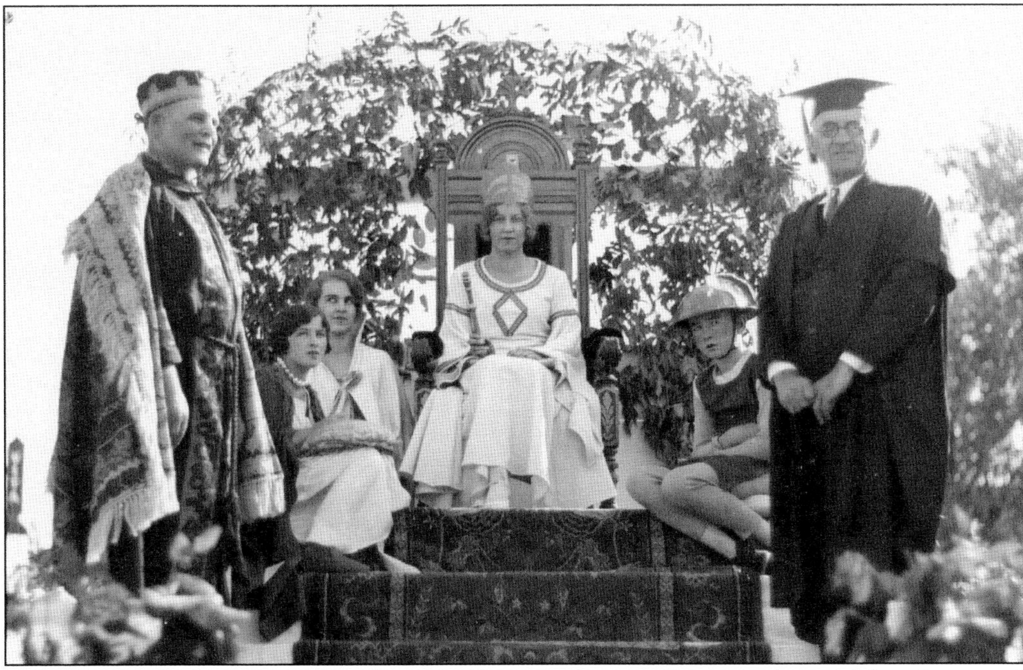

In keeping with the Swarm Day theme, each year a Swarm Queen is elected. This photograph shows Swarm Queen Edith Nelson and Swarm Day royalty during the coronation ceremony in 1932. (Courtesy of the University Archives.)

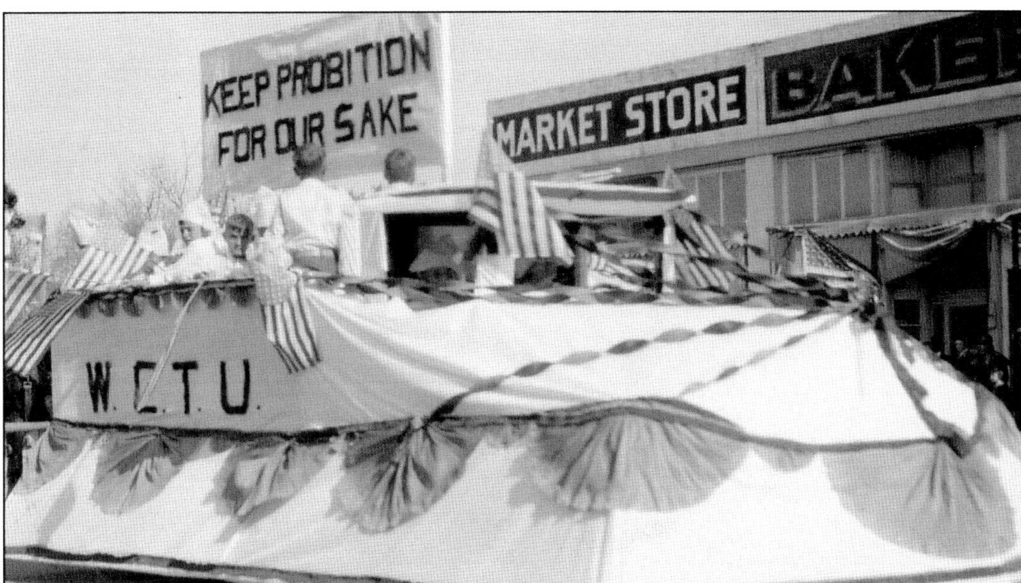

Many student organizations as well as community organizations and businesses participate in the Swarm Day parade. Pictured here is a Swarm Day float from 1930 supporting prohibition by the Women's Christian Temperance Union. The Women's Christian Temperance Union is not listed as a student organization in the 1930 college catalog. "Boosting a good cause," reads the caption for this picture in the school yearbook titled *Eociha*. The name *Eociha* is an adaptation of a Lakota word meaning "link" or "friendship." (Courtesy of the University Archives.)

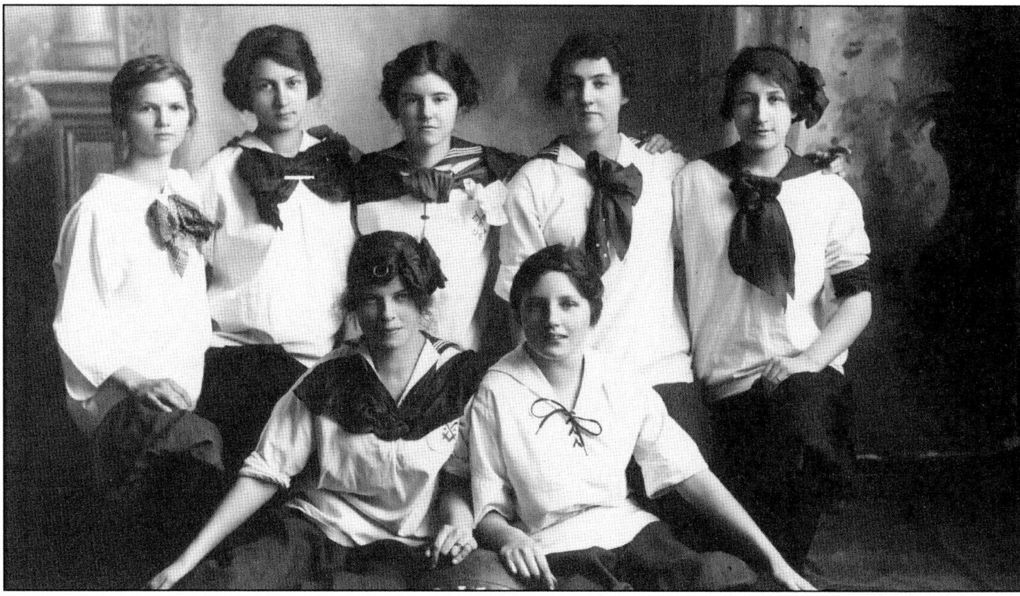

P. F. McCormick brought basketball to the State Normal School in 1903 when he convinced Pres. Fayette L. Cook that the girls needed some form of vigorous excise. McCormick took on the duties of coach and the president purchased the equipment. In addition to several student teams for girls, faculty women also formed a team. Games were intramural as well as played with teams from several area towns. Men's basketball began in 1906 with John Bender as coach. (Courtesy of the University Archives.)

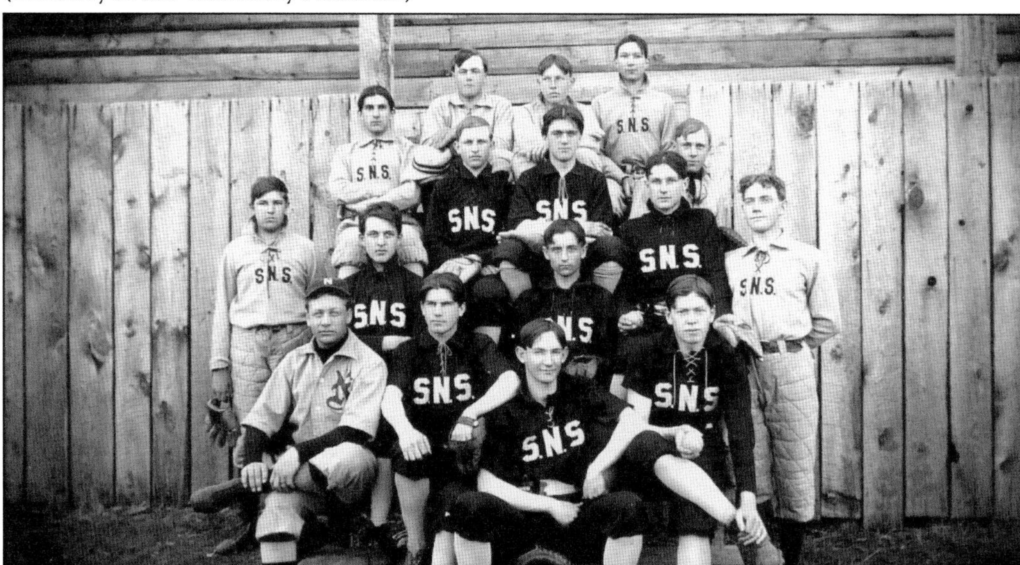

Baseball had a somewhat fitful start at the normal school. Two teams were formed in 1899; however, they only played practice games between each other. Indoor baseball was played throughout 1900, and in the spring of 1901 the baseball team was organized once again. It was not until 1904 that games were played with out-of-town teams. But after that the team flourished and remained very popular until World War II. This photograph shows the 1906 baseball team. (Courtesy of the University Archives.)

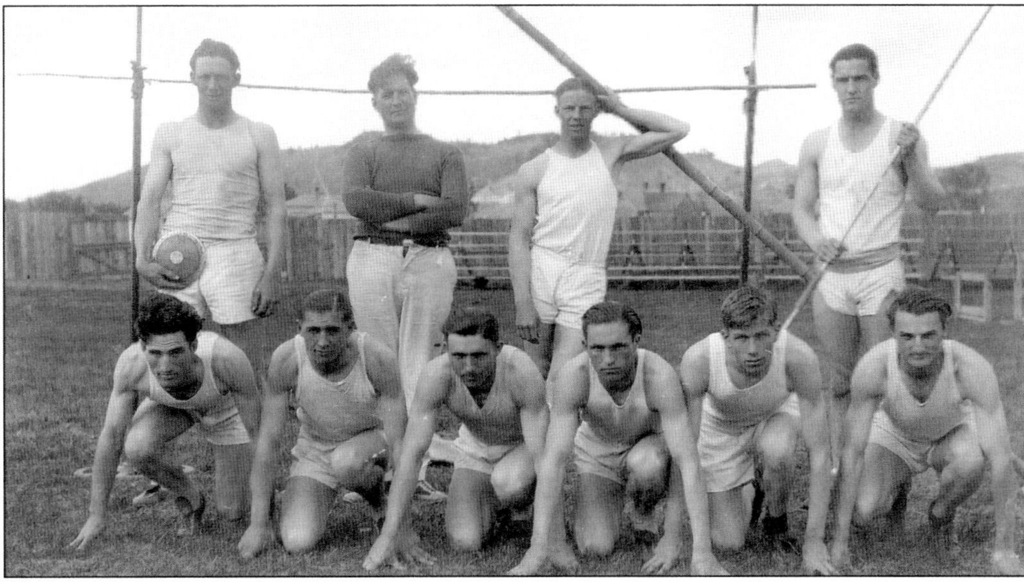

The Black Hills Athletic Association sponsored the first track and field competition in 1902. Sturgis, Deadwood, and State Normal School teams composed the association. Ward E. Bell coached the 1926 track team pictured here. From that team, five members who competed at the state track meet in Sioux Falls placed first and one placed third. Athletes in that meet were Allan Malcolm, discus; Elmer Murray, high jump; William Brown and Paul Beck, one mile; and Alvin Underhill, 440-yard dash. (Courtesy of the University Archives.)

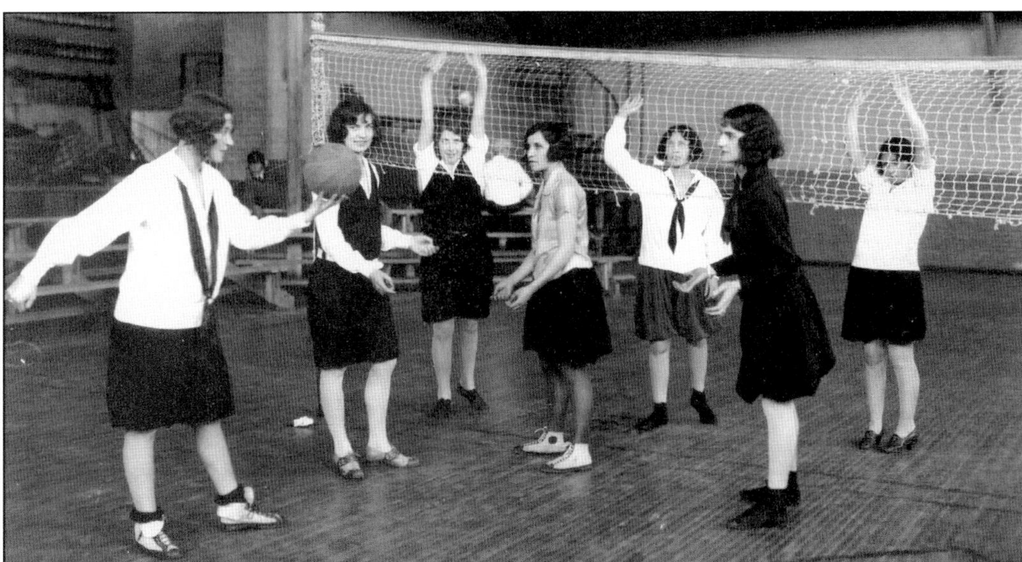

The Women's Athletic Association was formed in 1923. This student organization was in charge of extra-curricular athletics of the State Normal School girls. Members earned points for their participation in various events allowing them to earn awards from pins to the coveted sweaters. Students pictured in this 1929 photograph from Cook Gym are, from left to right, Thora Heggelund, Blanche Lampert, Millicent Troon, Lilian Gordon, Charlotte Wilson, Ruberta Wellman, and Margaret Rousseau. (Courtesy of the University Archives.)

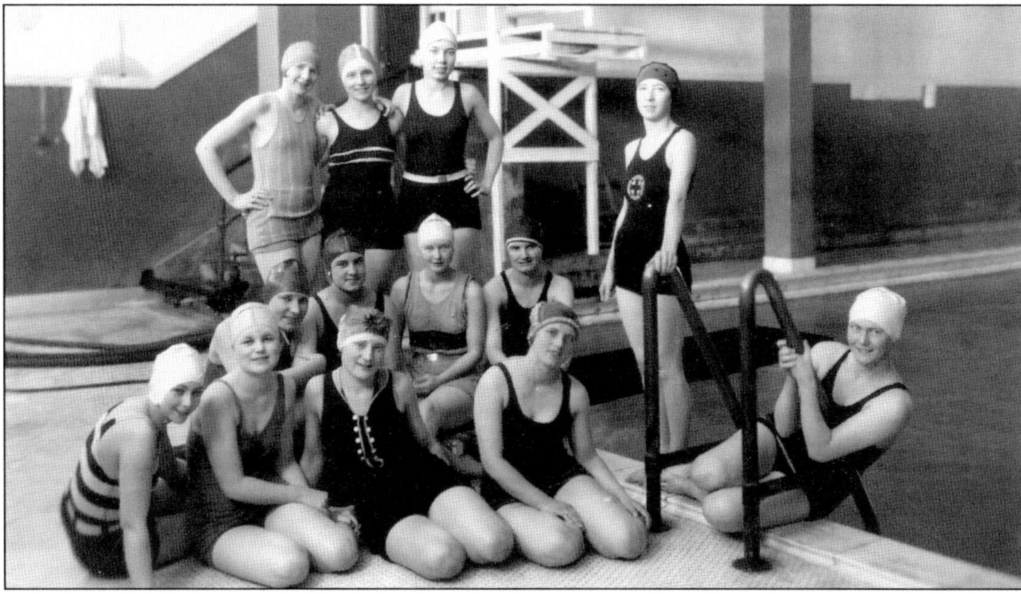

Women's Athletic Association or WAA sponsored numerous activities. These included tennis, basketball, volleyball, swimming, track, and soccer tournaments, as well as hiking and other activities. Members from the 1928–1929 school year pictured here are Velva Baker, Leone Whitlock, Dorothy Woodburn, Martha Mayer, Laura Lineau, Greta Osdale, Lois Phipps, Helen Painter, Margaret Rousseau, Marie Ford, Helen Kovaric, Mildred Bischoff, and Violet Olsen. (Courtesy of the University Archives.)

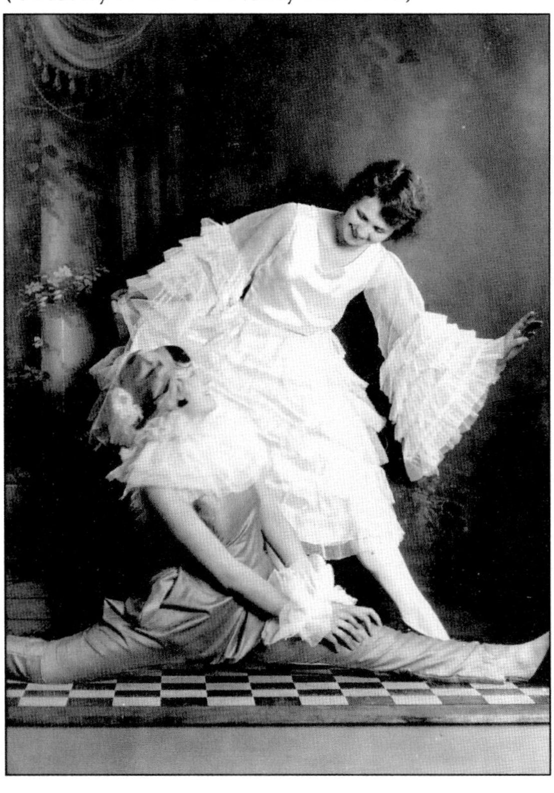

In addition to athletic activities, the WAA began producing a variety show in 1927 called the Follies. The 1929 yearbook gives a glowing review of that show coached by Edith Roeder Jacobs. One of the dance numbers is shown here. That yearbook further notes that the organization also sponsored a cabin to which members could go on weekends. Other events were a spring all-member picnic and a formal banquet closing the activities of the year. (Courtesy of the University Archives.)

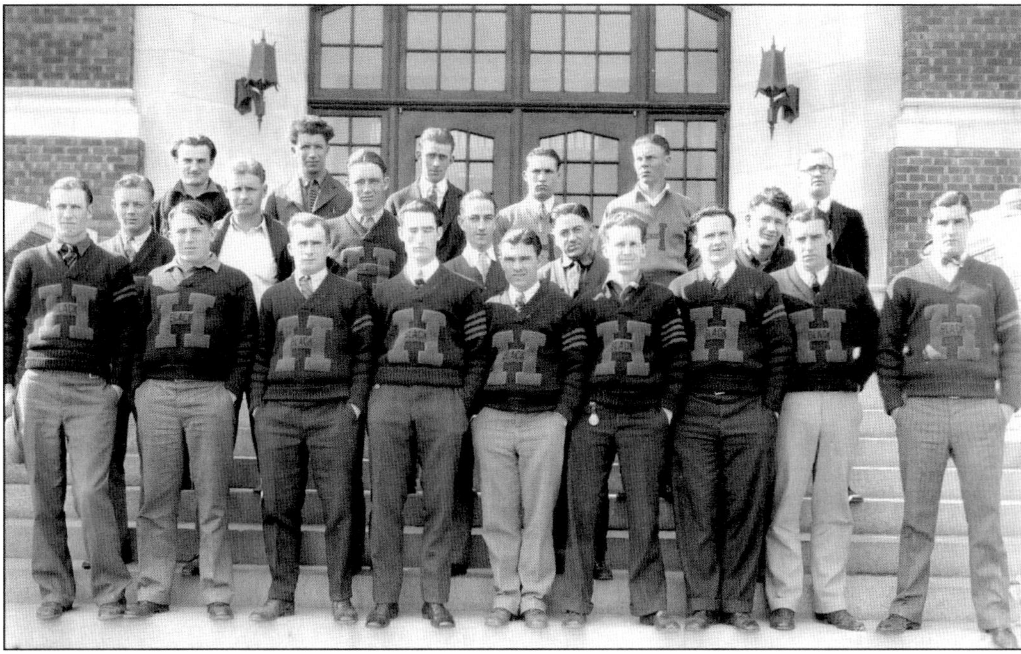

Coach Ward E. Bell formed the letterman club in 1923. All men who had received letters were eligible for membership. The club was named the N Club. The club's purpose was to promote the good of athletics in the school and create a closer feeling of friendship between lettermen. The men pictured were members of the organization in 1927. (Courtesy of the University Archives.)

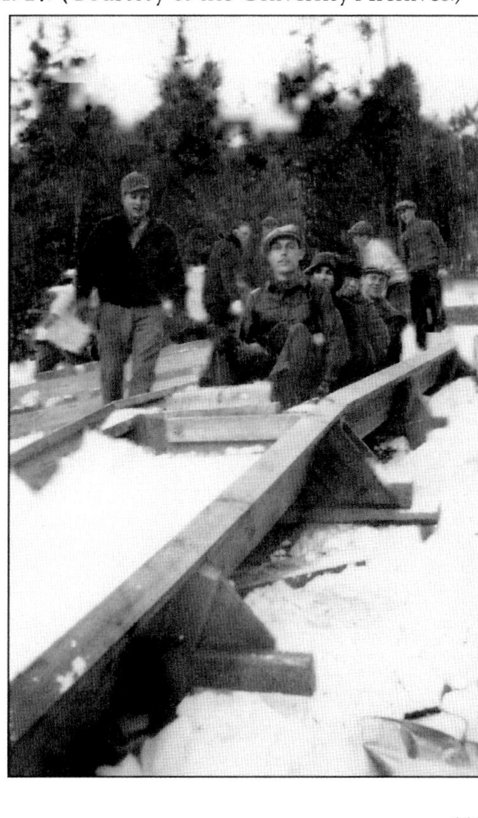

The Black Hills have long been a playground for winter sports enthusiasts. State Normal School students took advantage of all available winter activities such as skiing, and when available ice-skating. In an editorial in the *Anemone*, the writer laments the lack of an ice-skating rink in Spearfish. In this photograph from 1930, students are sledding on what appears to be something similar to a luge track. (Courtesy of the University Archives.)

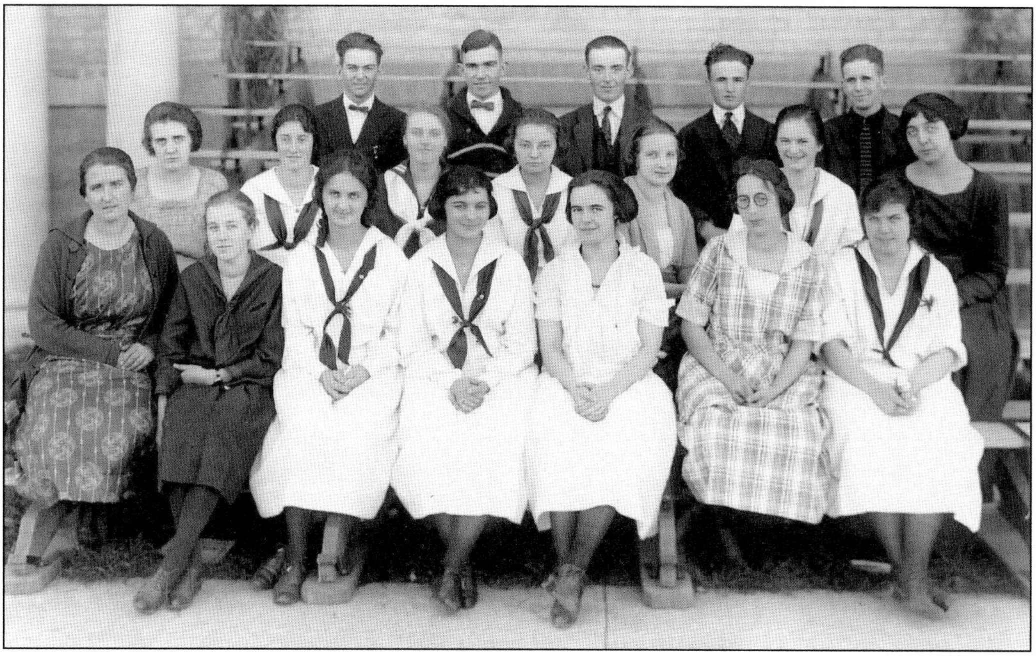

In addition to the student organizations previously mentioned, there have been many other groups on campus. The group shown here is the *Anemone* staff from 1922. The anemone was chosen for the campus newspaper, named after the state flower. It had previously been called the *Normal* and was part literary magazine. It was later renamed *Black Hills Today* and currently goes by the title of *Today*. (Courtesy of the University Archives.)

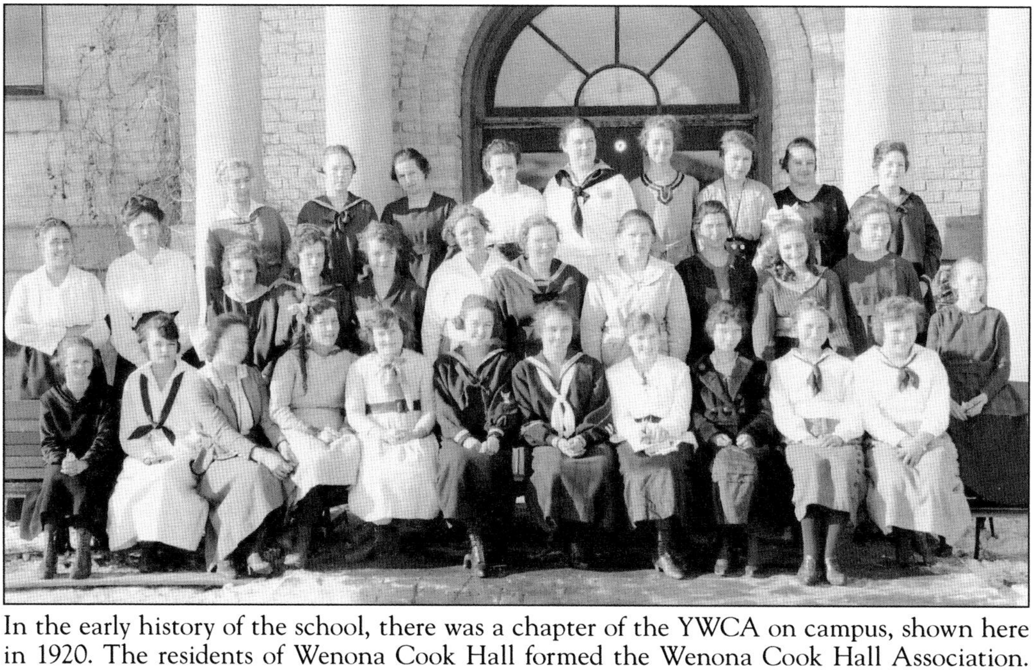

In the early history of the school, there was a chapter of the YWCA on campus, shown here in 1920. The residents of Wenona Cook Hall formed the Wenona Cook Hall Association. There was also a literary society organized in 1898. It consisted of two debate groups called the Ciceronians (male) and the Minerva Society (female).

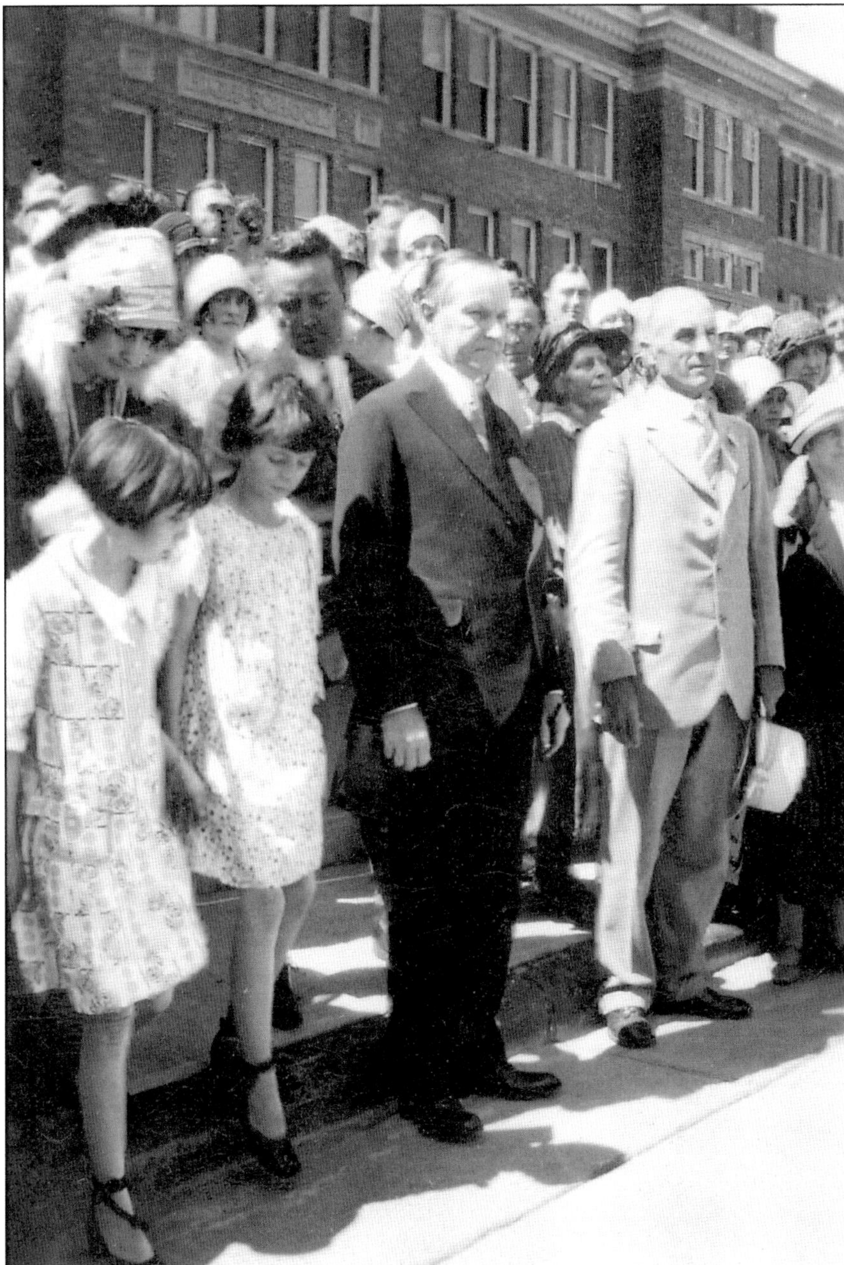

At the urging of Sen. Peter Norbeck, former superintendent of the Custer State Park, Pres. Calvin Coolidge spent the summer of 1927 in the Black Hills. He stayed at the State Game Lodge in Custer State Park and had offices in Rapid City. The State Game Lodge is referred to as the "Summer Whitehouse" in some photographs from that time. The president stayed for three months and was persuaded to dedicate Mount Rushmore National Memorial on August 10. On the Forth of July, Coolidge and Norbeck attended the Belle Fourche Round-up, a prominent rodeo across the west, in Belle Fourche, South Dakota. Coolidge is seen here with a delagation from the State Normal School in Rapid City on July 12, 1927. Next to Collidge is normal school president E. C. Woodburn. (Courtesy of the University Archives.)

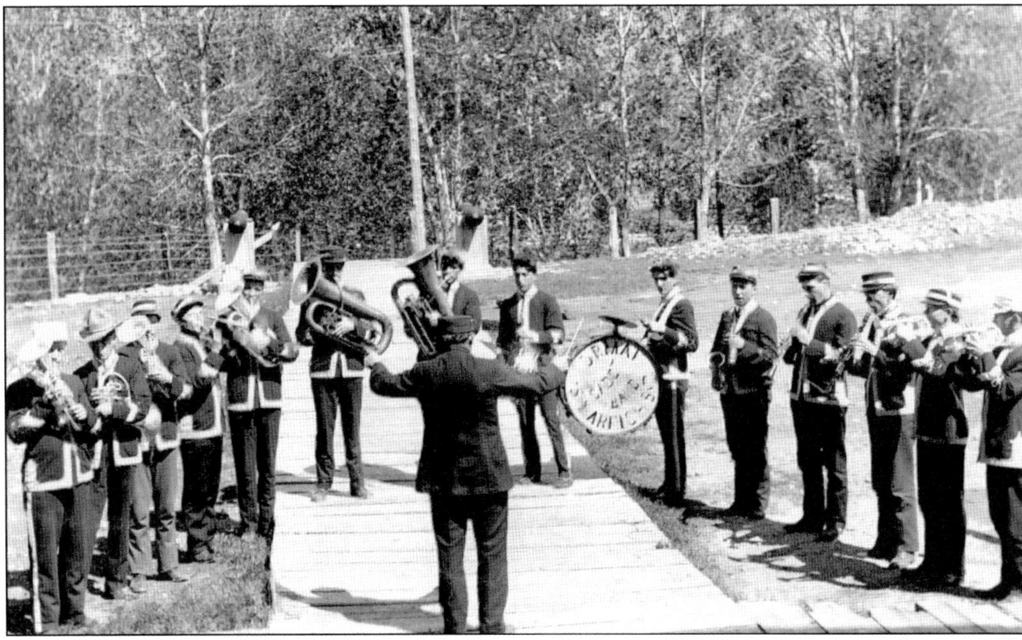

In addition to starting the basketball program at the normal school, P. F. McCormick started the first band in 1903. Music had been offered from 1898. The band started with 11 members but grew quickly. The band pictured here, from about 1909, is shown at rehearsal in front of the old main building. The conductor is facing the orchard. (Courtesy of the McClung collection.)

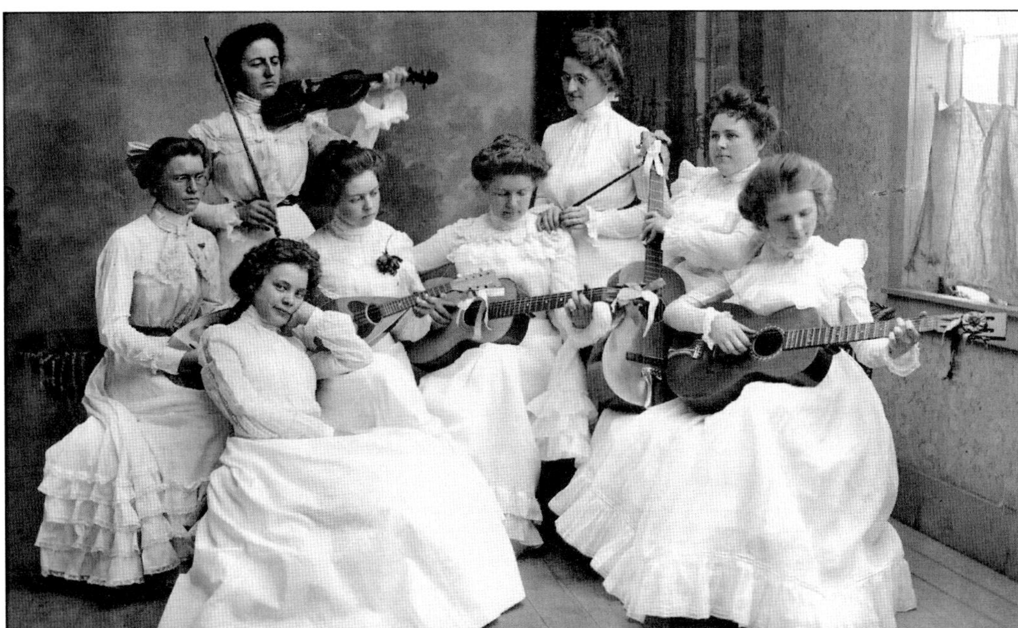

McCormick started the first orchestra, the women's mandolin and guitar club in 1904. They chose the name the Philharmonics from the Greek word for "friends of music." Their diligence paid off and they soon were playing for commencement, the alumni banquet, and other important events. (Courtesy of the University Archives.)

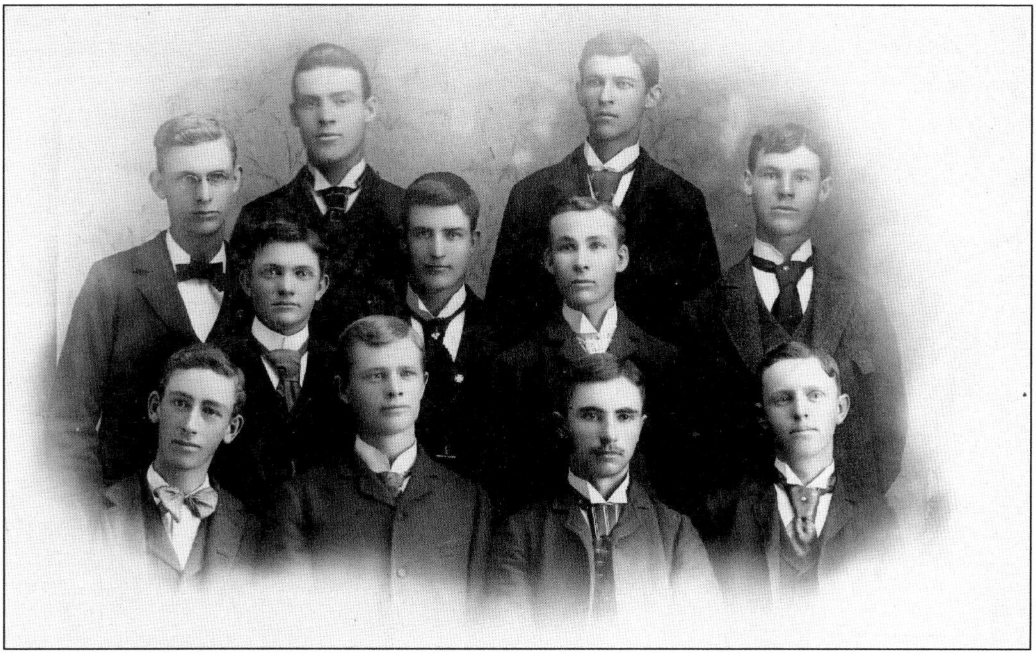

Some members of the 1896 boys glee club are (first row) Herbert Pratt, Roy Phillips, Carl James, and Arthur Deffenbach; (second row) unidentified, Cyril Miler, and Joe Lodel; (third row) Thomas Deffenbach, Arthur McCrady, Bert Robins, and Fred McCrawly. There was also a girls glee club, and for special events such as Easter, they would sing together. (Courtesy of the University Archives.)

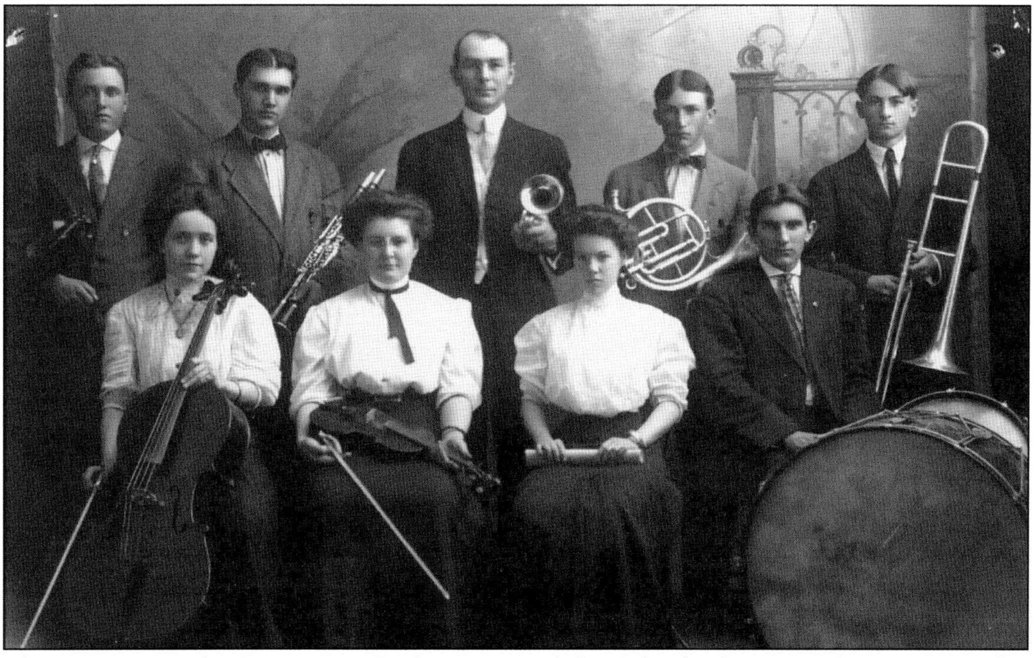

The 1910–1911 school year saw the beginning of the School of Music. The course catalog announced the presence of two new music teachers: Anna McCarthy, teacher of vocal music, and Helen Fowler, piano teacher. The group shown here is a coed orchestra from 1910. (Courtesy of the University Archives.)

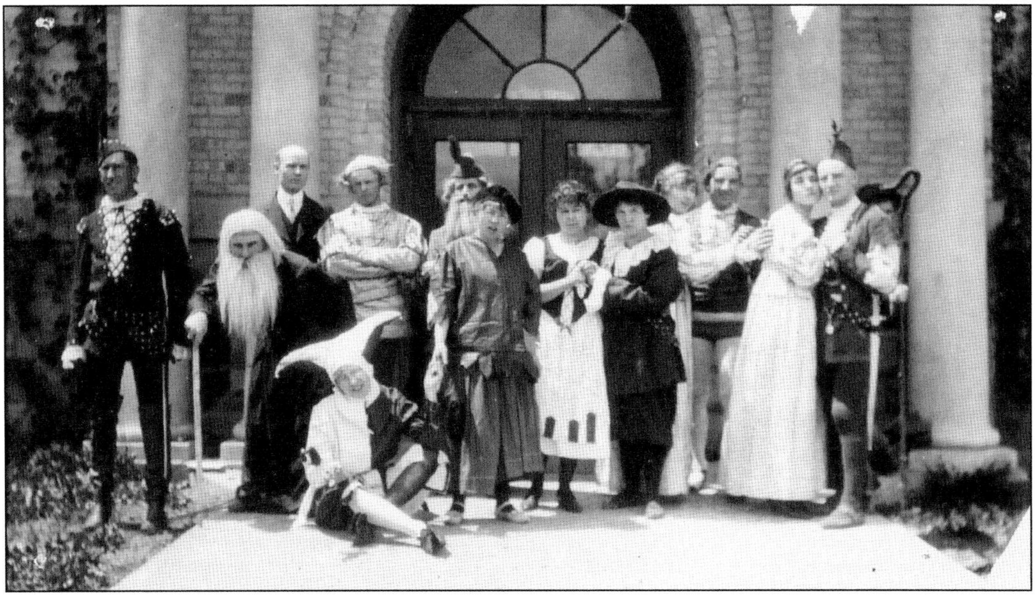

The *Anemone* reported in the March 1917 issue that it had been a "rule for the last twelve years" that the senior class present a Shakespearean play during commencement week. A teacher, J. C. Lindberg, directed this and all previous productions. The cast pictured here is from that year's production, *As You Like It*. The article concludes that the "dramatic possibilities" of the current cast equal that of past classes and that it promised to be a good show. (Courtesy of the University Archives.)

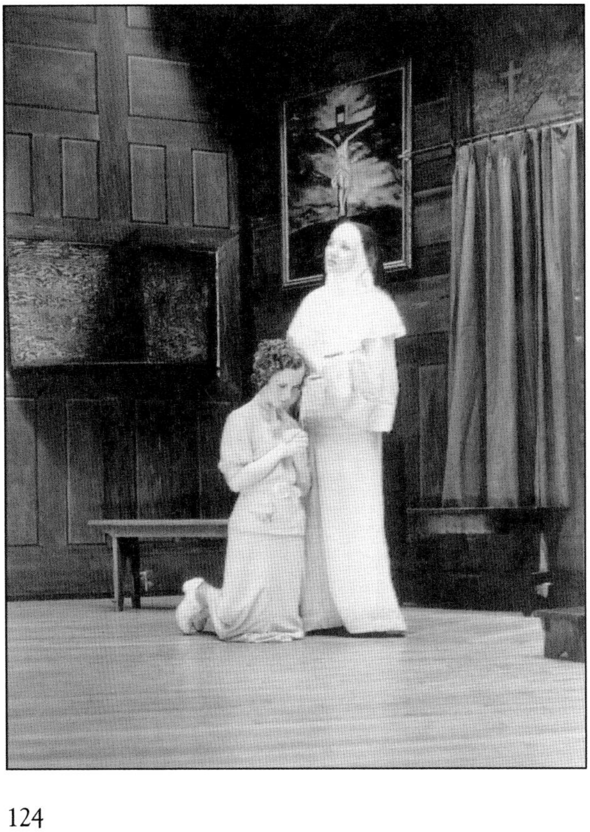

Props and Liners, the campus dramatic club, was formed during the fall semester of 1921. The name comes from the theatrical terms for stage properties and makeup. The commencement production in 1934 was *The Cradle Song*, a two-act Spanish play written G. Martinez Sierra. The play, directed by Lavina J. Humbert, received a rave review in the May 25, 1921, issue of the *Anemone*. Shown here are Evelyn Doody (kneeling) and Bernice Lown. (Courtesy of the University Archives.)

Like the rest of the nation, World War II had a profound effect on Black Hills Teachers College. Necessities such as food and paper were in short supply. The food service staff canned local produce for use in the Wenona Cook Hall dining room throughout the year. Two canons, a gift to the campus after the Spanish American War, were donated to the war effort for scrap metal. The *Eociha* was not published during the 1943–1944 school year, and in its place was a souvenir booklet. (Courtesy of the University Archives.)

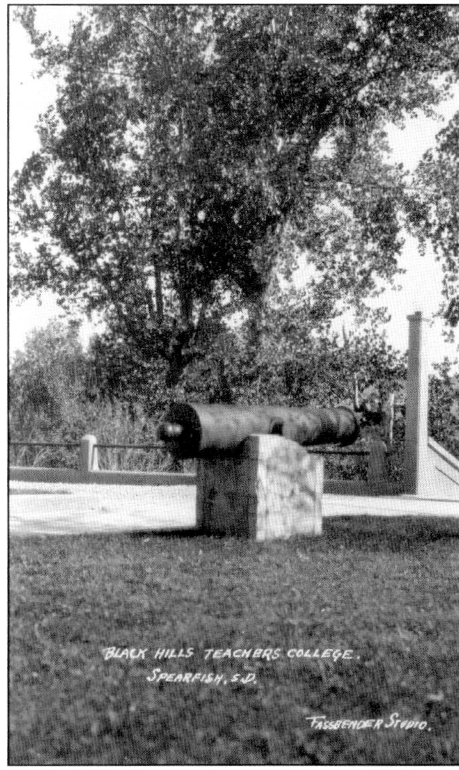

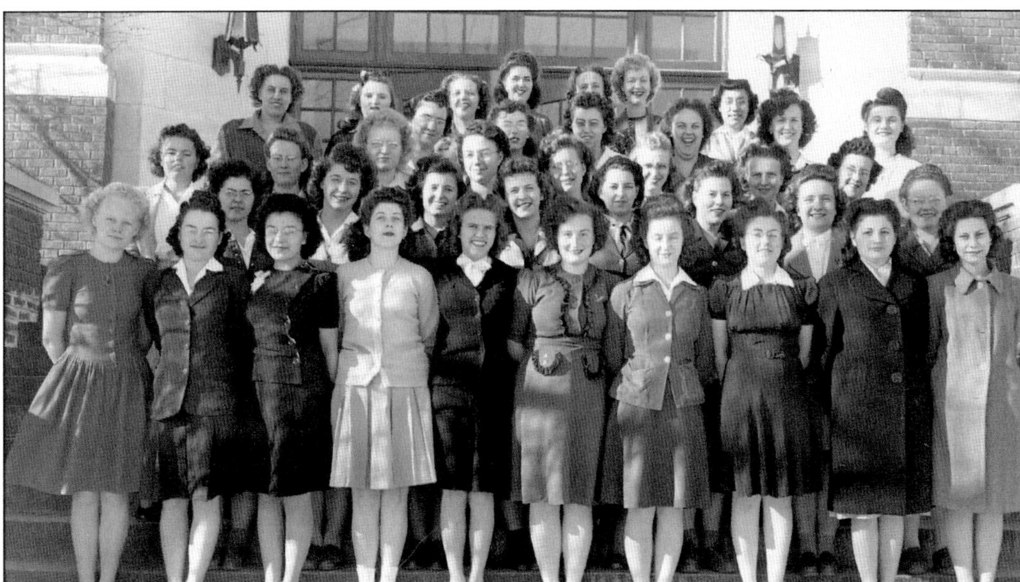

During World War II, enrollment dropped. Educational endeavors turned their focus to the needs of the war. The Civilian Pilot Training Program, a new deal program to train pilots for the fledgling aviation industry, became the War Training Services. Wenona Cook Hall was converted to an army barracks and mess hall. The students were moved to private residences. Thirty-nine nursing candidates came to Black Hills Teachers College from Saint John's McNamara Hospital in 1944 to complete a portion of their coursework. (Courtesy of the University Archives.)

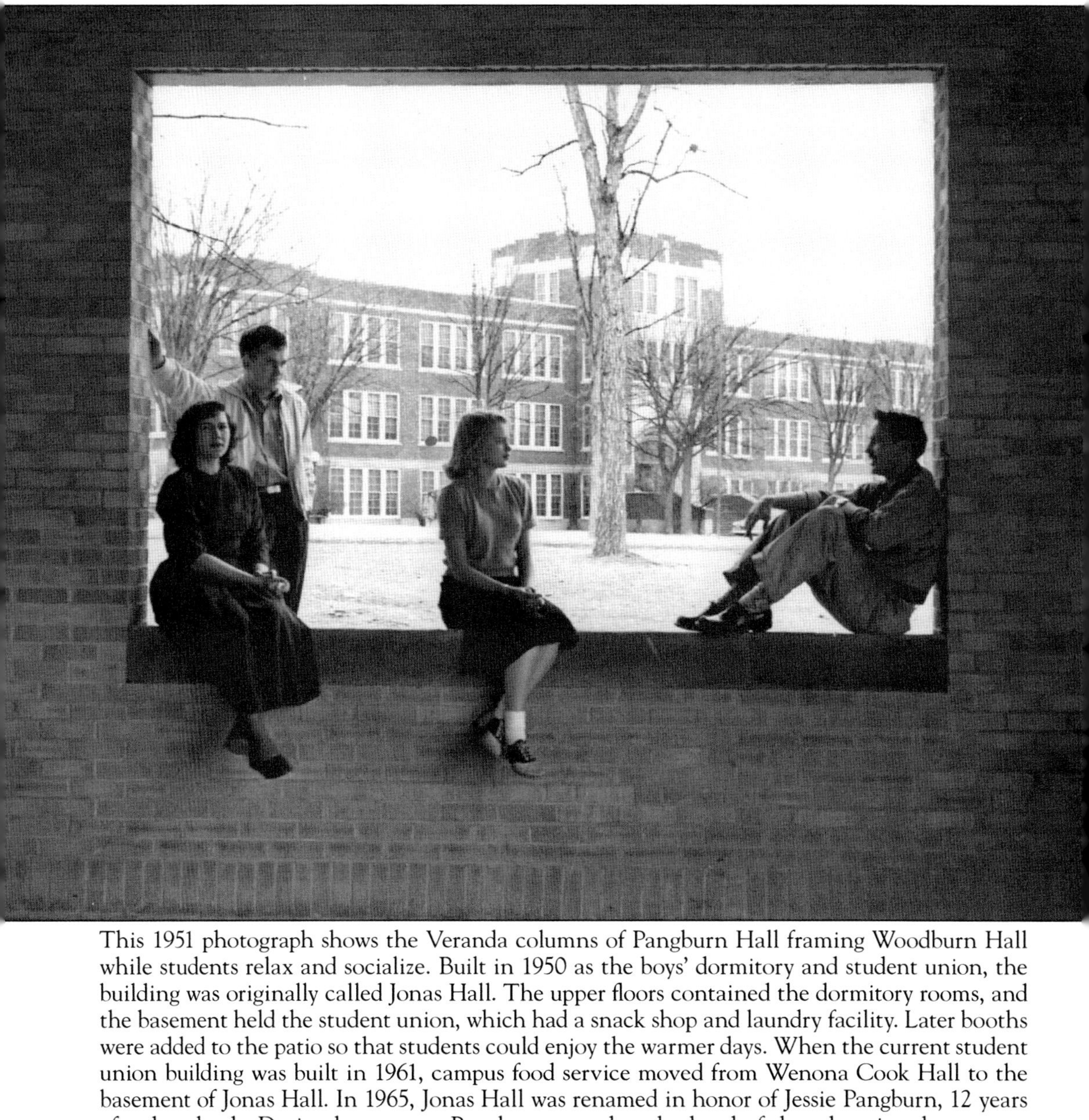

This 1951 photograph shows the Veranda columns of Pangburn Hall framing Woodburn Hall while students relax and socialize. Built in 1950 as the boys' dormitory and student union, the building was originally called Jonas Hall. The upper floors contained the dormitory rooms, and the basement held the student union, which had a snack shop and laundry facility. Later booths were added to the patio so that students could enjoy the warmer days. When the current student union building was built in 1961, campus food service moved from Wenona Cook Hall to the basement of Jonas Hall. In 1965, Jonas Hall was renamed in honor of Jessie Pangburn, 12 years after her death. During her tenure, Pangburn served as the head of the education department and as dean of academic affairs. Pangburn came to the State Normal School in 1920 and served until her death in September of 1953. (Courtesy of the University Archives.)

Bibliography

Bennett, Estelline. *Old Deadwood Days*. Lincoln, NE: University of Lincoln Press, 1982.

Black Hills Daily Times. Deadwood, SD.

Fielder, Mildred. *A Guide to Black Hills Ghost Mines*. Aberdeen, SD: North Plains Press, 1972.

———. *Lawrence County for the Dakota Territory Centennial*. Lead, SD: Seaton Press, 1960.

Haivala, Paul. *The Friendly College: The First Hundred Years of Black Hills State College, 1893–1993*. Spearfish, SD: Black Hills State College, 1983.

Higbee, Paul, and Kathleen Aney. *Spearfish*. Spearfish, SD: Black Hills and Bighorns History Project, 2000.

Higbee, Paul, and Les Voorhis. *Spearfish Canyon: A Journey Beyond the Rim*. Belle Fourche, SD: Royal Tine Images Inc., 2006.

Klock, Irma. *Yesterday's Gold Camps and Mines in the Northern Black Hills*. Lead, SD: Seaton Publishing Company, 1975.

Lee, Bob, ed. *Gold, Gals, Guns, Guts: A History of Deadwood, Lead, and Spearfish, 1874–1976*. Deadwood-Lead, SD: '76 Centennial Inc., 1976.

Parker, Watson, and Hugh K. Lambert. *Black Hills Ghost Towns*. Chicago: Swallow Press, 1974.

Rezatto, Helen. *Tales of the Black Hills*. Rapid City, SD: Fenwyn Press, 1989.

Thomson, Frank S. *The Thoen Stone: A Saga of the Black Hills*. Detroit: Harlo Press, 1966.

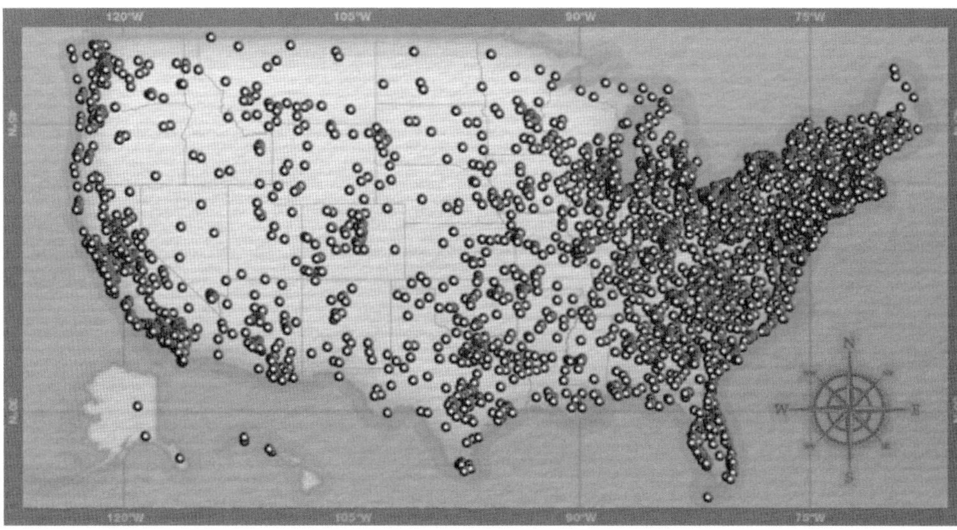

Consistent with our mission to preserve history on a local level, this book was printed in South Carolina on American-made paper and manufactured entirely in the United States. Products carrying the accredited Forest Stewardship Council (FSC) label are printed on 100 percent FSC-certified paper.

MADE IN THE USA